DESPOTISM IN AMERICA:

AN INQUIRY

INTO

THE NATURE, RESULTS, AND LEGAL BASIS

OF THE

SLAVE-HOLDING SYSTEM

IN THE UNITED STATES.

BY

RICHARD HILDRETH,

AUTHOR OF THE HISTORY OF THE UNITED STATES, THEORY OF
POLITICS, WHITE SLAVE, ETC.

BOSTON:

PUBLISHED BY JOHN P. JEWETT AND COMPANY.

CLEVELAND, OHIO:

JEWETT, PROCTOR, AND WORTHINGTON.

LONDON: LOW AND COMPANY.

1854.

Entered, according to Act of Congress, in the year 1854, by

JOHN P. JEWETT AND COMPANY,

In the Clerk's Office of the District Court of the District of Massachusetts.

STEREOTYPED AT THE
BOSTON STEREOTYPE FOUNDRY.

" The impression which has gone abroad of the weakness of the South, as connected with the slave-question, exposes us to such constant attacks, has done us so much injury, and is calculated to produce such infinite mischiefs, that I embrace the occasion presented by the remarks of the gentleman from Massachusetts, to declare *that we are ready to meet the question promptly and fearlessly. It is one from which we are not disposed to shrink*, IN WHATEVER FORM, OR UNDER WHATEVER CIRCUMSTANCES IT MAY BE PRESSED UPON US. *We are ready to make up the issue as to the influence of slavery on individual and national character—on the prosperity and greatness either of the United States, or particular States.* Sir, when arraigned at the bar of public opinion, on this charge of slavery, we can stand up with conscious rectitude, plead not guilty, and put ourselves upon God and our country."—*Speech of* ROBERT Y. HAYNE, *of South Carolina, in reply to Mr. Webster, delivered in the Senate of the United States, Jan.* 21, 1830.

CONTENTS.

CHAPTER FOURTH.

PERSONAL RESULTS OF THE SLAVE-HOLDING-SYSTEM.

CHAPTER FIFTH.

LEGAL BASIS OF THE SLAVE-HOLDING SYSTEM.

INTRODUCTION.

It has been said, and is often repeated, that the United States of America are trying a great social experiment, upon the result of which hangs the future fate not of America only, but to a certain extent, of all mankind.

The consequences likely to flow from the success or failure of this experiment, are doubtless exaggerated; for those universal laws which regulate the feelings and the actions of men, will ultimately produce their necessary effects, in spite of narrow systems of policy and morals, founded upon the success or failure of any single experiment.

But whatever we may think of its probable consequences, however fancy may magnify, or reason may diminish them, the experiment itself is a great one. It is in fact far more complicated and more critical, and therefore greater and more interesting, than it is commonly represented.

The American experiment is usually described, as purely an experiment of democracy; an attempt to establish a perfect equality of political rights; an essay towards the equal distribution among all the members of the community, of freedom, property, knowledge, social advantages, and those other good things which make up the mass of human happiness. And this experiment—as we are assured by every writer, native, or foreign, who has touched upon the subject, owing to the peculiar circumstances of the country, is carried on to the greatest possible advantage, not being compelled to encounter a multitude of hostile influences, by which such an undertaking, any where else, would be most vigorously opposed.

This is not a true representation of the case. If in certain parts of the American Union, the experiment of Democracy be steadily and quietly pursued, and with an influence and a feeling in its favor which have at length become predominant, in certain other parts of the country it is quite overshadowed, and is reduced to creep pale and sickly on the ground, by another experiment, less talked about, less celebrated, but not the less real or important, to wit, the *experiment of Despotism.*

The Northern States of the Union are unquestionable Democracies, and every day they are verging nearer and nearer towards the simple idea and theoretic perfection of that form of government. The Southern States of the Union, though certain democratic principles are to be found in their constitutions and their laws, are in no modern sense of the word entitled to the appellation of Democracies: They are Aristocracies; and aristocracies of the sternest and most odious kind. Property, and all the rights, advantages and enjoyments which the laws bestow, are limited to certain families and their descendants. Certain other families and their offspring, to the latest generation, are not only deprived of all political privileges and social advantages, but they are the hereditary subjects, servants, bondsmen of the privileged class. Every man of the privileged order who is possessed of any property at all, is apt to own at least one slave; if he is rich, he may own a thousand; but whether one or a thousand, of those he does own, the laws create him with but a single slight, and in fact merely nominal exception, the absolute master, lord and despot. In their relation towards each other, the members of the privileged class are nominally equal; and in that aspect, it may happen that the lord of a plantation and five hundred slaves, shall be a great stickler for liberty and equality. But the liberty and equality for which he contends, is wholly confined to the privileged order; and the total subjection and eternal servitude of the unprivileged class is considered a matter of course, a first principle, a fixed and established ordinance, as inevitable and as incapable of alteration, as the laws of nature.

It is evident then, how complicated is the American experiment. If the democratical part of it, has hitherto been pursued in silence and quiet, and with such apparent success that the admirers of Democracy have been ready to cry out that the problem is already solved;—that quiet and silence have been merely accidental; that success has been only a progress which was comparatively speaking, but slightly opposed; and it is but now that Democracy and Despotism face to face, like Gabriel and the Arch-enemy, make ready for a desperate and dreadful struggle. The preparation, the courage, the arms, the loftiness of soul were not on the part of the " angelic squadron" alone :—

> ——— On t' other side, Satan alarm'd
> Collecting all his might, dilated stood
> Like Teneriffe, or Atlas, unremoved.
> His stature reached the sky, and on his crest
> Sat horror plum'd; nor wanted in his grasp
> What *seem'd* both spear and shield.———

The struggle that impends is of a nature to shake the country to the centre, and to end, if we believe the prophecies of our southern friends, in civil commotions, infuriated hostilities, and savage war.

So it may be. The event is in their power. Let them be wise in time. The balance of justice is stretched across the sky,—and is it not their scale that kicks the beam? Let them look up and read their lot in that celestial sign, and know themselves, how light, how weak, if they resist. Even the arch-fiend cared not to struggle against inevitable fate, and fled a strife in which he could but suffer.

That heterogeneous mixture of aristocracies and

democracies, which makes up the American Union; that strange compound of liberty and despotism, which pervades the laws of so many of the States, and lurks demurely, in the federal constitution; such hostile and repulsive elements having been so long quietly in contact without producing an explosion, it has thence been argued, and believed, that they might always remain so. But those who reason thus, have not well considered the history of the American States, nor the kind of progress which Democracy has hitherto made.

The dispute which severed the colonies from Great Britain, gave rise to constitutions in the northern States of the confederacy, which acknowledged to a greater or less degree, the leading principles of liberty and equality; principles which before hardly had an existence, except in the speculations of a few political theorists. In no part of the country, were the fundamental theorems of this modern system of policy, more generally received or more warmly maintained, than in the New England States, where the equal distribution of property seemed to open the way for the easy introduction of a purely democratical system.

But property is not the only source of political power. From the earliest settlement of those States, the Clergy had always exercised a predominant influence. They formed a distinct order, acting together with decision and promptitude, and monopolizing all the learning and no small share of the active talent of the community. The mass of the people, though all could read,—an inestimable accomplishment, and under favorable circumstances, capable in itself of becoming the foundation of the most liberal knowledge,—were yet extremely ignorant; for they had no book but the bible, and for the most part they relied upon their religious teachers with a submissive and superstitious dependance, for such expositions of its contents as they saw fit to give. In this state of the case, the power which the clergy exercised was very great. It was however for the most part a moral power, a power not over the bodies, but over the minds of men, and of course, it was least felt by those who yielded to it the most implicit submission. Some harsh acts of persecution and punishment were occasionally dealt out to such insubordinate persons as were bold enough to think for themselves, or to question the infallible and divine authority of the " standing order." But in general, that veneration which the " ministers" claimed, was spontaneously yielded, and the power thus conferred was judiciously fortified by being shared with such of the laymen as most excelled in shrewdness, ambition, and spiritual gifts.

The Revolution, and those questions of constitutional law to which it gave rise, and more yet, those extensive and iniquitous fluctuations of property which the paper money system produced, raised into consequence another body of men, superior to the clergy in active talent; almost their equals in learning; and if they were not regarded with the same affectionate awe, yet both feared and respected by the people. These were the Lawyers.

This new order did not hazard its influence nor waste its strength in a struggle for power, with the clergy. On the contrary, the clergy and the lawyers soon formed an intimate union; and though these latter were sometimes a little wanting in respect for the theological dogmas, and the austere morality of their allies, these deficiencies of faith and practice were more than made up for, by the zeal and subtlety with which they defended the legal privileges of the clergy, and labored to uphold their influence and authority.

This double hierarchy of law and divinity, long maintained a predominating influence over the yeomanry of New England. Bred up on their farms in the simplest way, and with a deep reverence for religion and the law, a reverence easily and naturally transferred to the clergy and the lawyers; depending upon the pulpit for their weekly supply of knowledge and opinions, or if they read a newspaper,—and American newspapers in those times were but small affairs—choosing such an one as the minister recommended; the Legislature filled with lawyers, whose superior information, eloquence and adroitness, put every thing in their power; the judges, secure in the tenure of their office, and the profound respect with which it was regarded, contributing by their decisions, to uphold a system of which they formed a part; thus beset, hemmed in, controlled and over-awed, all the weaker spirits and more submissive tempers, that is to say, the mass of the community, cowered and submitted to a power, so boldly claimed, so vigorously enforced, and exercised on the part of those who held it, with a serious and sincere belief that superior knowledge, virtue and capacity justly entitled them to pre-eminent authority.

But notwithstanding this moral oligarchy to which New England was subjected, the spirit of democracy had nestled in the bosoms of her people; and cherished by degrees into energy and strength, it presently began to plume its wings, and to make ready for asserting its just dominion.

The history of the contest in New England, between Democracy on the one hand, and the priestly and legal alliance on the other, has never yet been written. It is not adorned with any of those palpable acts, those scenes of devastation and slaughter, which have hitherto formed the chief topics of historic narration; and though a most violent and bitter struggle, so little has it attracted the attention of political writers, that the progress of American Democracy, thus far, has been generally described as quiet, silent and almost unresisted.

. To one, who from the the array of the combatants, had divined the probable termination of the conflict, the speedy discomfiture of the democratical party would have appeared inevitable. Behind the legal and clerical champions who proudly led the van of the opposing forces, there followed a goodly host, including by far the most respectable, and apparently the most worthy portions of society. The wealthy, almost to a man, enlisted in behalf of the established order of things, which having made them rich, in their estimation, could not but be good. Besides, their wealth enabled them to purchase by gifts to pious uses, and without any special personal merit, high seats in the synagogue; and sufficed to enrol them in the list of "gentlemen," with whom the ministers and the lawyers were accustomed to share their authority. Next followed the great mass of the religiously disposed; for it requires an unusual degree of discernment and decision, to escape from the influences of education and habit, and to distinguish between a reverence for religion, and a blind submission to spiritual guides. The literature of the country, such as it was, naturally appeared on the side of those who were its principal patrons; and crowding in the rear, came the young talent and ambition of the times, anxious to sustain a system, which seemed to offer a rightful preeminence to talent, and to ambition a station above the vulgar level.

The array upon the other side, was contemptible in comparison. Some leaders there were, "sons of liberty," who had been nursed in the cradle of the revolution, whose character, whose honor, whose patriotism was unquestionable, and upon whose clear reputation not all the outrageous calumny of their opponents could fix the shadow of a stain. And there were some followers too, who seemed to love democracy for itself; men enamoured of the idea of equality, who sought no private advantage, but only the public good. But these, whether leaders or followers, were comparatively few. The mass of the party seemed made up like the band of David, when he rose in rebellion against the Lord's anointed;—all who were in debt, all who were in distress, all who were discontented, enlisted beneath this banner; and to believe the account of their opponents, not the tatterdemalions of Falstaff's enlistment were more idle, vicious, dishonest and dangerous.

The truth is, that so stern, severe, active and influ-

2

ential was the authority which the allied hierarchy
exercised, that few men who had property, standing,
character, friends, to lose, cared to risk the consequences of those bulls of excommunication which were
fulminated from the pulpit and the press, and those
torrents of calumny, denunciation, and abuse, poured
forth by a thousand fluent tongues, against whomsoever deserted the ark of the covenant, and allied himself to the uncircumcised Philistines.

The democratic party were not wanting in efforts
to enlist the powerful aid of religion upon their side.
They made friends with the Baptists and other dissenters from the established creed, who cherished an
hereditary hatred toward the congregational priesthood, and who were struggling to escape from the legal disabilities with which their heresies still continued
to be visited. These clerical allies, in imitation of
their opponents, mingled religion with politics, and
sought to turn the excited feelings of their hearers,
into political channels. They were denounced by the
regular order, as hedge-priests, sectarians, wild enthu-
siasts, puffed up with a ridiculous over-estimate of
their spiritual endowments, ignorant, turbulent, bad
men, who in attempting to overturn the platform on
which was raised the sober edifice of congregational-
ism, sought to destroy the foundations of society, and
to mix up all things in chaotic confusion.

In this situation of affairs, democratical principles
were still enabled to gain the ascendency in New England, and to become the prevailing creed, by the joint
effect of two separate causes, each of which was perhaps potent enough in itself to have ensured the victory.

Though the professors of these principles were proscribed by the New England oligarchy, declared destitute of any claims to attention or indulgence, represented
as wild political fanatics, the disciples of Robespierre,
desirous to abolish religion, and to root up morals, to
destroy the natural instincts of humanity, and to sprin-
kle the land with fire and blood; they found encourage-

ment, support and aid, where there was the least reason to expect it, to wit, at the hands of the southern slave-holders. Who could have anticipated that the apostle of American democracy should himself have been an aristocrat and a despot! Yet so it was. Jefferson is revered, and justly, as the earliest, ablest, boldest and most far-going of those who became the expounders and advocates of the democratical system in America. Most of the others, whether leaders or followers, seemed driven on by a blind instinct. They felt, but did not reason. Jefferson based his political opinions upon general principles of human nature. Men were supposed, in other systems of politics, to be helpless, blind, incapable children, unfit to take care of themselves, and certain, if the experiment were tried, to do themselves presently some dreadful and irreparable harm. Jefferson argued, that however weak and blind men might be, yet their own strength and eye-sight were still their surest hope, and best dependance. If aid were elsewhere sought, whence could it come? These guides, these guardians, these governors, who are they? Are they not men, weak and blind? Worse yet, men ready to betray the confidence placed in them, and under pretence of protection, themselves to plunder and oppress? It is therefore better to make each man, blind and weak though he be, the chief guardian of his own welfare. Subject no man to the arbitrary control of another, who if he may be wiser and better, may just as likely, be blinder and be worse. Such necessary rules of social conduct as the judgment of the majority shall approve, let them be laws, so long as that judgment continues to approve them; and let the laws govern, and the laws alone.

Such was the political creed of Jefferson. It is the creed of democracy; and he espoused it with a warm, an active, almost a fanatic zeal. The perfect political equality of all men; the absolute right of every man to be guided by his own pleasure and judgment, so long as he transgresses no law, and his equal claim to a fair participation in the enactment and repeal of every law; these were the very fundamental principles of this political system. Yet Jefferson remained all his life the tyrant of a plantation, in the enforcement of an usurped authority, either personally, or by his delegate, which he himself describes, as "a perpetual exercise of the most boisterous passions,—the most unremitting despotism on the one part, and degrading submission on the other." Ah Truth! 'Tis thee alone that men should reverence! Do they reverence men, it is an idolatry as base as if they bowed to stocks and stones. Men *are* blind and weak, the wisest and the best! But Truth,—it is unblemished, in itself complete, divine, pure, perfect!

Had Jefferson attempted to preach the full extent of his doctrines in his native state, he would doubtless have drawn down upon his head a storm of hatred and reproach, not rashly to have been encountered, nor easily to have been withstood. But that was an adventure of difficulty and peril, which he felt no call to undertake. Like Henry and Washington, and those other great men whose devoted patriotism and many virtues would make us willingly forget that on their own estates they were tyrants,—though he acknowledged the trampled rights and crying wrongs of the disenfranchised half of his fellow countrymen, he yet despaired to make any impression upon the ignorance, the prejudices, the blind and narrow self-interest of the privileged class, and he contented himself with now and then a protest against a system of tyrannical usurpation, which carried away by custom and convenience, he still continued to uphold through the support of his own example.

The democracy which he preached at home, was democracy among the aristocrats;—and the perfect equality of all the members of the privileged order, has ever been a popular doctrine in all aristocracies. The "love of liberty" is a phrase under which are included two feelings of a very distinct, and sometimes of an opposite kind. Each individual is always the ardent and zealous champion of his own liberty, because the hatred of all extraneous control, the desire to be solely governed by the free impulses of his own mind, is a part of the constitution of human nature too essential ever to be wanting. Hence it is that we find kings and emperors among the champions of liberty and equal rights, by which *they* understand, the liberty of governing their own realms without foreign control, and the absolute equality of all crowned heads. Have we not seen the Austrian and Russian despots, leaguing with the king of Prussia and the haughty aristocracy of England to vindicate the *liberties* of Europe against the usurpation and tyrannies of a Bonaparte? When the chains threatened to bind *them*, when they were like to be compelled to bow their necks beneath the yoke of a master, who more sensitive than they to the degradations of servitude? Who more zealous, more earnest, more sincere in liberty's cause? Alexander of Russia turned a demagogue, and the princes of Germany harangued their subjects, not in the dry and austere style of absolute authority, but with the supplicating tone, the humble and insinuating eloquence, the flattery and fair promises, with which ambitious men, in popular states, seek to inveigle the popular favor.

This passion for personal liberty burns fiercely in the soul of every human being, and no where fiercer than in the hearts of an aristocracy bred to its possession, and who have learned to estimate its value by having constantly before their eyes the terrible contrast of servitude.

But the "love of liberty" has also another meaning. It describes a passion not for individual freedom, but for the freedom of all men; a wide, expansive feeling, the offspring of benevolence, the height of philanthropy, the extension to others of that which we find best and most desirable for ourselves; its extension not only to those to whom we are bound by familiar ties of interest and sympathy, our friends and kindred, or those whom however otherwise unconnected with us, we still assimilate to ourselves by

2*

some real or fanciful analogies; but absolutely, its extension to all men,—the love of freedom wherever, by whomsoever, exercised, as an abstract good.

It is evident that the love of liberty in this high sense, can shine out in perfection only from hearts the warmest, souls the most cultivated, minds the most lofty, unclouded and serene. But fragments of it, sparks from this celestial flame, sometimes but dim, the smallest atom almost, and that too buried, and quite smothered amid the ashes of selfish passions,—yet dim or bright, smothered or burning clear, this passion for universal freedom is still a part of human nature, but a part of it which lies dead and dark in uncultivated souls, and which only begins to kindle and to blaze, in the forward and quick feeling minds of a polished and reflecting age.

To this latter feeling, noble and refined, and which lurks, however invisible, even in the hearts of a slave-holding aristocracy, Jefferson did not dare to appeal. He was content to act the humble and comparatively inconsiderable part of a champion for equality among the aristocrats; and laboring to forget that the unprivileged class—some of whom, to believe the voice of common report, were his own children,—had any greater capacities or rights than beasts of burden, he curtailed the expansive and universal clauses of his political creed, till the mantle of liberty which should have extended its protection to every citizen, embraced within its torn and mutilated folds only the privileged order.

The oligarchical party in the southern aristocracies, the aristocracy, so to speak, of the privileged order, though they were richer and better educated than their neighbors of the common sort, had no such moral hold upon men's minds as the hierarchy of the north. The prejudices in favor of family and rank to which they were indebted for the general acknowledgment of their superiority, had been shaken by the revolution, and after a short and ineffectual resistance, the oligarchical party in Virginia and the Carolinas was completely broken down by the vigorous assault which the Jeffersonians made upon them. Henceforward the most complete and democratical equality among all the members of the privileged class, became the settled and established creed of southern politics. But the Jeffersonian party, while it aimed at overturning the oligarchies of the southern states, aimed also at supremacy in the federal government; and the same victory which assured their ascendency at home, raised their leader to the presidential chair.

From that elevation, Jefferson stretched forth a helping hand to the struggling democrats of New England; and by means of the honors and offices within his gift, he enlisted into their cause divers mercenaries of courage and ability, who were seduced from the ranks of the hierarchy, and having taken pay at the hands of democracy, fought valiantly in her cause.

As the Jeffersonians continued for twenty-four years at the head of the federal government, and during all that time, consoled, comforted, aided and abetted the democrats of New England, the party began presently to grow somewhat more respectable; and as the advantages to be derived from belonging to it became more and more numerous, converts were multiplied, and presently there might be numbered among them even some of the clergy and the lawyers.

It is evident that this process alone would at length have given to democratical principles a nominal, if not a practical ascendency. But as I have mentioned, there was another cause in operation, in itself sufficient to have ensured an ultimate, and a more substantial triumph. Notwithstanding the grand array of followers mustered by the hierarchy, there were many among them who at heart were traitors to the cause. They had been bred up in a horror of democracy, which they were taught to regard as the concentration of all possible evil, and to the repetition of certain dogmas containing the substance of the oligarchical creed. Yet insensibly they became democrats themselves; and the superior order, to maintain its

influence and preserve its ascendency, was soon obliged to descend to all those arts of popularity, which
when practised by their opponents, they had denounced as fit only for demagogues.

The power of the priestly and legal hierarchy consisted in their monopoly of talent and education, and in a
certain superstitious reverence with which they were
regarded by the people. So long as these two sources
of power continued in full operation, their credit could
not be shaken, and their influence carried every thing
before it. But with the progress of time, and the increasing wealth of the community, education became
more general, books and periodicals were multiplied,
and knowledge was disseminated. The oligarchical
order lost their superiority in this respect, and with it,
they lost the awe and veneration of the people. To
complete their discomfiture, they quarrelled among
themselves on certain points of theology; and as the
dispute waxed warm, the parties to it became more intent upon destroying each other's influence, than upon
maintaining their own.

Such was the end of the oligarchical rule in New
England, of which some vestiges yet remain, but of
which the life and spirit has departed. The political
creed, generally and it may be said, universally, professed,—albeit the ancient regime has still many secret adherents,—is a purely democratic creed, and the
struggle for influence and office between contending
politicians, turns wholly upon the question, who among
them are the best democrats, who are most devoted to
the interests of the people?

Though the New England States formed that part
of the Union which held out longest against the general
reception of the democratic theory, yet the equal distribution of property, the more extensive diffusion of
knowledge, and that feeling of personal independence
and equality long cherished among the people, made
them from the beginning, the best adapted of all the
states, to enter fully into the spirit of democracy, and to
display, in the most striking light, the advantages of

that form of government. Accordingly it may be said that the New England States, notwithstanding some gross defects in their political and social system, afford, at this moment, the most remarkable approach, any where to be found, toward the theoretical perfection of ideal democracy.

But it was not in New England alone, that the progress of the democratical experiment met with opposition. The middle states—New York, New Jersey and Pennsylvania,—at the era of the revolution, contained an oligarchy of rich land-holders, who assumed, and for some time retained, the exclusive political control of their respective communities. To this landed aristocracy the lawyers joined themselves, as also the clergy, whose influence though by no means equal to that of their brethren in New England, was far from contemptible. The yeomanry of those states were in general, rude and ignorant. As there was no system of public schools, many of them were unable to read; and if they were free from some of the prejudices of the New Englanders, they were far behind them, in knowledge, industry, self-respect, and that sensibility of mind and heart, which civilization produces.

If the members of the oligarchical party in these states, could have agreed among themselves, they might long have maintained their influence and authority. But presently they quarrelled, and divided into hostile and bitter factions. Certain persons among them, whether to secure the popular favor by putting themselves forward as the champions of popular rights, or some of them perhaps, sincere converts to the creed, soon declared themselves the patrons and champions of democracy; but as they had a powerful resistance to contend against at home, and opponents who, though discomfited, still kept the field, they were fain to yield the precedence to Jefferson and his southern supporters, and to be content with the second part, where they would gladly have claimed the first.

As to the states north-west of the Ohio, which are now beginning to occupy so conspicuous a place in the

Union, their origin is so recent, and their population
has hitherto been so much engrossed with the cares
and occupations incident to new settlements, that as
yet, they have exercised but a limited influence upon
the sentiment and opinions of the country. That influence, however has been almost purely democratic,
and from the very birth of those communities, democracy has always been their prevailing political creed.

These slight and imperfect historical sketches lead
us to a fact of the greatest importance towards a correct understanding of the progress, present state, and
future prospects of political opinion and political action,
in America. Ever since the formation of the federal
constitution, down almost to the present moment,
strange as it may seem, the democratic party of the
Union has been headed, guided, governed and controlled by certain slave-holding aristocrats of the south;
—Jefferson, Madison, Monroe, and Jackson have been
successively, its leaders, and its idols.

Under Jefferson, theoretical democracy was a new
thing; and it was embraced with all the warmth which
novelty is apt to inspire. It formed a principal topic
of public discussion; and was defended, if not always
by sound reasonings and substantial arguments, yet
with the enthusiastic zeal of sincere conviction.

But presently the public attention was diverted into
other channels, and became engrossed by matters
with which democracy had little or no connection.
Under Madison, the great question was, whether the
United States should resent and repel the insults and
the wrongs heaped upon them by foreign powers, and
if so, whether they should make war against the
tyrant Bonaparte, or the English aristocracy. The
democratic party was in general favorable to Bonaparte, for he was the child, and he had declared himself the heir, and had seized upon the inheritance of
the French Revolution. But the very fact that they
were led by irrational sympathies, and the ardor of
political controversy, to wink at, to apologize for, and
almost to defend, the violence and outrages of a mili-

tary usurper, was so contrary to their principles, and produced such a confusion of ideas, that the great doctrines of their creed dropped almost out of sight, and whether or not one was favorable to a war with Great Britain, presently became the test of political orthodoxy,—a test altogether aside from the fundamental principles of the democratical system.

Under Monroe, the great controversies of the day, respected the protection of American industry; a pure question of national economy, upon which people took sides, for the most part, not according to their political opinions, but according to the views they entertained of the effect which this protection would be likely to have upon their own private pecuniary interests.

During the administrations of Madison and Monroe though the democratic creed was predominant throughout the greater part of the country, and though during the interval, it achieved its final triumph in New England, yet beginning in those states where it had earliest prevailed, and extending gradually to the rest, it degenerated almost into a mere form of words without force or vitality.

This state of things is easily explained. The leaders of the democratic, as of all other political parties, were for the most part adventurers,—mere soldiers of fortune, who sought credit, honors, office, and power, by the zealous advocacy of principles which they saw to have many adherents, but for which they themselves felt no very devoted love, apart from the advancement to which they hoped these principles might help them. That advancement attained, the party triumphant, themselves in office, they looked with feelings of contempt upon the ladder by which they had ascended, they were even desirous to cast it down, lest perchance stronger men might climb up thereby, and thrust them from their places.

The mouths of the prophets being closed, the people wandered as sheep without a shepherd; and though the democratic creed was publicly professed by all, there lurked in the hearts of many a cold indifference, a sneering scepticism, a silent disbelief.

With Monroe terminated the direct line of the Jeffersonian succession; and then began that struggle for the possession of the presidential chair, which has ever since been so pertinaciously kept up,—a contest in the earlier part of which no one had a larger share than John C. Calhoun, a person likely to figure in history, for the instruction and amusement of mankind.

That able, but restless and unprincipled man, first came into public life as a leading democrat; but that was at a time when democracy in its current sense, meant little more than hostility to Great Britain. Coming from South Carolina as he did, it was but natural that he should be, as he was, a thorough aristocrat; and that not content with the mere supremacy of one race over another, he desired to concentrate all political power in the hands of a chosen few, of whom he himself should be the chief and leader.

But satisfied by the result of his earlier experiments, that the aristocratical party was not strong enough to bestow that power at which he aimed, and that even if it were, he would encounter on that side, some dangerous competitors; he turned short about, and recollecting the success of Jefferson, resolved to try a new means of advancement, and to summon up, from the slumbers of some sixteen years, the genius of Democracy, which he fondly hoped to be able to convert into the mere servant of his political schemes.

The magician was able, and the charm worked well. Dimly in the distance, hazy and indistinct, appeared a figure, whose broad proportions told that time and slumber had but increased its stature and its power. One foot upon the western prairies, the other amid the snowy hills of New England, it strode across the land. The people saw and worshipped. A new enthusiasm was kindled in their hearts. Nothing could resist it. Those who put themselves forward as the priests, the favored, the chosen of this new avatar of democratical reform, were received with confidence, welcomed with acclamation, and entrusted with power. So far the thing worked well, and he who had called up this apparition of democracy, succeeded in installing, as its high-priest and chosen minister, a man who had been a slave-trader, a man who was a slave-holder, who preached liberty and equality at Washington, but who at home was the despot of the Hermitage!

His purposes thus far accomplished, he who had raised the spirit sought to lay it. But it defies his power. Among the crowd of hypocritical worshippers and blind devotees, there are found a few whose homage is at once enlightened and sincere. They look upon democracy not with a stupid gaze of admiration, unable to distinguish between the apparent and the real, but with a discernment, upon which the arts of political cunning will not easily impose. Democracy, in their estimation, is not a mere phantom by whose aid the credulous may be deluded, and offices and honors be secured to the deluders; it is a real existence, a substantial thing, a powerful and essential means of advancing the public welfare. It is to these adherents, that Democracy now entrusts herself. From being the nursling, the pupil, the instrument of Southern despotism, she is about to become a rival and an enemy. The allegiance she has so long yielded to Southern step-fathers, she will yield no longer. The alliance is broken; and conscious of superior power and higher claims, Democracy demands homage and submission, where hitherto she has paid them.

She prepares to act. She points in sorrow, shame and anger, to the capital turned into a slave market; to the broad plains of the south, watered with the blood of their cultivators; and to the thousand petty despots, each arbitrary lord and irresponsible tyrant, upon his own plantation.

3

It is in vain that southern oppressors console themselves with ideas of the insignificance of those who make the first assault. They may ridicule them as fools, fanatics, women. What of that? Does the result of an attack depend upon the prudence, or the wisdom of those who have volunteered for the forlorn hope? What matter who or what they are, those who rush blindly and devotedly upon the open-mouthed cannon, the leveled bayonets of the enemy? They are but food for powder, and they know it. In every great cause it is necessary that some should perish. But if the cause be great, for one that falls, ten will be found ambitious so to suffer!

It is in vain we at the North, cry out that the contest is unseasonable and premature. It has begun; it must go on. Grant that over-zealous and fanatical haste has precipitated a struggle which we would gladly have deferred, and slumbering out our own time in quiet, have thrust upon the days of our children. No matter. In this thing we cannot have our way. The trumpet has sounded; the bold and unquiet are rushing to the field. We may cry peace, peace,—but there is no peace. Fight we must, upon one side or the other. The contest is begun already, and will soon become general. In such a struggle there can be no neutrality. It is time to be choosing under which banner we will stand!

To every one at the North, Democracy is to some extent familiar. Many have doubtless viewed it through a deceptive medium, and have seen it only as it has been reflected by ignorance, or distorted by prejudice; all however have formed some opinion about it, and that opinion is founded upon knowledge either actual or imaginary. But Despotism, the despotism of the slave states, is a thing known at the north only by name, and in general. Few have seen it; fewer still have studied it; and the greater part are totally ignorant of its real character.

Before enlisting, it is well to know the cause in which we are to serve. It is the purpose of the following pages to exhibit the system of social polity established in the southern states, such as it is in its operation and effects; not in particular and accidental instances, but generally, and by virtue of those laws of human nature upon which the working of social and political institutions must depend.

This inquiry is necessary for our own satisfaction. Without making it, how can we act either reasonably or safely? Here is a question with two sides to it, and one side or the other, we must take. How can we choose without knowledge? Despotism may be an excellent thing, well entitled to our warmest support; but how can we know it to be so, without knowing what it is?

Yet are we stopped short, in the very threshold of this inquiry, by the threats and execrations of the south. Dare to inquire; dare look behind the veil that hides our private doings; dare question us, or any of our acts, and we dissolve the Union! Such an impertinence is lawful cause of war, and we will wage it! Indeed!—It is necessary then to weigh these threats.

The Union of the States has been made the occasion and the theme of a great deal of unmeaning declamation. An idea seems to prevail, that excellent a thing as the Union is, the people, ignorant and short-sighted, may sometime take it into their heads to think otherwise; and therefore it is necessary to create a *prejudice* in favor of the Union,—a sort of feeling for it like that feeling of loyalty, which has often upheld a throne in spite of the vices and the tyranny of him who sat upon it.

Under a democratic government, prejudices of this sort are not only useless, they are highly mischievous; they are but manacles and fetters put into the hands of the artful and designing, by means of which the people are bound, and shorn, against their interest, and against their judgment.

The men who formed the Union were neither better nor wiser than ourselves. For certain arguments and reasons in its favor, they formed it; for certain arguments and reasons in its favor, we should sustain it; not for itself; for in itself, it is neither good nor bad. It may be either, as circumstances are.

What are these reasons and arguments in favor of the Union? Briefly these; that the Union serves to protect us against aggressions from abroad, and civil war at home; that it is the best guarantee of our independence and our freedom.

But suppose this same Union to be made the pretext for a violent interference with our dearest rights? Suppose that under pretence of preserving the Union, we are to be deprived of the liberty of the press, the liberty of discussion, the liberty of thought,—nay more, the liberty of feeling, the right of sympathy with those who suffer? Suppose this Union requires to be cemented with blood, and that we are called upon to surrender up the noblest of our sons and daughters to be tortured to death by southern whips, for the grievous sin of having denounced despotism with the generous emphasis of freedom?

Are we ready to bow thus submissively before the grim and bloody shrine of this political Moloch? Are we prepared to make these sacrifices? When the thing has changed its nature, what though it still retain its former name? Though it be called a Union, what is it but a base subjection, a miserable servitude?

Some eighty years ago, we had a Union with Great Britain, a Union that had lasted for near two centuries, a cherished Union, the recollection of which kindled a glow in every American bosom; not a fraternal Union merely, but closer yet, maternal, filial. That connection had many things to recommend it. It sustained our weakness; it brightened our obscurity; it made us partakers in the renown of Britain, and part and parcel of a great nation. What curses, eighty years ago, would have blighted the parricide, who should have gone about to sever that connection, so dear, so beneficial!

The mother country, not satisfied with the affection of her daughter, sought to abuse her power, and to extort a tribute. But were all the advantages of our Union with Britain to be given up, merely to avoid the payment of a paltry tax on tea? Were all the calamities of civil war to be hazarded, all the miseries of a hostile invasion, intrigues with foreign powers, and their dangerous interference, public debts, standing armies, the risk of anarchy, and of military usurpation?

Yes, all, said our fathers, all is to be risked, rather than surrender our pecuniary independence, rather than become tributary to a British parliament; rather than be taxed at the pleasure of the mother country. A Union upon such terms is a mockery; it is not the Union we have loved and cherished. We scorn it, and we spurn it.

So our fathers said. And when it is undertaken to deprive us not of our money,—which, for the sake of peace, we might be willing to part with,—but of that whose value money cannot estimate; when it is attempted to shut out from us the atmosphere, the essential life-breath of liberty; when it is sought to gag our free mouths, to forbid and stop the beating of our free hearts; to subdue us by penal statutes into a servile torpidity, and an obsequious silence, shall we hesitate one moment to repel this impudent effort of despotism, because, if we refuse to submit, it will endanger the Union? Perish the Union; let it ten times perish, from the moment it becomes inconsistent with humanity and with freedom!

Should South Carolina declare that war, for which, as she asserts, she has such lawful cause, and march an army northward to enforce silence at the point of the bayonet, the sons of those men who fought at Lexington and Bunker Hill, will perhaps know how to repel the invaders; and those states which furnished soldiers, generals, arms and money, to re-conquer Carolina from Cornwallis and Rawdon, will be able, peradventure, to vindicate their own liberties against any force which Carolinian despots may be able to send against them.

In this matter, let us learn a lesson from these very

3*

Carolinians. It is now some twenty years since, that South Carolina considered herself aggrieved, by what she esteemed the usurpations of the federal government. She accused Congress of levying taxes, which the constitution did not authorize. No matter whether the charge were true or false; those who made it, doubtless were sincere. And did they quietly submit to this aggression, rather than endanger the Union by their resistance? Not they.

Though denounced at the north as rebels and traitors, though coldly looked upon even by those states which shared the grievance, and which had promised to assist in the redress; though unaided and alone, and harassed too by a large party at home, who threatened, in the event of hostilities, to take sides with the general government,—the South Carolinian leaders magnanimously dared to "calculate the value of the Union;" and they concluded, like brave men as they were, that rather than give place to what they esteemed oppression, rather than be ruled in a manner which no constitution authorized, rather than submit to an usurped authority, it were better to break the Union, and risk a war.

The bold are always less in danger than the timid. The strength and resources of South Carolina compared with those of the remaining states, were but as dust in the balance; yet rather than provoke violent resistance, by an exercise of doubtful authority, Congress yielded; the tariff was modified, and the principle of pure and unlimited protection was totally abandoned.

If South Carolina calculated the value of the Union, when it was only a question of tariffs and of taxes, shall we hesitate to calculate its value, when the dearest rights of manhood are in danger? when we are commanded to submit in silence, and not dare to criticise the despotism that controls us?

Let them break the Union, if they choose; it is a matter wherein they are free to act. But before they break it, they will do well to revise their calculations of its value. What the southern States would be, if they stood alone; what elements they have within themselves of civilization, greatness, safety, strength, and power; what sort of a nation they would form, if isolated, and cut off from intercourse with their northern neighbors, is an inquiry which will find its proper place hereafter. But there are some more obvious considerations, which our southern friends will do well deliberately to weigh, before they judge fit to dissolve the confederacy, and to break up those constitutional guarantees by which they are now protected. As sister states, talk as they may of the mischievous intermeddlings of the north, they enjoy privileges and an impunity, they never could expect from a foreign, an offended and a hostile nation. Those unhappy fugitives who had once reached the borders of States then truly free, could never be reclaimed; as between independent nations, the tortures and the death wantonly inflicted upon northern citizens would no longer be regarded with a careless unconcern; and how many forays from the frontiers, how many crusades of liberty would there not be undertaken, by men anxious to redeem from slavery, if not their own relatives, those at least whom they regard as brothers? These collisions, sooner or later, would inevitably bring on war; and the broad banner of emancipation, with fifty thousand men to back it, once displayed, and gayly flaunting on the southern breeze, farewell, and forever, to the despotisms of the south!

But here we are met again.

If you have no regard for yourselves, say our southern friends, fool-hardy and fanatical, if you do not tremble at that annihilation with which we threaten you,—pray, at least, have some consideration for us. Remember the delicacy of our situation. Do you wish to involve us in all the horrors of a servile insurrection? Why scatter "seed that will presently germinate, and sooner or later will ripen into a harvest of desolation and blood?"

How this solemn objurgation is to be reconciled with the loud threat of severing the Union, and enforcing silence and submission at the point of the bayonet, those can best tell who are accustomed to join that threat and this objurgation. In the mean time, we may remark a curious analogy.

When the Jeffersonian aristocrats of the south first began to preach the doctrines of democracy, it was in terms like these that they were greeted by the northern oligarchs. "Bad men, wicked, turbulent, seditious, fanatical, contrivers of mischief, what mean ye, what do ye desire? Would you uproot society from its foundations? Would you abolish religion? Would you overturn morality? Would you do away with government? Would you dissolve all ties? Would you put an end to the established order and rightful propriety of things?

"What?—Do you seek to elevate the most ignorant and abandoned of society to a level with us, their betters and natural superiors? Would you deprive us of that power and authority which God has seen fit to entrust to us, which is our natural right, and which we exercise so much to our own honor, and the benefit of those we rule?

"Yes:—and you talk of guillotines too; you dare to denounce us as tyrants; you are organizing a conspiracy for a general insurrection, and for the slaughter and destruction of all good men. Out upon ye, ye Robespierres, ye Dantons, ye blood-thirsty knaves! Democrats forsooth!—Jacobins, atheists, murderous villains! Why scatter seed that will presently germinate, and sooner or later, will ripen into a harvest of desolation and blood?"

So they preached, and so they prated, from pulpits and the press. Yes, and they passed laws too. There was the Alien Law, whereby all *dangerous foreigners* were to be excluded from the country; and there was the *Sedition Law*, intended to gag the press, and to subject those who spoke disrespectfully of the powers that were, to the penalty of fine and imprisonment.

When the southern aristocrats offered to our fathers the precious boon of democracy, such was the loathing, such the struggling reluctance, and such the passionate indignation with which they received, and would have rejected it. And now that we, in our turn, recollecting with gratitude, the good offices of the South, seek to repay the favor, and commend to their lips that same draught, of their own concocting, which however bitter to the taste has health and vigor in it, life and strength; they in their turn, with the rage and malice of spoiled and wayward children, reject the medicine, snap at the nurse, and load their best friends with frantic maledictions.

Let us be patient with them;—they are sick. Yes very sick; and when the fit is on, light-headed. Compared with their disorder, all the fierce fevers that infest their clime are mild and trivial. What angry passions, what tormenting fury, what anxious fears, what cares, forebodings, terrors, tremors, seize upon the despot, when he feels the sceptre slipping from his grasp, and sees his subjects ready to claim their freedom?

How he has governed; how he has trodden under foot men good as he; what wrongs he has inflicted; what cruel, bloody, barbarous, bitter wrongs, he knows full well. He dreads a retribution; he shakes and changes color when he thinks how just that retribution, and if complete, how ample! Though he be brave, a coward conscience chases away his courage; a cold sweat stands upon his brow; and he becomes as fearful as a child, while phantom images of guilty actions flit round his pillow,—

> By the apostle Paul, *shadows* to-night
> Have struck more terror to the soul of Richard,
> Than could the substance of ten thousand soldiers
> Armed in proof.

Those frightful visions which afflict the south; they are but shadows. One act of generous justice, of prudent justice, which yields what it can safely keep no longer, shall absolve the greatest tyrant of them all, and send him forth, a neophyte from the baptismal font of freedom, pure, washed, and spotless ; and he may walk, like Sylla the ex-dictator, through the streets of Rome, unguarded, undisguised, and meet at every turn one he has injured, yet never suffer harm !

But an act like this requires a moral courage a noble-ness of soul, not common.   That justice is the highest expediency, is a maxim which our southern friends sometimes repeat, but a doctrine which they have not the wisdom, nor the magnanimity to practise.

In the mean time they need our help, our most judi-cious care.   But to afford it, we ought to understand their actual condition ; we must make ourselves fa-miliar with that melancholy state of things, of which they are at once the champions and the victims.

And this knowledge is necessary to us not on their account only, but also on our own.   We form a part of the same nation.   It is hardly possible for one mem-ber to suffer, and the disease not to extend sympatheti-cally to the whole body.   Suppose a general insurrec-tion at the south,—who would be called upon for men, arms, and money, to put it down ?   Suppose the slaves rise upon their masters,—is it not the democrats of the north, who are constitutionally bound to draw their swords in behalf of despotism ?—those very democrats. who have said and sworn, that resistance to tyrants is obedience to God ?

Let us learn, then, the full extent of this obligation ; let us know what that system is, which we may thus be called upon to uphold !

CHAPTER FIRST.

THE RELATION OF MASTER AND SLAVE.

SECTION I.

The Origin of Slavery.

THE relation of master and slave, like most other kinds of despotism, has its origin in war. By the confession of its warmest defenders, slavery is at best, but a substitute for homicide.

Savages take no prisoners; or those they do take, they first torture, and then devour. But when the arts of life have made some progress, and the value of labor begins to be understood, it is presently discovered that to eat prisoners, is not the most profitable use to which they can be put. Accordingly their lives are spared; and they are compelled to labor for the benefit of their captors. Such is the origin of Slavery.

It was formerly a practice in America to sell as slaves such Indian prisoners as were captured during the frequent wars waged with the aboriginal inhabitants. But the great mass of those unfortunate persons held in servitude throughout the southern states, derive their origin from another source.

A Virginian planter deduces the legitimacy of his dominion by the following process. Your great-grandmother being captured by a certain African prince,—in a war, undertaken, doubtless, for the mere purpose of making prisoners,—was sold upon the coast of Guinea to a certain Yankee slave-trader; and being transported by him to James River, was there sold to

a certain tobacco planter. In time, your great-grandmother died; but she left children, to which as a part
of her produce, the owner of the mother was justly
entitled. From that owner, through diverse aliena-
tions and descents, the title has passed to me; and as
you are descended from the woman above referred to,
it is quite clear, how perfectly reasonable and just my
empire is.

Whether in point of logic and morals, the above
deduction is completely satisfactory, is not now the
question. The nature of the master's claim is stated
here, only as an assistance towards obtaining a clearer apprehension of the relations which must grow out
of it.

SECTION II.

General idea of a Slave-holding Community.

Slavery then is a continuation of the state of war.
It is true that one of the combatants is subdued and
bound; but the war is not terminated. If I do not
put the captive to death, this apparent clemency does
not arise from any good-will towards him, or any extinction on my part of hostile feelings and intentions.
I spare his life merely because I expect to be able to
put him to a use more advantageous to myself. And
if the captive, on the other hand, feigns submission,
still he is only watching for an opportunity to escape
my grasp, and if possible to inflict upon me evils as
great as those to which I have subjected him.

War is justly regarded, and with the progress of
civilization it comes every day more and more to be
regarded, as the very greatest of social calamities.
The introduction of slavery into a community, amounts
to an eternal protraction of that calamity, and a uni-

versal diffusion of it through the whole mass of society, and that too, in its most ferocious form.

When a country is invaded by a hostile army, within the immediate neighborhood of the camp it becomes impossible to make any effectual resistance. However fierce may be the hate with which they look upon the invaders, the inhabitants within the range of their scouting parties, are obliged to submit. They are made to furnish wood, forage and provisions; they are forced to toil in the entrenchment of the camp; their houses are liable to be ransacked and plundered, and their women to be subjected to the lusts of the soldiers. Upon certain emergencies, the ablest bodied among them will be armed, surrounded by foreign squadrons, and obliged to fight against their own countrymen. But though plundered without mercy, and liable to the most frightful injuries, yet as their services are valuable, and even necessary to the invaders, they must be allowed to retain the means of sustaining existence; and if under all the discouragements to which they are subjected, they neglect or refuse to cultivate their fields, they must be driven to work at the point of the bayonet, lest the invaders might suffer from their negligence, and fall short of forage and provisions.

Now every plantation in the slave states is to be looked upon as the seat of a little camp, which overawes and keeps in subjection the surrounding peasantry. The master claims and exercises over his slaves all the rights of war above described, and others yet more terrible. Consider too that this infliction is not limited to a single neighborhood, as in the case of an invading army, but is scattered and diffused over the whole extent of the country; nor is it temporary as in the other case, but constant and perpetual. It is by taking a view like this, that we are enabled to form a primary, general, outline idea of the social condition of a slave-holding community.

4

SECTION III.

The Empire claimed by the Master.

The relation of master and slave, as we may conclude from the foregoing statements, is a relation purely of force and terror. Its only sanction is the power of the master; its best security, the fears of the slave. It bears no resemblance to any thing like a social compact. Mutual interest, faith, truth, honesty, duty, affection, good-will, are not included, in any form whatever, under this relation.

But let us descend somewhat into particulars, and inquire more specifically what is the nature of the empire claimed by the master.

That empire is the most absolute and comprehensive which it is possible to imagine. The master considers his slaves as existing solely for his benefit. He has purchased, and he possesses them for his own sake, not for theirs. His sole object is to obtain the greatest possible profit out of them.

Perhaps to obtain this greatest profit, it may be necessary to feed them plentifully, and clothe them well, and to allow them certain intervals of rest, and other like indulgences. If the master is of that opinion, he acts accordingly. But in so acting he merely pursues his own advantage. If he has adopted the contrary opinion, if he imagines that he can save more by retrenchment than he can make by outlay, in that case he cuts down the allowance of rest, food, and clothing, and endeavours to supply the deficiency by the stimulus of the lash. It is a mere matter of calculation either way; not a question of morals, but a mere problem of domestic economy. The slaves are not thought of as sentient beings, but as machines to be kept in profitable operation.

One who visits a slave-holding community, for the first time, if he have any feeling of humanity and any spirit of observation, is puzzled and shocked, by what appears to him a series of distressing uncongruities. Men who in their relations towards those whom they acknowledge as fellow-citizens, fulfil with promptitude and exactness all the duties of benevolence and justice, in their conduct towards their slaves, often seem destitute of all human sympathies.

This course of action results from the very position of a master; and men naturally of the most benevolent dispositions, become reconciled to it by force of custom and education. The soldier, frank, generous, warm-hearted, ready to share his last dollar with his comrade, from the moment he enters an enemy's country becomes a violent, fierce, and brutal robber, who plunders whenever he has opportunity, without hesitation or remorse.

It is exactly so with the master of slaves. His conduct towards his fellow-citizens, and towards his servants, is regulated by rules and considerations totally distinct. In making this distinction, he is supported by the laws of the land, and the dogmas of the church; upheld by the example and countenance of his friends and neighbors; and encouraged by the approbation, open or implied, of all the world. If nobody finds fault with his conduct, why should he think of changing it? Why relinquish a lordship and a revenue, which every body tells him he does right to retain?

The value of this lordship, and the amount of this revenue, would be nothing at all, if instead of looking steadfastly, and with a single eye, to his own interest, the master should trouble himself about the well-being of his slaves. Their well-being evidently requires the liberty on their part of pursuing their own happiness, according to their own notions of it; and it clearly demands the disposal at their pleasure of the entire fruits of their own labor. That is, it requires the complete cessation of the master's empire. But it is impossible for the same thing to be and not to be at the same time; so that whoever wishes to retain the character of a master, and to exercise the prerogatives which that character confers and implies, is driven, by an invincible necessity, to disregard the well-being of his slaves, and to consider solely his own profit. Whether indeed that profit is best promoted by retaining the character of master at all; whether the master's interest, upon a full and comprehensive view of it, might not best be advanced by ceasing to be a master, is a question not now under discussion.

But in communities where all are free, how many are there, who regard any interest except their own? And wherein is the particular evil of slavery in this respect?

The peculiar evil of slavery consists in the very fact, that the slaves do not stand in this particular on a level with other men; they are not allowed to pursue their own interest. Not only is the well-being of the slaves disregarded by the masters, it is deliberately sacrificed. Left to themselves, like other men, they would pursue their own happiness, with success, less or greater. But their own happiness is a thing they are not suffered to pursue; and if yielding to the instinctive impulses of nature, they make the attempt, they are thwarted and driven back at every turn. Their own comfort or pleasure is a thing they are not allowed to think of at all; or to think of only at the risk of the lash.

In free communities, selfishness itself is enlisted into the service of benevolence. In order to obtain favors, it is necessary to confer them. Mutual services are secured by the attraction of mutual interest. But mutuality is a thing which slavery knows not. The master does not say, "Work for me, and I will give you in return wherewith to feed and clothe yourself and family." "Work for me," he says, "or I will torture you with the lash!" If the master supplies the slave with food and clothes, he does not do it by way of compensation for labor. It is a necessary expenditure, grudgingly laid out, in order to keep these human machines in motion. So far from being in the nature of a bargain or contract, slavery is nothing but violence upon one side, and compulsive obedience upon the other.

SECTION IV.

Means of enforcing the Master's Empire.

To sustain an empire of the kind above described, it is evident that the most vigorous means must be essential.

The means employed are chiefly three, to wit: *force, terror, fraud;* and according to the different tempers, talents, habits and notions of the master, one or the other of these three means, is made the key of his system.

I. Force. Those masters whose tempers are harsh, violent, and brutal, especially those who have never been softened by education, and who are strangers to the refinements of cultivated life, and others who are endowed with a firm, decided vigor that moves directly to the point, and by the shortest way, rely principally upon force.

Is the slave late in coming into the field? Twenty lashes. Is he idle? Thirty lashes. Does he disobey or neglect an order? Forty lashes. Does he negligently waste or destroy his master's property? Fifty lashes. Is he detected in a lie? Sixty lashes. Is he strongly suspected of theft? Seventy lashes. Does he say or do any thing that can be construed into insolence? Eighty lashes. Is he guilty of the slightest act of insubordination? One hundred lashes. Does he venture to run away? Let him be pursued by men and dogs, disabled by small shot, and so soon as he is taken, be flogged till he faints, then be worked in chains, locked up every night, and kept on half allowance, till his spirits are broken, and he becomes obedient and *contented.* Should he dare, upon any occasion, to offer any resistance? Let him be shot, stabbed, beat to the ground with a club, and should he not be killed in the process, as soon as he is so far recovered as to be able to stand, let him be subjected to all the discipline mentioned in the preceding sentence, and in addition, be flogged every night, for thirty days in succession.

4*

Such is a brief specimen of this system of plantation management, which some call cruel, but which those who follow it, merely describe as vigorous and efficient.

II. TERROR. But there are many men, naturally soft-hearted, who cannot look without some feelings of sympathetic pain, or at least of instinctive disgust, upon the body of an old man, or a woman perhaps, cut up with the lash, and scored with bloody gashes. The screams and outcries of the victims affect them disagreeably. They lack that harsh, unfeeling vigor, that stern promptitude, tyranny's steadiest and most efficient support. They endeavor to avoid the actual use of the whip, and to govern as far as possible, by the fear of it. They utter most tremendous threats, and strive to supply by bitter and alarming words, the place of action. But words, when they are found to be intended only as scare-crows, soon lose their efficacy. It is therefore necessary to maintain a steady stream, and the master who governs upon this wordy plan, soon comes to keep both himself and his slaves, in a constant state of irritation and ill feeling, by a process of fault-finding, scolding and threats, which becomes a habit, and goes on from morning to night, from day to day, from one year's end to another.

The slaves, who are thus made to feel every moment the weight of tyranny, and the humiliation of servitude, contract towards these snarling masters, the sincerest hate ; and from hating, being soon satisfied that with all their bluster, they have not the vigor to act up to their threats, they come presently to despise them. Whether they do well or ill, it is much the same, the master scolds on by habit ; but though he scolds, as yet he does not punish; and the bolder among the slaves soon begin to try experiments upon his patience. They are encouraged by the impunity of first transgressions to take greater and greater liberties. Their example finds imitators, till presently the whole plantation falls into a state of idleness and insubordinacy, which cannot be longer overlooked or endured.

The master must now give up the hope of revenue

from his slaves, or he must re-establish his authority.
He begins with moderate whippings. But his first attempts in this way are laughed at, or perhaps resisted.
He is alarmed and inflamed. Anger and fear supply
a vigor he does not naturally possess. He storms and
raves; flogs without mercy; shoots, stabs, chains, imprisons, starves, tortures. His nature seems to be
changed, and for a while he acts out the tyrant, in the
most savage and vindictive spirit of despotism. The
slaves bend and bow beneath this whirlwind of tyranny. The most turbulent and unmanageable,—those
of them at least, who have escaped with their lives,—
are sent off and sold; and presently things subside into their former state. The master grows ashamed of
his violence, and perhaps endures some twinges of remorse; the lash is disused, and the tongue supplies its
place. The discipline of the plantation is presently
relaxed; the servants become idle and insubordinate as
before; but this flattering calm cannot be relied upon;
a new storm of tyranny is secretly brewing, which
will burst at a moment when it is least expected.

III. Fraud. There are some masters, who pride
themselves upon their cunning and superior knowledge
of human nature, who make considerable use of fraud,
in the management of their slaves; but this is a means
employed only occasionally, and of which the efficacy
is not great.

One of the most usual applications of it, is the attempt to take advantage of the religious feelings of
the slaves, and to impress them with the idea, that
obedience, honesty towards their masters, humble submission, and other like plantation virtues, are religious
duties, which God commands, under the penalty of
damnation.

This stratagem is chiefly practised by slave-holding
clergymen and church members. The religious people of the South have been at the pains of preparing
a slave catechism; in some places they have established slave Sunday schools; and meetings for slave-worship are regularly held. The immediate agents

in these proceedings, are generally men of good intentions, but of very feeble understandings. They are mere tools in the hands of crafty hypocrites. The motive of their labors is doubtless the spiritual welfare of the slaves; but those by whom they are supported and encouraged, however tender a regard they may have for the salvation of their own souls, look upon religion among slaves merely as a means of plantation discipline; and please themselves with the idea that the more religious their slaves are, the easier they may be managed.

The agents employed in this double service of christianity and despotism, often succeed in kindling a warm spirit of devotion in the hearts of the slaves; but they have often occasion to deplore the inconsistency, the back-sliding, the delusion of their converts, who cannot be made to realize in its full extent, the enormous sinfulness of any attempt to elude that tyranny under which providence requires them patiently, and even joyfully to submit.

Deeply sympathizing with the sad, and almost angry feelings, with which these pious people are accustomed to lament the small success of their labors, and to accuse that stony-heartedness and inherent depravity which prevents even the converted slaves from attaining to the perfection of humility and obedience, the remark nevertheless may with all due deference, be permitted,—that so long as these pious teachers are able to construe ·the generous precepts of the gospel into an apology and a justification for tyranny, it cannot be considered very surprising that their pupils among the slaves, should instinctively acquire the art of reconciling with christian patience and submission, any and every means, whereby they can shake off, alleviate, or elude the usurped authority of their masters.

But this piece of pious fraud is falling into bad odor at the South. It has been found that religion causes an excitement among the slaves, both dangerous and troublesome. The rascals preach and pray when they

ought to be working. Besides, that religious enthusiasm, which kindles so readily in the most ignorant as
well as the most cultivated minds, gives rise to a dangerous exaltation of soul which makes the subjects
of it obstinate and unmanageable. Religion once
awakened in such savage and untaught bosoms, is apt
to degenerate into a superstitious fanaticism. The
gifted and the artful begin to see visions, and to dream
dreams. They are not content with being hearers
and pupils, they aspire to be speakers and teachers.
In their sermons and exhortations, it is the vices, the
luxury, the cruelty, the wickedness of the masters,
upon which they principally dwell, and whence they
draw examples and illustrations; and who knows but
some one more enraptured than the rest, may imagine
himself called, like Moses of old, to smite the task-
master, and to lead forth the oppressed children?

For these reasons the bible has been proscribed at
the South, as an incendiary publication; a book not
fit for slaves to read or hear. In some parts of the
country the catechism is looked upon with almost equal
suspicion; and many masters forbid their slaves to
hear any preacher, black or white, since they consider
religion upon a plantation as quite out of place, a thing
dangerous to the master's authority, and therefore not
to be endured in the slave.

Another stratagem, occasionally employed, when it
is desired to stimulate the efforts of the slaves, is the
distribution of little prizes among those who accomplish the greatest labor in the shortest time. This
contrivance works wonderfully well for a few days;
but as soon as it is discovered who are the ablest work-
men, the emulation is confined to them, and the greater
number, who have no chance to win the prize, presently relapse into their former apathy. Besides, this
distribution of prizes, is apt to give rise among the
slaves to the inconvenient notion, that they ought to
be paid for working, and the moment it ceases, they
work more grudgingly, unwillingly and negligently
than ever. Moreover it is expensive; in the minds of
most planters, a decisive objection against it.

But there are cases when force and terror cannot be employed, or fail to answer the purpose, and where stratagem is necessarily resorted to. The most common of these cases, are the detection and prevention of theft, and the recovery of runaways.

Upon these occasions, the most respectable and religious masters do not hesitate to descend to every petty art of fraud and falsehood. They have hired spies and informers among the slaves; they blacken their own faces, and lurk in disguise about the cabins, peeping through the cracks, and listening at the doors. They lure the fugitives back into their power, by the most ample promises of pardon, which they break with as little hesitation as they make them. Not uncommonly they attempt to take advantage of the superstitious ignorance of the slaves, and pretend to magical and supernatural powers, in hopes of frightening the culprit into confession. They exult over the success of these fraudulent arts; and in all transactions with their slaves, their total want of respect for their own word has given ample occasion for the proverb common among the unprivileged class, which describes white men as "mighty uncertain."

Of the three principal means above enumerated, and briefly explained, upon which the sustentation of the slave-master's empire depends, it is evident that the first involves the second; for the surest way of striking a deep terror into the heart is, to punish every transgression with a stern and unrelenting severity.

It accordingly happens that those who act upon this plan not only have the least trouble upon their plantations, but are often comparatively popular, so to speak, with their servants. The certainty of punishment greatly diminishes the necessity of its frequent infliction. The slaves know exactly what to expect; how far they can go; and what is the limit they cannot safely transgress. If the rule is an iron one, it is nevertheless steady and sure. It does not partake of that uncertainty, which besides being a dangerous temptation, is in itself one of the greatest of evils. Slaves are like other men; and in general, they far prefer to take a punishment, and have it over, to being perpetually scolded, threatened, cursed and stormed at, even though there may be hope that the storm will end in words, and pass over without raining blows.

But this regular and systematic discipline, resembling the despotic precision of a well drilled army, is to be found only upon a very few plantations. Most masters and most overseers are too negligent, or too good humored for their business, or else are ignorant of the real nature, and only sure support of the authority they exercise. They overlook some offences because they do not want the trouble of punishment; some they permit to go unnoticed, because they hate to flog a woman, or a child; some allowances they make for the petulance of old age, or the hot temper of youth. But every liberty that goes unpunished is made a pretence for yet greater liberties; the slaves, always eager and watchful to regain any particle of freedom, perceive in an instant, and with unerring sagacity, every indication of weakness, or want of vigor on the part of their master; they artfully break, now this link, and now that, from their chains; till at length, beginning to feel something of the spirit of liberty, their "insolence," to use the master's phrase, becomes intolerable, and waking from his dream of indulgence and good nature, their despot is obliged to vindicate his authority, and to repress the licentiousness of his slaves, by a sudden outbreak of violence and cruelty, which, however he may excuse it by the plea of necessity, he cannot think of, in his sober moments, without some disagreeable feelings of self-condemnation.

Thus it is that the greater part of Southern plantations are the scenes of a constant struggle; idleness, encroachments, a passive resistance upon one side; negligence and yielding first, then passion, violence and cruelty upon the other.

SECTION V.

Means of resistance on the part of the slaves.

We come now more minutely to consider, with what feelings the slaves look upon their own lot, and what resistance they make to the usurped authority of their masters. For by the very constitution of human nature, it happens of necessity, that such an authority must be resisted, in some shape or other.

As to escaping from a condition to which they seem to have been born, and in which they are held by the joint interest, real or supposed, of all the members of the privileged class, that is, of all those who make and enforce the laws, and who alone possess knowledge, wealth and influence in the community ;—such a deliverance appears impossible, and rarely enters into their thoughts. It is true that running away is extremely frequent ; but in ninety-nine cases out of a hundred, the runaway is speedily retaken and severely punished ; and the attempt is generally made, not with any hope of ultimate escape, but as a means of eluding for the moment some threatened misery, which the unhappy fugitive has not the courage to face.

However, if a door were opened for their escape ; if by any circumstance they were induced to entertain the idea of it, and if that idea budded into hope, it is not to be supposed that they would stickle, or hesitate at any means, however horrible, that seemed necessary or convenient, towards the accomplishment of that great end. Prisoners of war, if they can but take their guards at unawares, are accustomed to stab them with their own bayonets, and by that bloody means, to break away. Captives, such as slaves are, must be expected to act upon the same ideas ; but with a promptitude the readier, and a hate the more earnest, in proportion to their longer restraint and their greater provocation. When has the master respected the person of his slaves? Would he hesitate one moment to stab, shoot, hang, or burn the best beloved of his servants, if he supposed that servant's life inconsistent with his safety, or with the security of that tyrannical empire, upon which depends his condition of master? Let there be the whisper of an insurrection, and the old trees of the plantation, shall dance with dying men strung thick as acorns. This the slaves know; and knowing it, what wonder, when the desperate project of insurrection is resorted to, what wonder, if they grant no mercy where they can expect none? What wonder, if with the torture of death by a slow fire, or by some other means equally cruel, before their eyes, they feel no clemency? What wonder, if they steel their hearts to pity, and emulate their masters in bloody cruelties and barbarous revenge? In so doing, they merely practise a lesson they have been all their lives learning; all their lives, the sword has been pointed at their hearts, and if they in any way succeed in grasping it by the hilt,— what wonder if they use it?

If it were possible to speak otherwise than seriously upon so grave a matter, it would be difficult to point out any thing more ridiculous than the frantic fear, the panic terror, the ineffable alarm spread throughout the South, by the slightest suspicion of insurrection among the slaves. That the women and children should be terrified, is natural enough; but that men, men of violence and blood, accustomed to go their daily rounds with the pistol in one hand and the whip in the other, men who have every advantage on their side with the single exception of justice,—an exception however, which they affect to deny and disregard;— that such men should stagger and turn pale at the mere report of a distant insurrection, can only be, because a guilty conscience disturbs their reason, and frights away their courage.

Do they not know the stake for which they play? Have they not considered the conditions of the game? What!—Do they entertain the puerile notion, that an eternal war can be waged, and all the blows, the thrusts, the cuts, the wounds, the danger, be only on

5

one side? Is it so terrible and atrocious a thing, that my enemy dares to struggle in my grasp? What though I have him on the ground, my knee upon his breast, and a dagger at his throat, is it so strange that even in that position, still he resists, and strives to push his weapon to my heart?

Slavery being in its nature, a permanent state of war, although the overwhelming force of the masters restrains the slaves for the most part to an apparent submission, yet occasional outbreaks must from time to time be expected. The ignorance in which the slaves are kept, makes them incapable of perceiving the utter hopelessness of success; and there are some hot tempers, and enthusiastic minds, which, though they did perceive it, would still be ready to risk any thing and every thing, for the most trifling chance of freedom and revenge. The danger from these outbreaks is extremely small. They will cost the masters now and then a few lives; but that is the fortune of war, and those brave soldiers who can slaughter the enemy with such perfect indifference, if not with absolute gusto, ought to be able to lose a few of their own number, without being so wholly carried away with panic terror.

An intended rising requires preparations, means, and an extended combination, which generally lead to its detection before the conspirators are ready to act. Besides, it is only under peculiar circumstances, that any thing of the kind can be attempted. The slaves are so much in the power, and at the mercy of their masters, that they seldom venture upon any thing like violent opposition; they content themselves, for the most part, with a passive resistance.

The master claims, and endeavors to possess himself of the whole time, capacity and labor of the slave. The slave does not venture openly to resist this robbery; but he attempts, by all the silent and quiet means in his power, to evade it, to escape the exactions, and to diminish the plunder of his master.

He yields his time from day-light, until dark; or rather he seems to yield it; for if he be not constantly watched, he contrives to regain hours and moments, which as he can apply them to no better use, he spends in idleness or sleep. His capacity is a thing more in his own power. It is in general, only certain simple acts of manual labor that can be extorted by force. The mind is free. A master cannot force his slave to reason, to remember, or except in certain cases, to hear, or see. If he is sent with a message, he forgets it. He never considers that if the fence is broken, the cattle will get among the corn; and if they do, he neither sees nor hears them. The thing he is commanded to do, that single thing he does, and nothing else. The master would go hunting, and he sends his slave to bring his powder-flask. The slave sees there is no powder in it;—but what is that to him?—he does as he was bid, and carries the flask. When the gun is to be loaded, it appears then there is no ammunition. "Go home," says the master, "in the closet on the upper shelf there is a canister of powder; fill the flask, and bring it to me." As it happens, there are two canisters, one good, the other damaged. The slave takes down the damaged canister first, and without further examination fills the flask with powder that cannot be used, and carries it to his master. He is set to planting corn. The seed, it chances, is worm-eaten and decayed. What is that to him? He goes on planting. It is just so in every thing else. He neglects to exercise his reasoning faculties at all. He becomes apparently as stupid and thoughtless as the mule he drives. Whatever capacity or understanding he may have, he sinks it, hides it, annihilates it, rather than its fruits should be filched from him by his owner.

He is compelled to labor so many hours; but he takes care to labor to the least possible advantage. Nothing stimulates him but the fear of the whip; and under the show of diligence he proceeds with the greatest possible dawdling and deliberation. Is he a brick-layer? He selects a brick with caution and solemnity; he turns it over a dozen times; he looks as carefully at every side of it as if it were covered with intelligible hieroglyphics; he feels the corners and the edges; he fits it to its place; removes it; takes up the mortar; spreads and slowly arranges it with his trowel; and at last—lays the brick.

In all those processes which require any thing of skill or judgment, it is impossible to extort a large amount of labor from a slave. He conceals his idleness so cunningly, any attempt to drive him seems to put him into such a flutter and confusion, that he bungles or spoils his work, and it becomes necessary that it should be done over again, allowing the workman his own time. The master can only insist that he shall devote his whole time to the work, but he must be content to let him dally and trifle with it as he chooses.

Hence it is that slave labor is only profitable for those rude and simple processes, which demand nothing but an exertion of muscular strength. A slave may be driven by the whip to cut up grass with the hoe, or to pick cotton with his fingers, nearly or quite as fast as a freeman, who labors for himself; but to compel this labor he must be constantly watched and pressed; and if the whip is not used upon his shoulders, he must at least see it brandished in the air as a spur to his activity.

The day, from earliest dawn oft times till long past dark is all the master's; but the night, since the human machine requires some rest and relaxation, is principally yielded to the slave. He is thus transformed into a nocturnal animal. During the day, he appears a dull, stupid, sleepy, inanimate thing, without sense or spirit, little better than an idiot, and neither so sprightly nor so sensible as the horse he drives. At night, he becomes quite another creature. He runs laughing, singing, jesting, to his cabin. With his calabash of corn, he hastens to the hand mill; and as one grinder succeeds another, the rumbling of the stones is heard all night, a doleful sound, mixed with the curses and execrations of those who grind. But it rumbles on with a steadiness which shows with what incessant industry the mill is plied, and which is evidence enough that those who grind, labor not for their master, but themselves. His corn cracked into hominy, or ground to meal, he kindles up a fire, and prepares his simple, and too often scanty supper; his family gathers about the smoking dish; they eat with lively talk and laughing repartee; and as no whip cracks in their ears, they readily forget that such a thing exists.

The meal ended, they do not think of sleep. They meet for talk and dances. The more daring secretly mount their master's horses and ride to visit their cronies upon some neighboring plantation. One goes courting, another to see his wife; some with dogs and axes hunt the opossum, a night-walker like themselves; some meet to preach and pray; others prowl about to see what thing of value they can lay their hands upon. Others yet, with bags of stolen corn or cotton on their heads, secretly set off to visit some petty trader, who receives their stolen goods in exchange for whiskey. Some have a bottle on hand, and collecting their intimates about them, they drink, and emboldened by the liquor, they discuss the conduct of their masters, or the overseer, with a keen freedom, a critical observation, an irony as bitter as it is just;—happy if a prowling overseer, or some false-hearted spy does not stand listening, and make them presently pay the penalty of free discussion. It is only toward morning that they think of sleep; and it is surprising with how little sleep they exist. But in fact, their day time is but a lethargy, during which, though the body be active, the mind slumbers.

But as the slaves become more numerous, and the masters more timid and more exacting, tyranny takes possession even of the night. At dark, the slaves are penned up like cattle, and forbidden to leave their huts, lest they should employ themselves in plunder, or in plotting insurrection; or if merely indulging in sports and amusements, lest they should exhaust that strength and vigor, which the master claims as wholly

5*

his. The dance is forbidden; no merry laugh is heard, no torch-lights are seen glancing and streaming on the darkness, or eclipsing the splendor of the moon, as the slaves pass from one cabin to another. All is still as night and tyranny can make it; and if the slaves, spite of this despotism, yet have their meetings, for talk, for drinking, for plunder, or for prayer, all are equally prohibited, and they steal forth with slow and stealthy steps, watchful and cautious as the midnight wolf.

The masters grievously complain of this night-walking propensity on the part of the slaves. Besides the efforts of each planter to suppress it on his own estate, and the barbarous severity, with which it is customary to punish slaves for being found visiting on a plantation to which they do not belong,—public patrols are established for the purpose of arresting, flogging, and sending home, all slaves caught wandering at large without a pass, that is, a written permission.

The two grand charges, however, brought against the slaves, and which are quoted by the masters as decisive proofs of their lamentable depravity, and total destitution of all moral principle, are the accusations of *lying*, and of *theft*.

1. The slaves, we are told, are arrant liars. They lie for themselves; they lie for each other; and to deceive their master or the overseer is esteemed among them as an action, not blameless only, but even praiseworthy.

Well,—why not? Falsehood has ever been considered a lawful art of war; and slavery, as we have seen, is but a state of protracted hostilities. Do we not applaud a general for the stratagems and arts by which he deceives, misleads, entraps his enemy? Do not the very masters themselves, chuckle and exult over the ingenious falsehoods by which they have detected a theft, or recovered a runaway? Though they be tyrants let them use a little philosophy. Dionysius did so, and so did Pisistratus. With their masters, enemies who have seized them, and who keep them by force, the slaves are not connected by any ties of social duty. It is a condition of open war; and as in point of strength, the slaves are wholly overmatched, stratagem and falsehood are their only resource; and if by bold lying, vociferous protestations, and cunning frauds, they can escape some threatened aggression, if they can so secure some particle of liberty from the prying search and greedy grasp of despotism, why blame them for acts, which in like cases, all the world has justified, and has even exalted to the character of heroism?

In a slave, considered as a slave, cunning is almost the sole quality of mind which he has any occasion to exercise; and by long practice it is sometimes carried to an astonishing perfection. Under an air of the greatest heedlessness and stupidity, and an apparent apathy more than brutal, there is occasionally veiled a quick and accurate observation, a just estimate of temper and disposition, lively and ardent feelings, and a loftiness of spirit, which some day perhaps, will burst its ordinary cautious bounds, and terminate the life of its possessor, by bullets, knives, the gibbet, or the flames.

2. It is astonishing say the masters, how destitute of all conscience these rascals are. The best among them, the most pious and obedient, are no more to be trusted than so many foxes. Even our domestic servants steal every thing they can touch. There must be a lock on every door, every trunk, every closet. But even the strictest watchfulness is no match for their arts; and the sternest severities cannot repress their spirit of plunder.

The slaves it seems then, however overmastered and subdued, do still, in a silent and quiet way, and to the best of their ability, retort upon their masters the aggressions and the robbery that are perpetrated on themselves.

Property, it is to be recollected, is a thing established among men, by mutual consent, and for mutual convenience. The game I have killed, the fish I have caught, the vegetables I have cultivated, are decided to be mine, and are secured to me by the consent and warranty of all my tribe, because the security and comfort of each member of it requires for himself the like privilege and protection. But between slaves and masters, there is no such compact, no such consent, no such mutual arrangement. The masters claim all; and so far as they are able, they take all; and if the slaves by stealth, by art, by cunning, can secretly regain the possession of some gleanings from the fruits of their own labor, why should they not? It is in their eyes a spoiling of the Egyptians; it is a seizure and appropriation of things to which they surely have a better title than the masters.

Is it to be supposed that in the prosecution of a perpetual war, the plunder will be all upon one side? The disproportion is doubtless very great; the aggressors, as their strength and means are so superior, carry off rich trophies and abundant spoils; the conquered are well pleased to gather some fragments, to filch some trifles from the over-loaded stores of the triumphant invaders, who plundering upon a great scale themselves, are yet astonished at the depravity of those who plunder on a small one. To expect, as between masters and slaves the virtues of truth, probity and benevolence, is ridiculous. Slavery removes the very foundation of those virtues.

SECTION VI.

The treatment of American slaves considered as animals.

The slave-master desires to look upon his slaves as he does upon his horses; to persuade himself that his empire over both is equally just; and that the claims and rights of horses and of slaves, are confined within the same limits.

But even in this view of the case, narrow and false as it is, the slave-holder too often falls lamentably short of what common humanity, and ordinary good nature require.

A slave is an expensive animal, since he must be supplied not only with shelter and food, but with fire, and clothing. There are however several circumstances in the condition of the southern states, which operate at present to reduce these expenses to a minimum.

The houses of the slaves for the most part, are little miserable log cabins, with chimneys of sticks and clay, without windows, and often without a floor, but one step in advance of the primeval wigwam. They contain but one room, in which the whole family is huddled together without any regard to the privacies or decencies of life ; nor are they in any respect superior, if indeed they are equal, to the stables or the cow house. The furniture is as rude as the dwelling, and betokens the lowest state of poverty and destitution. When these cabins have become thoroughly rotten, and ready to tumble to the ground, they are rebuilt at no other expense except a few days labor of the plantation carpenter. Other things have undergone great improvements ; but in the construction and comforts of a slave's cabin, there has been little or no change for upwards of a century.

Clothing, especially in the more northern of the slave states is an expensive item ; but as its necessity in those parts of the country is the more apparent, the good economy of furnishing a tolerable supply is more generally acknowledged, and the suffering of the slaves from deficiency of clothing, is probably much less than in the more southern states, where the mildness of the climate encourages the masters to stint the allowance, and where the numerous deaths among the slaves from quinsy, influenza, and pleurisy, are a proof how insufficiently they are guarded against the sudden changes from heat to cold, to which the whole climate of the United States is so liable. The children, till they reach the age of twelve or fourteen, run about almost naked, being covered, if at all, only by an unwashed shirt of tattered osnaburgs. Their sufferings from cold must sometimes be excessive.

Firewood is still so abundant throughout all the southern states, as in most parts of the country to have no exchangable value; or to owe that value entirely to the labor expended in preparing it. The slaves are at liberty to take from the woods on Sundays, or by night, such supplies as they choose. For the most part, they carry it on their heads; though sometimes on Sunday, they are allowed the use of a pair of oxen and a cart. To save steps and trouble, if they can do it without detection, they generally prefer to lay their hands upon the first fence they come to.

Very different opinions prevail in different portions of the southern states, as to the quantity of food which it is necessary or expedient to allow a slave. In Kentucky, Missouri, and Tennessee, where corn and bacon are produced in great abundance, and where their value is small, the slaves are allowed as much coarse food as they desire; and the plump condition and buoyant vivacity of the children are an evidence that they seldom suffer from hunger.

In Virginia, Maryland, and North Carolina, where corn is seldom worth above fifty cents the bushel, some sixteen bushels of it is considered a competent yearly supply for a slave, to which is generally added, a weekly allowance larger or smaller, of fish or meat.

In the states further south, which may be properly designated as the cotton growing states, where corn is generally worth a dollar or upwards the bushel, and where provisions of all sorts are comparatively scarce and high, twelve bushels of dry corn by the year, without any allowance of meat or fish, or any thing beside, is esteemed a large enough supply of food for a working hand. Sweet potatoes, are sometimes served out during the fall and winter months, instead of corn; and on the rice plantations, broken or damaged rice furnishes the chief supply of food; but whether it be corn, potatoes, or rice, the allowance is often scanty enough; and the starved, shriveled, peaked condition of the children upon many plantations, are too evident proofs how cruelly they are stinted.

With respect to this subject, the following observation is worthy of attention. A certain quantity of food may suffice to sustain life, and even strength, yet not be enough to appease the cravings of appetite, nor to stay or prevent the torments of hunger. Most laboring men at the North, might probably live and enjoy health, though their daily food were diminished in quantity one half, or even more; yet this is a sacrifice they would very reluctantly make; and the certainty of life and health would be no sufficient consolation for the gnawings of hunger, and the disquietudes of an unsatisfied appetite.

It happens very unluckily, that the slaves in that part of the country where they are worst supplied with food and clothing, are yet subjected to the severest and most unremitting labors.

In Missouri, Kentucky, North Carolina, Virginia and Maryland, except in those limited tracts in which the culture of tobacco is pursued, there are considerable intervals in every year, when the labor of the slaves is little needed, and when the tasks imposed are sufficiently light. But the cultivation of tobacco, and still more, that of rice, sugar and cotton, is an incessant round of labor, from one year's end to the other. These plants are a long time in coming to perfection. The labor of securing the crop, and preparing it for market, is very great; and one year's work is hardly ended, before it is time to begin upon the next. Winter or Summer, there is no rest nor relaxation from constant, steady toil.

On the whole, it may be stated that the physical condition of the slaves throughout the southern states, is far inferior in every respect, to that of the unfortunate men, confined for the punishment of their crimes in our Northern prisons and penitentiaries. Their food is less savoury, less abundant, and far less various,—and a certain variety of diet seems as essentia to health as it is agreeable to the taste. The work demanded of them is far more fatiguing and severe, the time of labor is longer, the clothing with which they are supplied is far less comfortable; and their exposure far more trying. That sort of discipline which we have fixed upon as the most terrible and exemplary punishment of crime,—or rather a discipline much more severe than that,—is the regular, constant, perpetual condition of a large proportion of our fellow-countrymen at the south.

What has been observed with respect to food, applies with equal force to physical condition in general. That which is sufficient to sustain existence, is by no means sufficient for comfort, or for pleasure. Life may be supported, and protracted under such a series of privations that it ceases to be any thing but a continuity of suffering.

That the physical condition of the slaves is far inferior on an average to that of the free, may be made evident by some statistical considerations. During the fifty years from 1790 to 1840, the white population of the United States had a uniform increase at the rate of thirty-five per cent. in each period of ten years; while during the same time the slave population increased at the rate of only twenty-nine per cent. In the period of ten years, from 1830 to 1840, while the free population increased 34.6 per cent., the slave population increased only 23.8 per cent.; a striking proof of the alteration for the worse, in the condition of the slaves, produced by their transfer to the cotton fields of the far south. The increase of the white population, by immigration from abroad, could not have amounted, during those ten years, to more than five per cent.; still leaving a balance of increase over the slave population of more than seven per cent. An examination of the returns of the recent census of 1850 would afford results not materially different.

Now it is to be recollected that there are certain prudential checks, as they are denominated, constantly operating to retard the increase of the white population. The extent to which these checks operate, even in those parts of the country in which the white population increases with the greatest rapidity, will be obvious, when it is considered, that in the state of New York, as appears from the results of the State census, in 1825 and in 1835, out of all the women in the state between the ages of sixteen and forty-five, that is, of an age to bear children, *two fifths* are unmarried.

Among the slaves, these prudential checks are totally unknown. There is nothing to prevent them from yielding to the instincts of nature. Child-bearing is stimulated and encouraged by the masters, and so far as it depends upon the mere production of children, the slave population ought to increase, two fifths faster than the free. Instead of doubling once in twenty-five years, it ought to double once in fifteen years. If the increase is kept down to the former level, it is only because disease and death are busier among the slaves than among the free; and as the slaves escape all those kinds of disorders which spring from luxury and over-indulgence, this greater mortality can only be ascribed to greater severity of labor, and to destitution of the physical supports of life.

It is often argued that self-interest alone is enough to make the master attentive to the lives and health of his slaves; on the same principle that he provides corn for his horses, and fodder for his cattle. But that provident and enlightened economy which makes a present sacrifice for the sake of avoiding a future greater loss, however it may be generally recommended and applauded, is but seldom practised; and he who is familiar with the domestic management of the southern states, must know that of all places in the world, it is least practised there.

An anecdote is related of a Virginian planter, who discharged his overseer, because sufficient cattle had

6

not died during the winter to furnish leather enough to supply the slaves with shoes. This story though perhaps a little exaggerated, will serve to give an idea of the domestic economy of the south; and he who knows how many mules and horses yearly drop in the furrow, through starvation, over-work, and the abusive treatment which the slaves, emulous of their masters, heap upon the only creatures in their power; he who has seen the condition of southern cattle in the month of March, hundreds actually starved to death, and those which are alive, a mere anatomy of skin and bones, with hardly substance enough to cast a shadow, searching with feeble steps, and woeful countenance, for a spear or two of withered grass, wherewith to protract their miserable existence; he who has seen these things, would not much care to have his life or his sustenance dependent upon the good economy of a management so utterly thriftless and unfeeling.

SECTION VII.

The treatment of American slaves, considered as men.

There are some people whose sympathies have been excited upon the subject of slavery, who if they can only be satisfied that the slaves have enough to eat, think it is all very well, and that nothing more is to be said, or done.

If slaves were merely animals, whose only or chief enjoyment consisted in the gratification of their bodily appetites, there would be some show of sense in this conclusion. But in fact, however crushed and bruti-fied, they are still men; men whose bosoms beat with the same passions as our own; whose hearts swell with the same aspirations,—the same ardent desire to improve their condition; the same wishes for what they have not; the same indifference towards what they have; the same restless love of social superiority; the same greediness of acquisition; the same desire to know; the same impatience of all external control.

The excitement which the singular case of Casper Hauser produced a few years since, in Germany, is not yet forgotten. From the representations of that enigmatical personage, it was believed that those from whose custody he declared himself to have escaped, had endeavoured to destroy his intellect, or rather to prevent it from being developed, so as to detain him forever in a state of infantile imbecility. This supposed attempt at what they saw fit to denominate, the *murder of the soul*, gave rise to great discussions among the German Jurists; and they soon raised it into a new crime, which they placed at the very head of social enormities.

It is this very crime, *the murder of the soul*, which is in the course of continuous and perpetual perpetration throughout the southern states of the American Union; and that not upon a single individual only, but upon nearly one half the entire population.

Consider the slaves as men, and the course of treatment which custom and the laws prescribe, is an artful, deliberate, and well-digested scheme to break their spirit; to deprive them of courage and of manhood; to destroy their natural desire for an equal participation in the benefits of society; to keep them ignorant, and therefore weak; to reduce them if possible to a state of idiocy; to crowd them down to a level with the brutes.

A man, especially a civilized man, possessed of a certain portion of knowledge, and well skilled in some art or science, is a much more valuable piece of property, and capable of producing for his master a far greater revenue, than a mere, two-legged human animal, with all the failings and defects, and none of the virtues of a savage. But if such a slave is more valuable, he is far more dangerous, and far more dif-

ficult to manage. To extort the services of such a
slave, by mere severity, would always be hazardous,
and often impossible. Drive him to despair, of which
such a man in such circumstances, is easily suscepti-
ble, and he might violently end a life from which he
derived no enjoyment, and court a death which offered him, at least, the pleasure of thwarting the hopes
of a too greedy master. With such slaves, it has always been found necessary, to enter into a sort of
compromise,—a treaty of peace, in which, if the claims
of the conqueror were largely provided for, some respect has also been paid to the rights and the happiness of the conquered. The claims of the master
have been commuted for a monthly or daily tribute;
and what else the slave could make or gain, has been
relinquished to his own use. He has been further encouraged by the prospect of presently purchasing his
freedom ; or of obtaining it by the free gift of a master well satisfied with his services.

But though such slaves are very profitable, they
are also, as has been above observed, very dangerous.
Put thus upon a level with their masters, in all that
constitutes the moral strength of men ; keenly sensitive to the injustice that is done them, and to the un-
fair advantage that has been taken of their weakness,
—they have ever been ready to burst into rebellion,
have sometimes succeeded in overpowering their masters, and have often maintained a long, a bloody, and
a doubtful contest.

All this is perfectly well understood at the south.
A slave who can read is valuable on many accounts,
and will sell for more money than one who cannot.
A slave who can read, write, and compute, and who
by reason of these accomplishments is able to fulfil
the duties of a merchant's clerk, is plainly far more
valuable than a mere field hand. One who under-
stands the art of printing, an armorer, an apothecary,
are evidently capable of performing more profitable
operations, than he who knows only how to handle a
hoe.

But well aware how dangerous such slaves would be, the privileged order have preferred to sacrifice profit to safety. In most of the slave holding states, it is specially enacted that no slave shall be taught to read. This inability to read, disqualifies them at once for all the higher occupations. Some few are rudely instructed in those simple handicrafts indispensable upon every plantation; but custom and public opinion, if not the law, imperiously forbid, that any slave should be bred up to the knowledge or practice of any of the superior arts. Some publishers of newspapers, in defect of white journeymen, introduced slaves into their offices as compositors; but the experiment was pronounced too dangerous, and they were obliged to relinquish it.

With the exception of those employed in domestic service, and in the few mechanic arts above mentioned, the great mass of the slaves are occupied in agriculture, which, for the most part, is prosecuted in the rudest possible way. This is a subject which will be more fully considered in a subsequent chapter. Every thing is done by main strength, and under the direction of an overseer. The slaves are confined to the constant repetition of a few simple mechanical acts; and continually employed as they are in this constant round of stupefying labor, which is not enlivened by hardly a single glimpse of art or intellect; thus shut out from the means and opportunity of exercising their higher faculties, no wonder that the soul falls into a deep and death-like slumber. Drugged with such a stupefying cup, so artfully administered, the *soul murder* if not complete, is closely approximated. The man loses his manhood, and is a man no longer. Those mental and moral capabilities which are his pride and glory, fall into abeyance, and apparently he dwindles down into something little better than a mere animal.

The domestic slaves, being constantly attendant upon their masters, and listeners to their daily conversation, cannot but pick up some crumbs of knowl-

edge, and acquire a certain habit of reasoning and reflection. In consequence of these accomplishments
they are feared, suspected, and very narrowly watched. In all the towns and villages of the south, the
strictest regulations are established and enforced, by
which among other things, the slaves are forbidden to
leave their master's houses after an early hour in the
evening, and in many other respects, are subjected to
a constant system of the most prying and suspicious
espionage.

Some writers misled by a spirit of patriotism, or de-
ceived by views too superficial, have represented the
system of American slavery as extremely mild, and
quite a different thing from slavery in any other age
or country. There is a difference it is true; but that
difference is not favorable to us. It is easy to show,
that in certain most essential points,—those fundamental points by which alone a social system ought to be
judged,—American slavery is a far more deadly and
disastrous thing, more fatal to all the hopes, the sentiments, the rights of humanity, than almost any other
system of servitude which has existed in any other
community.

Slavery as it existed among the ancient Greeks and
Romans has been often referred to, as a system of the
extremest severity, cruel beyond any thing to be found
in modern times.* No doubt that system was bad
enough. It would be well however, if other systems
were not worse.

The Roman master had the power of life and death
over his slaves; but the slaves, in this respect, stood
upon a level with the freemen; for the Roman husband and father had the same power over his wife
and his children, and he might claim and exercise it,
long after those children had passed the age of puber-
ty, and even after they had attained to the highest
honors and distinctions of the state. It is true that the
laws do not confer an equal authority upon the American master; but it is equally true that the lives of his

* See Channing on Slavery.

slaves are not the less in his power. It is easy for the master to invent a thousand pretences for taking the life of any slave, against whom he may have conceived a prejudice. If he does not think it prudent to use the pistol or the knife, he needs only to have recourse to a somewhat more lingering process of torture, or starvation.

But the great distinction between the slavery of the ancient world and that of America is this. The Greek and Roman slaves, in the estimation of their masters and themselves, though slaves, were yet men. It was true doubtless, as Homer says, that the day a man became a slave he lost half his manly virtues. From the nature of things it must have been so; but manhood or a portion of it, remained, though darkened and eclipsed, still visible. To a certain extent at least, in point of knowledge, accomplishments, and the development of mind, the slaves stood upon a level with the free; and if there be something terrible in the idea,—terrible because we need no preparation to comprehend it,—of a city sacked and plundered, and all its inhabitants, the noblest, the wealthiest, the delicate women, as well as the hewers of wood and the drawers of water, sold under the hammer of a military auctioneer, and thence dragged into servitude,—we must recollect that the accomplishments, the knowledge, the refinement of these unhappy captives, furnished also many means of alleviating the calamity of servitude, and presently of escaping it altogether. The Athenian captives taken in the unlucky expedition against Syracuse, purchased their liberty by reciting the verses of Euripides. Slaves first cultivated the art of Latin poetry, and introduced at Rome an imitation of the Grecian drama. Such were Plautus and Terence, and almost all the elder Roman poets. All the arts which give comfort and refinement to life, and the mere practice of which confers a certain social distinction, music, poetry, literature in general, painting, medicine, education, and many others, were principally, or commonly practised by slaves, who thus acquired favor, fame, freedom, and finally wealth and social elevation. Horace, educated at Athens among the sons of Roman nobles, and afterwards the friend and intimate of the lords of the empire, and the delight and pride of the Roman people, was the son of a freedman. Emancipations were frequent and were favored. The slave constantly had before his eyes the hope and the prospect of liberty; he thus had a noble object for which to live; and although there were in general, some political disqualifications which he could not expect to shake off from himself, wealth, consideration, and all the more common objects of human hopes and wishes, were still spread out before him; and for his children—and men live as much for their children as for themselves,—he had every thing to anticipate.

Undoubtedly the condition of the country slave, employed in agriculture, more nearly resembled that of slaves with us. But still there was an opening for talent and for hope. No slave was so low or miserable, that he might not aspire to freedom and to social elevation.

Under this system, there existed that compromise between the master and the slave, which has been explained above. If the slave lived and labored for his master, he also lived and labored for himself. He was secured by custom, which is stronger and more effectual than law, in the enjoyment of a *peculium*, or property of his own. The relation of master and slave lost to a certain degree, the character of pure despotism, and approached towards that of lord and vassal, patron and client; while the frequency of emancipation introduced into the relation of servitude, sentiments totally opposite to those which naturally spring from it. There were gleams of benevolence and of gratitude; there was a twilight of good-will. Compared to a condition of freedom, it was as the gray morning dawn to the brilliancy of noon. Compared to the system of our own country, it is as that same morning dawn to the blackness of midnight.

It is true that we read of savage atrocities, exercised in those ancient times, by masters towards their slaves. The Spartans, we are told, were accustomed from time to time, to send out assassins who put to death the boldest and most intelligent of the Helots; and it is undeniable that the frequent servile insurrections which took place in the ancient states, were suppressed and punished by a series of the most dreadful cruelties.

But these fierce acts ought to be regarded as proofs not so much of the degradation of the slaves, as of an approach on their part, towards an equality with their masters. No repose is so perfect as the repose of absolute despotism. The unfrequent and always trifling disturbances among the slaves of America furnish palpable evidence how sunk they are. It is only where a certain portion of liberty is enjoyed, that more begins to be strenuously claimed, or boldly sought. To him that hath, shall be given; from him that hath not, shall be taken away, even that which he hath. Such servile insurrections as take place in America, are faint flashes of folly or despair. The insurrections of slaves in ancient times, were the promptings of genius and of hope.

Had the Greek and Roman masters been the same indolent, scattered, untrained, unready people as are the American planters, such were the means, the courage, the spirit of their slaves that they could not have retained their dominion for a day. In those times the free were all soldiers. War was their constant study and pursuit. They lived too in cities, ready to combine and act at a moment's warning. Thus they were able, by constant preparation, and superior means, aided as they were by the moral causes above enumerated, to maintain their authority over slaves, enjoying an intellectual equality with themselves. Under the Roman empire, the standing army by which the emperors maintained their authority, served also to hold the slaves in subjection. Besides, the masters had a strong body of firm friends and

allies in the numerous class of freedmen. The emancipations constantly going on would soon, in fact, have
put an end to the condition of servitude, had not the
numbers of the enslaved been kept good by fresh importations and purchases. When at length these importations ceased, slavery in towns and cities soon
came to an end; the slavery of the country was
changed into villanage, and villanage ended at last, in
liberty.

To a certain extent, many of these observations apply to slavery as it exists in Brazil and Spanish America. However disastrous may be the social condition of those countries, it is not destitute of allevia-
tions. The slave is at least regarded as a man, and
is always cheered by the prospect and the hope of freedom. His efforts to obtain it by purchase, by gaining
the good - will of his master, or by other peaceable
means, are encouraged by the laws and by public
opinion; and if he attempt to qualify himself for the
more advantageous possession of it, so laudable an
ambition is approved and applauded.

In the United States, with all their democracy, there
prevails a totally different system. It is laid down,
as an indisputable maxim, that the freedom, the equality, the moral and social elevation of the servile class,
or any of its members, are totally inconsistent with
the dignity, the interest, the existence even of the
privileged order. That contempt, that antipathy, that
disgust which the degraded condition of servitude naturally inspires, is sedulously aggravated by the whole
course of education, and is artfully, though impercep-
tibly, transferred from condition to race; and to crown
the whole, the idea is earnestly and industriously incul-
cated, that these suggestions of prejudice and ignorance, are the very innate promptings of nature.

In consequence, the natural sympathies of humanity are first smothered and then extinguished. The
privileged cease to consider the servile class as belonging to the same scale of being with themselves. The
slaves in the estimate of their masters, lose all the at-

tributes of humanity. The kindest, the most tender-hearted, the most philanthropic of the privileged order, learn to be perfectly satisfied when the animal wants of the servile class are tolerably provided for. To make any account of their mental wants,—that is, to entertain the idea that they are men,—is considered an absurd, a misplaced and a fanatical tenderness, certain, if persevered in, to uproot the foundations of society, and to end in results indeterminate, but terrible.

For the slaves are regarded not merely as animals, but as animals of the wildest and most ferocious character. They are thought to be like tigers, trained to draw the plough, whom nothing but fear, the whip, and constant watchfulness, keep at all in subjection; who would take advantage of the slightest relaxation of the discipline that restrains them, to break away from their unwilling labors; and who if left to themselves, would quickly recover their savage nature, and find no enjoyment except to riot in blood.

Whether or not there is any thing of reason and truth in these ideas, is not now the question. Suffice it to say, that they are universally prevalent throughout the southern states. They are the received, the authorized, the established creed. They are interwoven into the very frame-work of society; laws, customs, charities, morals, and religion, all are modified by them. Doubtless there are men of reflection and discernment, and men in whom a warm benevolence supplies the place of reflection and discernment, who perceive more or less clearly, the monstrous and extravagant absurdity of these popular ideas. But for their lives they dare not whisper the suspicion of a doubt. To do so would be high treason against the authority of the privileged order,—an order as jealous, fretful and suspicious as ever was the aristocracy of Venice; and as apt to punish too, on vague suspicion, without a trial, or a responsible accuser.

It is plain that emancipation can form no part of such a system. In South Carolina, Georgia, Alabama and Mississippi, no master can emancipate his slave, except with the express permission of the state legislature, a permission not easily to be obtained. In North Carolina and Tennessee, the emancipating master must have the approbation and consent of the County Court. In Virginia, he must remove the emancipated slave, beyond the limits of the State. In Maryland a similar law prevails. In Kentucky, Missouri and Louisiana, the master still retains the right of emancipation under certain restrictions. But throughout all the slave states, this exertion of power—the only act of justice which the owner of slaves, in his character of owner, is able to perform—is totally discouraged by public opinion. The emancipated class is studiously subjected to mortifications and disabilities without number. They are considered as noxious vermin whose extermination is required for the comfort and security of the privileged order. They are hunted down by legislative enactments as bears and foxes are in other states; and by depriving them of all the rights of citizenship, advantages of society, and opportunities for labor, the attempt is made to render them if possible, even more miserable than the slaves. These efforts have been to a certain extent, successful. The condition of the emancipated class, would seem to be wretched enough to satisfy their worst enemies. Yet wretched as they are, still they are envied by the slaves. What conclusive evidence of the miseries of servitude !

Some few emancipations occasionally take place; but it is obvious that the value of the boon is exceedingly diminished, by the miserable condition to which the emancipated class is studiously reduced. As to passing from the unprivileged into the privileged order, that is a thing entirely out of the question. No slave can expect it for himself, for his children, or even for his remotest posterity. The feeling which exists upon this subject throughout the South, is a perfect fanaticism. In one or two rare instances, a good-natured master has attempted to elevate his own

children, born of slave mothers, to the rank of freedom. But in every such case, the penalty of setting
public opinion at defiance, has been dearly paid. The
transgressor has been assailed in every form of ridicule, and reproach; he has been pursued with the
most inveterate malice; has been overwhelmed with
torrents of obloquy; and held up to public scorn and
indignation, as a blasphemous violator of the decencies of life and the sacred laws of nature.

Here is the point at which the slaves of the United
States sink into a depth of misery, which even the
imagination can hardly measure. What is life without hope? All men of reflection, whether poets or
philosophers, have agreed, that life even in the better
aspects of it, if we did but see things as they are and
as they will be, would be a dreary and a worthless
thing. It is hope that cheers, supports, sustains us.
It is in the anticipation of future joys, that we are
happy. But what hope, what anticipations has the
American slave? His hopes are all fears; his anticipations, if he has any, are anticipations of suffering.
This is a state of existence which could not be endured by cultivated or reflecting minds. The slightest
gleam, the faintest and most uncertain glimmer, a
hope, a chance which to all beside ourselves may appear but the faintest, will suffice often to lead and
guide us on, through defiles dark and gloomy as the
valley of the shadow of death. But when that light
goes out, that glimmer ceases, that hope expires, what
shall save us from the horrors of despair?

7

SECTION VIII.

Wealth and luxury of the masters, as it affects the condition of slaves.

It is a fact well worthy of consideration, that with the progress of wealth and luxury among the masters, the sufferings, the misery, the degradation of the slaves have been steadily aggravated; till at length, in the wealthiest and most refined of our slave holding communities, a point has been reached, both in theory and in practice, beyond which it does not seem easy to go.

The mildest form of American slavery is to be found, not among the polite and well educated citizens of Richmond and Charleston, but amid the rude and wild abodes of the Creeks, the Choctaws, the Seminoles,—tribes whom we describe and stigmatize, as savages.

The indian slaves, are in many respects, almost upon a level with their masters. The wants of savage life are few and simple. The avarice of the master is not stimulated by the greediness of luxury. He is content with a moderate annual tribute of corn and other provisions; and provided this be paid, the slave is left at liberty to procure it as he pleases, and to employ his time and strength as he best sees fit. It thus happens that an indian slave is sometimes richer than his master; and if he have talents and ambition, though still a slave, he may become one of the most influential persons of the tribe.

The indian slaves are well aware how superior is their condition to that of the miserable sufferers, who labor for white masters, upon cotton and sugar plantations; and the dread they have of that lot, as well as the influence they are able to exercise, may be clearly illustrated by the case of the Seminole war. That war, according to the statement of those best acquainted with the subject, had the following origin. It was not that the indians themselves had such serious objections to removal; but as the time for the execution of the treaty approached, their country was overrun with speculators and adventurers from the states, who came partly to set up claims, true or false, to certain indian slaves, on the ground that they were runaways, or the children of runaways, who had years ago fled to the Seminoles for protection ; and partly to set on foot a slave trade with the indians, who, it was hoped might be induced at the moment of their removal to part with their servants for little or nothing. The indian slaves were filled with terror and alarm at this prospect of falling into the hands of white masters; and it is believed to have been by their instigation and encouragement, that the Seminoles were induced to resist the execution of the treaty, and to commence the war.

The small planter, who can neither read nor write, who has been bred up in poverty and ignorance, but who has wandered into some new settlement and has earned by his own personal labor, the means to purchase two or three slaves, next to the wild indian, is the most mild and indulgent master. He works with his slaves in the field, he converses with them and consults them. If either of them exhibits any peculiar shrewdness or good judgment, the master perceives it, and avails himself of it; and such a slave often becomes his owner's chief confidant and adviser.

In his fits of drunkenness, or those bursts of passion to which the rude and uneducated are peculiarly liable, such a master beats and abuses his slaves. But he does the same thing to his wife and children. In general he treats them with a certain degree of tenderness and familiarity; and as they are always about him, by flattery, management and importunity, they are able to carry a thousand points, and to secure a thousand indulgences.

But as such a planter grows rich, and increases the number of his slaves, his feelings and his conduct change with his condition. He appears in the field, not as a laborer, but on horseback, whip in hand. He begins to copy the airs and to imbibe the sentiments of his aristocratic, refined, and educated neighbors. He forgets the equal terms upon which he once lived with his slaves; he feels himself transmuted into a being of a superior order, born to be idle while they were born to work. He ceases to have any sympathies for them. He learns to despise them; to hear their complaints and appeals with indifference; and to push them to labors, which when he worked by their side, he did not exact.

Under this new discipline, and with the frugal habits which he acquired in his youth, this planter's property rapidly increases. He becomes one of the wealthiest men of the neighborhood; and his son and heir takes rank with the choicest aristocracy. Conscious of his own deficiencies in education and manners, the father secures for that son, the best instruction he can obtain. He is sent early to school, and perhaps to some northern college to finish his education. He returns well mannered, and accomplished, with the refinement of sentiment and the gentle bearing which education and good company impart. The father dies, and the son succeeds to the inheritance. He has no taste for agriculture; or if he has, he cannot bear the constant annoyances of a plantation. He leaves every thing in the hands of an overseer; and is almost a perpetual absentee.

Every reduction in the allowances to his slaves, is so much net addition to his own revenue. He is always in want of money; and as he finds it less disagreeable to retrench the comforts of his slaves than his own luxuries, the slaves are soon reduced to the merest subsistence. What are their sufferings or complaints to him? He is not at home to witness or to hear them. He leaves the execution of his orders to an overseer. This overseer is desirous to secure the good graces of his employer. The surest way of doing so is, to make a great crop. For this purpose the quantity of land in cultivation is increased. The tasks are extended, and the additional labor necessary to their execution, is extorted by the whip. Between this new labor and these new punishments, the slaves grow insubordinate and discontented. The boldest and most enterprising take to the woods. They are pursued with guns and dogs; retaken; mangled with the lash, and loaded with fetters. These examples terrify the others. They submit in silence. Order is restored. The discipline of the plantation is spoken of with admiration. The crop is unusually large. The owner is delighted with the result, and urgent for its continuance, and thus extortion and severity are carried to their highest pitch.

At the same time that the physical comforts of the slaves are diminished, all their moral qualities are deteriorated. Every bad passion is called into play. That state of hostility and warfare in which slavery orginates and consists, from being lulled, and half-quiescent, becomes open and flagrant. The masters learn to hate the slaves, as fiercely as the slaves hate the masters. Presently they begin to fear them. Fear and hate upon both sides! God have mercy upon the weaker party!

———

SECTION IX.

Improvement in physical condition, as it affects the condition of servitude.

Benevolence is one of those native impulses of the human heart, which never can be wholly eradicated; and which may be seen mingling itself with actions that proceed from motives of a totally opposite character.

It is plain that the whole system of slavery is in violation of the dictates of benevolence; yet no impartial observer, who has resided in the southern states

7*

of America, attempts to deny, that mingled with all its wrongs and crimes, there may be perceived, in many cases, much kind feeling on the part of the masters. Indeed it is out of this fringe of benevolence with which the dark garment of slavery is more or less scantily ornamented, that most of its defenders have woven the frail texture of their apologies.

This benevolence however is of a very limited character. It is confined almost entirely to physical condition. It conforms itself to the established sentiment of the country; it considers the slaves not in their character of human beings, of men, but merely as animals.

It is asserted that within the last twenty or thirty years, as the tobacco cultivation has declined in Virginia, there has been a great amelioration in the treatment of slaves. Many benevolent individuals have exerted themselves to bring about this state of things, by creating in the public mind a spirit of reprobation against instances of excessive cruelty. It may be observed in passing, that this amelioration in the treatment of the Virginia slaves, is a strong confirmation of the doctrines of the preceding chapter. As the masters have grown poor, and have been obliged to retrench their splendors and their luxury, at the same time, they have grown comparatively humane.

The Kentuckians boast, that of all the American masters, they are the kindest and the best; and they take to themselves no little credit, for the liberal supply of food and clothing which they bestow upon their servants, and the moderate labor which they demand.

This course of treatment, so much applauded by its authors, is worthy of all approbation on the score of domestic economy. It is also gratifying to the humane feelings of all those persons of sensibility, to whom the constant presence of visible suffering, is the source of emotions far from agreeable. But when we consider the matter a little deeper, when we see how this merely physical kindness operates upon the intellect and the heart, we may well doubt whether this sort of benevolence, however well intended, and however on that account worthy of applause, does not in fact, greatly aggravate the miseries of servitude.

So long as men are constantly pressed by merely physical wants, those wants absorb almost their whole attention. The peculiar attributes of humanity are scantily, or not at all, developed. They have the form and the aspect of men, but in character they are little more than mere animals; and the gratification of their animal wants occupies their total attention.

But so soon as these merely physical necessities are satisfied, the mental and moral attributes begin to unfold themselves. The passions bud and blossom; the feelings, the desires, the aspirations of manhood display their various forms and colors. If they might bear their natural fruits, those fruits would be good and wholesome. But crushed, withered, blasted, plucked up as it were by the roots, their premature decay evolves a deadly miasm, which poisons the soul, corrodes the heart, and sets the brain on fire.

Let us consider this matter more minutely. We read in ancient fables and eastern tales, of men transformed by the power of magic into beasts. Here is an operation of an analogous kind. Here are men who have advanced so far as to feel that they are men, whom law, custom, prejudice, and the potent force of public opinion, confine to the condition of mere beasts of labor. The more their humanity develops itself, and the more conscious of it they become, the more irritating and oppressive this condition must be. To be penned up, driven to labor, and foddered by the hand of a master,—and what consequence is it though the fodder be plentiful, and the labor be light?—to be repulsed from that condition of manhood to which they now begin ardently to aspire; to be expelled from the circle of social emulation and made mere counters in a game, of which they so long themselves to be the players; to be despised, scorned, and degraded into a fellowship with

the beasts they drive; forbidden to indulge their natural and irrepressible inclinations; prisoners though
at large; forever watched; forever thwarted; aggrieved still further by the constant spectacle of
privileges, enjoyments, objects and pursuits to share
in which they cannot even dream, but which increase
in estimated value, with the hopelessness of their at-
tainment;—what wonder, if in souls so beset with
grievous temptations, there should spring up and
grow, a fierce envy, a desperate hate, an impotent indignation preying on itself, a dark, ferocious, restless
spirit of revenge, which delay irritates, concealment
sharpens, and fear embitters? What wonder, if all
the mild feelings which soften man, and make him capable of happiness himself, and of conferring happiness
on others,—are choked and blasted by a rank
growth of deadly passions; and that he, who under
better auspices, might have been an ornament and a
benefactor to society, becomes a plague to others, a
torment to himself?

Such are the effects which must inevitably be produced upon that sensitive and irritable disposition,
the usual accompaniment of genius; and the same
effects, to a greater or less extent, may be expected to
result in the case of every slave, whose physical wants
are so far satisfied, that he becomes capable of reflection, and passes from the narrow circle of animal
desire, into the boundless amphitheatre of human
wishes.

Would it promote the happiness of our domestic
animals, our horses and our oxen, supposing them to
remain in their present external condition, to endow
them with the passions and the intellect of men? Who
will maintain the affirmative of a proposition so absurd? Yet the attempt to alleviate the condition of
slavery, merely by improving the physical condition
of the slaves, is an attempt, the absurdity of which,
if it be less obvious, is precisely of the same nature.

Keep your slaves pinched with hunger and worn
down with fatigue, and they remain merely animals,

or very little more. They suffer it is true; but they suffer as animals. There is a certain fixed limit to their misery. It has its intervals of cessation. The imagination has no power over it. What it is, it is. The present is the whole; for the past is forgotten, and the future is not anticipated.

But satisfy their hunger; put them physically at ease; give them leisure for thought,—and you create new sufferings more bitter than those you have removed. The man finds that yoke intolerable, of which the animal hardly perceived the existence. For two or three wants that you have relieved, you have created twenty others, or caused them to be felt, wants incessant, unquiet, unappeaseable; and for these wants there is no remedy,—no remedy, while you remain a master, and they slaves! After the sybil had cast two volumes into the fire, the third remained, as costly and as precious as all the three. In like manner, the chain of servitude loses none of its weight, by parting with a portion of its links. While one remains, that one is heavy as the whole! Nay, heavier;—and as it dwindles to the sight, still it pierces deeper to the soul; it frets and ulcerates the heart. At first it only bound the limbs; but now it penetrates, and with its murderous touch, tortures the vitals!

It is a common remark at the South, that the more intelligent a slave is, the more unquiet, dangerous, and troublesome he is. The remark is just. The more intelligent a slave is, the more grievously he feels the yoke of slavery. If a master then, through indulgence towards his slaves, has placed them in a situation of comparative physical comfort, so far from having a reason for stopping at that point, it becomes more imperatively his duty to go on. By doing what he has done, he has sharpened the appetite for liberty; and this appetite which he has sharpened, is he not the more urgently called upon to gratify?

Let it not be said that this argument is no better than an apology for a system of hard labor and starvation, nor let any man so use it. God forbid! Those are obvious cruelties; and so clearly perceptible to the senses, that no man of common humanity, however thoughtless and unobservant, can fail to perceive them ; and no man of common sensibility can bear to inflict them. I have desired to call attention to sufferings of another kind—mental sufferings,—not so obvious, yet far more excruciating; slavery's second growth, a rank and poisonous growth, more deadly than the first.

I have desired to point to the slave-holder, the fearful dilemma by which he is hemmed in. The moment he ceases to inflict tortures at which his sensibilities revolt, the moment he yields to those prayers for mercy which his own heart re-echoes to him, at that very moment he becomes the author of new sufferings ten times more severe, than those he puts a stop to. He irritates while attempting to soothe; and the oil which he drops into the wounds of servitude becomes a bitter and acrid poison.

This is one of those cases in which all must be done, or nothing. Half measures, palliatives, do but inflame the disease. The only cure for slavery, is, freedom !

CHAPTER SECOND.

POLITICAL RESULTS OF THE SLAVE-HOLDING SYSTEM.

SECTION I.

General View of the Subject.

The great objects aimed at, or which should be aimed at, in the political constitution of a government, are 1st, *Security*, 2nd, *Freedom*, 3d, *Equality*.

Security has two principal branches, of which one relates to the person, and the other to property. A good degree of security in both these respects, is essential to the comfort, and to the advancement of society.

Freedom is either political or civil. *Political Freedom* consists in a participation, more or less direct, in the appointment of magistrates, the enactment of laws, and other public acts. *Civil Freedom* depends upon the supremacy of the laws. It guarantees every citizen against arbitrary and capricious interference. It admits of no punishments except according to existing statutes; and it allows the enactment of no law founded upon any other reason than the public good.

Equality divides itself into three sorts; 1st, *Political Equality*, or the equal participation in political privileges, and the equal chance to enjoy political power;—in other words the perfection of political freedom; 2nd, *Equality of property*, or the most equal distribution, consistent with security, of the wealth already existing, and the equal chance to produce or acquire new wealth; 3d, *Social Equality*, or the equal chance of acquiring estimation and regard by the exhibition of amiable and useful qualities, or the performance of meritorious actions.

Now so far as regards the unprivileged class of the community, it is obvious at a single glance, that the constitutions of the Southern States fail totally, in securing any one of the above objects. They not only fail, but they do worse; they make a deliberate sacrifice of them all.

This sacrifice is said to be necessary in order to secure the well being of the privileged class. If in fact it is so, it must needs be confessed that the alternative is very unfortunate. The Southern people, if we allow this necessity, are in the unhappy predicament of a savage tribe of which one half, in order to sustain existence, are driven to kill and to devour the other half. Before we can admit the necessity of any such horrible experiment, every other means must first have been tried, and must have failed. What should we think of a tribe of savages who lived fat and comfortable upon the blood and flesh of their brethren, without the slightest attempt to devise any other means of subsistence; and who repulsed with impatient anger and bitter reproaches, the benevolent efforts of those who would point out to them a more decent and innocent way?

It is clear that so far as the unprivileged class are concerned, the political results of slavery are most disastrous. Slaves suffer at one and the same time, all the worst evils of tyranny and of anarchy. The laws so far as they are concerned, are all penal; they impose a multitude of obligations, but they create no rights. The compendious definition of a slave is, a man, who has no rights, but with respect to whom the rights of his owner are unlimited. If the law in some respects, seems to protect him, it is not in his character of a man, but in his character of a thing, a piece of property. Exactly the same protection which the law extends to a slave, it extends to a dog, a horse, or a writing desk. The master does as he pleases with either. If any other person undertakes to damage, steal, or destroy them, he is answerable to the owner, and is punished not as a violator of personal rights, but for having disregarded the laws of property.

The constant sacrifice of so many human victims, amounting in several states of the American Union to a majority of the population,—such a sweeping deprivation of rights as the slave-holding states exhibit, if it can be justified at all, must find that justification in some vast amount of good, which that sacrifice produces. This good must be principally sought for among the privileged class. If it exist at all it must be either political,—by increasing the security, freedom and equality of the privileged class; economical, —by increasing wealth, comfort and civilization; or personal,—by its beneficial influences on individual character. When Mr. McDuffie pronounces slavery the best and only sure foundation of a free government, if he has any meaning at all, if this declaration be any thing more than a passionate paradox,—he must mean to imply, that the political consequences of slavery are of a kind highly beneficial to the master; in fact so beneficial to the master as to form a counterpoise, and more than a counterpoise to all the evils it inflicts upon the slave. It becomes then an important question, what are the effects which slavery produces upon the political, economical, and personal condition of the privileged class? And in the first place of its political results.

8

SECTION II.

Slavery, as it affects the security of the privileged class.

I. We will consider in the first place how the security of property is affected by the institution of slavery.

Property is better secured in proportion as a greater part of the population is made to feel a direct interest in its security. The moral force of opinion in this as in other cases, has an efficacy greater than law. Laws unsustained by public opinion can only be enforced by a great and constant exertion of physical power.

1. With regard to the slave holding states, a large part of the population, to wit, the slaves, so far from having any personal interest in upholding the laws of property, have a direct and powerful interest the other way. The laws of property in their eyes, so far from being designed to promote the public good, and to confer a benefit upon all, are but a cunningly devised system by means of which the character and the name of *Right* is bestowed upon the rankest injustice, and the most flagrant usurpation. This attempt to monopolize the benefits of property, this system by which a large portion of the community are not only deprived of those benefits but are actually themselves converted into articles of property, has the necessary effect to create in the very bosom of the community, a state of feeling utterly hostile to security. Slaves are universally depredators upon the property of their masters. Such depredation they regard as perfectly justifiable and even praiseworthy. It requires the most incessant vigilance to guard against it, nor will the most incessant vigilance always suffice. The security of the slave-master is the security of a housekeeper who knows that he entertains a gang of thieves upon his premises, and who is in constant apprehension of being robbed.

Nor is this systematic spirit of plunder confined to

the unprivileged class. It embraces also the large class of free traders who gain their livelihood by a traffic in stolen goods. It is these persons who offer inducement for a large part of the depredations which the slaves commit upon their masters. These depredations, though small in the individual instances, are enormous in the total amount. The extreme severity with which the laws of the southern states visit the offence of trading with slaves in articles suspected to be stolen, and the terrible outrages occasionally committed upon this sort of offenders by planters who think the inflictions of the law to be too mild, or too uncertain, are a sufficient proof in how serious a light these depredations are regarded.

2. By the institution of slavery, the slaves themselves become the chief article of property. Property of all kinds has a certain tendency to take wings to itself and fly away. This is peculiarly the case with slave property. In addition to all the other accidents to which slaves, in common with other species of property, are exposed, they have a propensity to impoverish their masters by absconding. How frequently this propensity comes into exercise, any body may learn by examining the columns of the southern newspapers. Of the slaves that run away, the greater part are recovered: this is true, but still the master is a loser. He loses their services during their absence,— often at the most critical moment of the crop,—besides the expense of their apprehension and conveyance home, including the reward offered, which in itself is often equal to half the money value of the slave.

3. Many slaves submit with great reluctance to the station and duties which the law assigns to them. To keep these unquiet creatures in due subordination, it becomes necessary to wound, to maim, and sometimes to kill them. This chance of loss takes away in a certain degree, from the security of this kind of property.

4. We come now to a cause of insecurity of a more serious character than any yet enumerated. Property

in slaves is not a kind of property generally acknowledged. There are whole nations who deny that any
such kind of property ought to exist. All the most
enlightened people in the world are precisely of that
opinion. Within the last fifty years, an effort has
been begun,—an effort which every day gathers new
force and earnestness,—for the total abolition of this
kind of property. The alarm which this effort produces among the holders of slaves is natural, and it is
great. An alarm exists at all times among slave-
holders, because there is always a certain apprehension lest the slaves themselves may reclaim their
liberty by force. But that alarm reaches an extreme
height when it is known that there are other persons,
over whom the slave-masters have no control, who
sympathize with the slaves, and who profess the intention of using every moral means to bring about their
emancipation. *Moral means* is a phrase which slave-
masters find it difficult to understand. *Force, violence*,
is the only means with which they are familiar; and
this means which they themselves so constantly employ, they naturally apprehend, will be used against
them. The degree of alarm thus produced, is sufficiently indicated by the ferocity with which the persons called abolitionists have been assailed by the
slave-holders, and by the savage barbarities exercised
upon such abolitionists, or supposed abolitionists, as
have fallen into their hands; exercised generally upon
mere suspicion, and with hardly any evidence that
the sufferers were guilty of entertaining the opinions
ascribed to them.

Thus it appears that under a constitution authorizing slavery, one of the chief items of property, namely, slave property, from its very nature, its total want
of any foundation of mutual benefit, is peculiarly insecure; and this insecurity spreads to every other kind
of property, because the institution of slavery, by its
necessary effect destroys all respect for property of
any kind, in a large part of the population, and also
creates a vast number of depredators.

II. We come now to that branch of Security, which relates to the person.

Here again the privileged class of a slave holding community are beset with alarms and dangers. These dangers and alarms are of two kinds,—dangers from the slaves, dangers from one another.

1. Dangers from the slaves. The master retains his authority only by the constant exercise of violent means. This violence is liable at any time to be retorted upon himself. The subjugation and cowardice of those over whom he tyrannizes, afford the master a certain degree of security. But passion often supplies the place of courage; and we frequently hear of terrible acts of vengeance committed upon the person or family of the master, by outraged and infuriated servants.

But this danger is trifling compared with that anticipated from a rising of the servile class. Every two or three years the report of an insurrection, real or imaginary, spreads the most frantic terror through the southern states. The antics enacted upon such occasions, would be in the highest degree farcical, did they not generally terminate in bloody tragedies. Men who are individually brave, and who would march to the assault of a battery without flinching, work each other into a complete paroxism of fear. A single negro seen in the woods with a gun upon his shoulder, suffices to put a whole village to flight. Half-a-dozen unintelligible words overheard and treasured up by some evesdropping overseer, or invented perhaps by some miscreant, who delights himself with the public alarm, are enough to throw all the southern states into commotion, and to bring nights of agony and sleeplessness to hundreds of thousands. But this is not the worst of it. When terror makes cowards it always makes bloody-minded cowards.

Blood! blood!—nothing else can appease the general alarm. Committees of safety with the most absolute authority, are every where established. On these committees sit many a village Tinville, many a rustic

Danton. Before these tribunals the unhappy victims are dragged; accusation and condemnation keep close company. Hanging, shooting, and burning become the order of the day. The headlong ferocity of these proceedings betrays the greatness of that alarm which produces them.

It has been shown in another place, that notwithstanding the extreme degree of terror to which the apprehension of slave vengeance gives rise throughout the south, the actual danger is by no means proportionately great. Many causes contribute to this disproportion, of which one leading one is, a secret consciousness of the cruel injustice of slavery. Tyranny is ever timid, always full of fears.

2. Danger from one another. In this case, the alarm is less, but the danger is more real. Throughout the greater part of the southern states it is considered essential to personal safety, to carry concealed weapons. This single fact shows that personal security is at the lowest ebb. When a man must protect himself, for what is he indebted to the laws? These weapons are no doubt carried partly as a protection against the slaves; but they are chiefly used, in quarrels between freemen. Of these quarrels the laws take but little notice. In such a case it is considered the mark of a mean spirit to appeal to the law. If I am assaulted or beaten, it is expected that I stab or shoot the aggressor. In several of the southern states it seems to make very little difference, whether I challenge him to a duel, or assault him without previous notice given, in a tavern, or the streets. Murders are constantly committed in this way. For the most part they go entirely unpunished, or if punished at all, it is only by a short imprisonment, or a trifling fine. They fix no imputation upon a man's character. Persons guilty of homicide are to be met with in the best society of the southern states. If it be inquired what is the connection between this condition of manners and the existence of slavery, the answer is, that the imperious ferocity of temper which the exercise of despotic

power produces or inflames, is the main cause of the existence and the toleration of an insecurity of person and a recklessness of human life, such as hardly elsewhere prevails in the most barbarous countries.

But even this is not the worst aspect of the case. The panic terror which the rumor of an insurrection produces at the south has been already mentioned. That terror levels all distinction between slaves and freemen, and so long as it lasts, no man's person is secure. During the period of the Mississippi insurrection, or pretended insurrection, in the summer of 1835, the committee of safety appointed upon that occasion, by a tumultuous popular assembly, were vested with ample authority " to try, acquit, condemn, and punish white or black, who should be charged before them." By virtue of this commission, the committee proceeded to try a large number of persons, principally white men, accused of having instigated, or favored the alleged intended insurrection. Many of those tried were found guilty, and were hung upon the spot. A great many others were cruelly whipped, and were ordered to quit the state in twenty-four hours.

The case of Mr. Sharkey will clearly exhibit the degree of personal security existing in the state of Mississippi at that time. Mr. Sharkey was a magistrate, and in the exercise of his legal authority, he set at liberty three men, of whose entire innocence of the charges alleged against them he was well assured, although they had been seized by the pursuivants of the committee of safety. This gentleman was a planter, a man of property, a large slave-holder, brother to the chief justice of the state,—a person not very likely to be implicated in a slave insurrection. But his opposition to the despotic authority of the committee was considered to be plenary proof of guilt, and a large party was sent to arrest him. Mr. Sharkey had no relish for being hung upon suspicion; so he barricadoed his doors, built fires about his house, in order that the darkness of the night might not conceal the approach of the pursuivants, wrapped his

infant child in the bed clothes to save it from the bullets, loaded his muskets, and quietly waited the attack.   His left hand was dreadfully shattered by the
first fire of the assailants; but he succeeded in killing
their leader, in wounding several of the rest, and in
compelling a retreat. By this time his friends and
connections began to collect about him, and a party
was formed in his favor.   Had he been less wealthy,
or less influential, he would inevitably have perished.

SECTION III.

Slavery as it affects the liberty of the privileged class.

One of the chief branches of civil liberty consists
in the unrestricted disposal of one's property.   There
are restrictions which are necessary; but the more
these restrictions are multiplied, the more is liberty
restrained.

By the institution of slavery, slaves become one of
the principal kinds of property; but in the free disposal of this kind of property, the slave-master at the
South is very much restricted. The "sacred rights
of property," as to which he is apt to be so eloquent,
with regard to that very subject-matter with respect
to which he considers them most sacred, are closely
restrained by laws of his own enacting.

To set a slave free, is certainly the highest act of
ownership; the only one indeed which a truly virtuous
man ought to exercise; and certainly the last one
which a person of any manly spirit would be willing
to surrender. But in the greater part of the southern
states, the master is deprived by law of the right of
emancipation. Here certainly is a most grievous infringement upon liberty.

The right to improve one's property so as to increase

its productiveness and give it an additional value, is an essential part of civil liberty. But this is a right of which, as respects his slaves, the southern master is in a great degree deprived. In most of the slave states it is a highly penal offence to teach a slave to read. Now reading and writing are essential to many employments. These accomplishments, and others which by their means the slave might acquire, would greatly tend to enhance his value, by making him capable of more valuable services. But the master is not allowed to improve his property in this way. The law interferes to prevent it.

Considering slaves merely as property, here are two grievous infringements upon the master's liberty. But consider them as men, and the infringement upon the master's freedom of action is still more intolerable. I am deprived by law of the capacity to be benevolent and just. I am ready to confer upon a fellow being the highest boon which man can give or receive;— but the laws do not permit me to confer it. Perhaps the slave is my own child. No matter; he shall remain a slave to the day of his death, unless I can obtain as a particular grace and favor, a special permission to set him free. Is this liberty? Is not the servitude of the father as miserable almost as that of the son?

The authors of these laws have plainly perceived that the natural dictates of humanity are at war with the institution of slavery; and that if left to their own operation, sooner or later, they would accomplish its overthrow. To perpetuate the slavery of the unprivileged class, they have fettered up those sentiments of the human heart, which are the foundation of morality and of all the charities of life. For the sake of brutalizing others, they have sought to barbarize themselves.

Liberty of opinion, liberty of speech, and liberty of the press do not exist in the southern states of the American Union, any more than under any other despotism. No doubt there are some subjects which

may be very freely discussed there; but the same is
the case under all despotisms. Any body may freely
discuss at Rome or Moscow, the merits and demerits of
American slavery. The only prohibited subjects are,
the plans of government and systems of policy upheld
by the pope or the czar. So at Charleston or Richmond, one is at full liberty to discuss subjects having
no obvious bearing upon the political system and
social condition of Virginia or South Carolina. But
approach *that* subject, lisp the word, slavery; dare to
insinuate that the existing system of southern society
is not the best possible system; assail ever so cautiously the tyranny of the slave-masters; point out
ever so temperately the inevitable wretchedness of
the slaves, and you will soon be taught that despotism
is as jealous, as watchful, and as fierce, in America
as in Europe.

The discussion of this prohibited subject is not only
visited by severe legal penalties, under pretence that it
has a tendency to produce insurrections,—the same
reason, by the way, which is given at Rome and Moscow,—but it is still more effectually suppressed by the
terrors of Lynch law, a system of procedure, which
in cases of this sort is either openly countenanced, or
secretly abetted by the gravest jurists of the South.

Not only is discussion prevented, but it is dangerous
to receive, to read, even to have in possession, any
book, pamphlet or newspaper which has been en-
rolled in the *Index Expurgatorius* of the slave-holding
Inquisition, or which, though not proscribed by name,
appears to treat upon the evils of slavery and their
remedies.

The United States post-office at Charleston was
violently assaulted by a mob, headed by the principal
inhabitants of the city, and a large part of its contents publicly burnt, under pretence that among the
newspapers and pamphlets contained in it, there were
some of an *insurrectionary* character.

At Richmond a bookseller received a box of books
containing copies of a certain work compiled by a

Virginia clergyman, to aid the Colonization Society. It was principally made up of extracts from speeches delivered in the Virginia House of Delegates in favor of a project for the gradual abolition of slavery by shipping off the slaves to Africa, broached shortly after the Southampton insurrection. This book was denounced as *incendiary* by the Richmond Committee of Safety, and by their order all the copies were delivered up, and burnt in the public square.

In the District of Columbia an unlucky botanist happened to have among his papers used for the preservation of plants, some copies of a prohibited newspaper. He was arrested, almost torn in pieces by the mob, thrown into prison where he lay upwards of six months, and it was with great difficulty that his acquittal was obtained.

It is a curious fact that at the very moment at which the *Richmond Whig* was assailing Louis Phillippe and his ministers for their restrictions upon the French press, the *Journal des Debats* was defending those restrictions by the example of Virginia! It must be confessed that the French restrictions are perfect liberty, compared with the law and practice of the southern states.

The Secret Tribunal of Venice, which received anonymous accusations, and which proceeded to judgment without notice given to the culprit, has been always denounced as an institution the most hostile to liberty that can possibly be imagined. Tribunals very similar, and in many respects much more to be dreaded, exist throughout almost the whole of the slave-holding states. They pervade the country and hold all the citizens in awe. The punishments inflicted are of the most dreaded kind,—death by the gallows or a slow fire, banishment, scourging, tar and feathers. This jurisdiction is known as *Lynch law*, and the accusers, judges and executioners are generally the same persons. As was the case with the Secret Tribunal, it confines itself principally to state crimes, that is, to such actions as are supposed to have a tendency to overthrow the existing system of despotism. This system of Lynch law which sprung into existence among the barbarous settlers of the backwoods, where no law existed, and which was invented by them as a substitute for law, has of late been introduced into the oldest and most civilized of the slave states, and has been made to supersede the regular administration of justice in a variety of the most serious and important cases. The terror of this tribunal is sufficient to preserve a dead silence at the South, and to produce an apparent unanimity of opinion. There are no doubt numbers who still entertain the opinions of Washington, of Henry, and of Jefferson upon the subject of slavery; but no one dares in public or in private to utter those opinions. No one known or suspected to be an abolitionist,—and this word at the South obtains a very extensive signification,— can reside or even travel in the slave states without imminent danger. Such, under a system of despotism, is the liberty even of those called free.

SECTION IV.

Slavery in its influence upon Equality.

Equality it has been stated, may be considered under three points of view, *Political Equality*, *Social Equality*, and *Equality of Wealth.*

Political and social equality are essentially dependent upon equality of wealth. The truth of this observation is confirmed by universal experience. Those who possess the property of a country, have always succeeded in obtaining the political power. Revolutions of property have always produced political revolutions.

Look for example to the history of England. So

long as the wealth of that country consisted principally in land, and that land was possessed by a few feudal and ecclesiastical barons, the whole political power of the country was in their hands. Towns having sprung into existence, inhabited by artisans and traders, whose industry created a new species of wealth, these towns presently attained a representation in the national legislature. Their influence at first was trifling; but it has steadily increased with the increase of manufacturing and commercial wealth, till now it has become almost predominant.

The history of France furnishes proof to the same point. So long as the nobility, the clergy and the magistrature, possessed the larger portion of property, they found no difficulty in maintaining their political superiority. But no sooner had the progress of events thrown a preponderancy of wealth into the hands of the *tiers etat*, than they began to devise means for obtaining political power. Hence the French Revolution; which, after immense struggles, resulted in putting the government into the hands of the more wealthy proprietors. The unfortunate adoption of too narrow a basis led, in the end, to the present imperial usurpation, which, however, could not stand for a moment, did not the French property holders support it as a means of defence against those who have no property.

If in the Northern States of the American Union there exists a degree of political equality of which the world offers no other example on so large a scale, the equal distribution of property throughout those states, is not less striking and remarkable.

It is an observation as curious as it is important, that in countries in which industry is respectable, and where the fruits of labor are secure, property always tends towards an equal distribution. Every man possesses as a means of acquirement, his own labor; and though there be a very considerable difference in the capacity, the industry, the good fortune of individuals, yet this difference has its limits; and diversities of acquisition are still more limited; for in general the in-

9

dustry of the rich man is relaxed; he is more inclined to spend than to accumulate; while the poor man is still stimulated by the desire of acquisition.

It appears then that in civilized communities, the natural tendency of things is towards equality. Inequality can only be maintained by artificial means; by laws which give to some individuals exclusive advantages not possessed by others, such as laws of primogeniture, of entail, laws conferring hereditary rights and privileges; laws creating monopolies of any and every kind.

If political equality be dependent upon equality of wealth, social equality is equally dependent upon it. Social distinctions which appear to spring from other sources, rise in fact from this, and by means of this are kept in activity. Blood and family are esteemed of great importance, and according to a vulgar notion which we hear every day repeated, are said to afford a much nobler and more respectable aristocracy, than that of mere wealth. But the founder of every noble family was first rich before he became noble. It is his wealth transmitted to his descendants to which they are principally indebted for distinction. When they become poor they soon fall into contempt. This is so well understood that whenever a Marlborough or a Wellington is raised to the highest rank of the peerage for services or supposed services rendered to his country, an *estate* is bestowed by parliament, to accompany the *title*.

Equality in general, may be resolved into equality of wealth. All depends upon that.

Now it is a fact clear and indisputable, that the existence of slavery in a country, is the surest and most inevitable means of producing and maintaining an inequality of wealth. This is not said with any reference to the unprivileged class, who are to be regarded in this view not as men, but merely as things. Reference is had only to the free. Slavery necessarily produces a great inequality of wealth among the free.

The method of this operation is obvious. The labor of each individual, is as we have seen, the natural and original source of individual wealth. But when a man is enabled to possess himself of the fruits produced by the labor of a large number of individuals, *to whom he is not obliged to make any compensation beyond a bare support*, his wealth tends to increase in a vast and disproportionate ratio, over the wealth of that individual who relies solely upon his own labor.

Moreover slaves are a sort of property much less valuable when held in small portions, than when possessed in masses. Where four or five hundred slaves are owned together, the doctrine of chances may be applied to the numerous casualties to which this kind of property is liable. The average annual loss and gain under ordinary circumstances will be pretty regular, and may be made a subject of calculation. But the owner of only four or five slaves may at any time lose them all by a sudden disorder. They may all be taken sick at the same time, and the crop may perish for want of hands to tend it. They may all run away together. The income expected from them is thus liable to fail entirely, and the poor man is constantly thrown back in his attempts to accumulate, by the necessity he is under of investing his gains, or a considerable part of them, in a species of property which when possessed in small quantities, is peculiarly insecure.*

But there is another effect of the existence of slavery in a community, much more extensive and powerful in its operation. Wherever slavery exists, labor comes to share the degradation and contempt of servitude, while idleness is regarded as the peculiar badge of freedom. But when idleness is general, the great mass of the community must inevitably be poor. In every country the number of those who inherit any considerable portion of wealth, is small. Personal industry is the only resource of the great bulk of the citizens. Where labor is honorable, it proves

---

* See Chapter III. Sec. II. for additional and important reasons of the tendency of slave-holding property to accumulate in a few hands.

to the prudent and industrious, a resource sufficient not only for support, but for the accumulation of wealth. When labor is not honorable, the mass of the citizens rather than degrade themselves by submitting to it, will be content with the merest subsistence. Thus it happens that in countries in which slavery has existed for a considerable length of time, the citizens are divided into two classes, of which the first and much the smaller, comprises a few rich proprietors who at the same time are large slave-holders, while the second class contains the great mass of the free people, persons of little property, or none at all.

This was the state of society in all the republics of ancient Greece. Those republics were constantly divided into two parties or factions. The oligarchical or aristocratic party, composed of the few rich and their immediate connections and dependents, and the democratic party, as it was called, composed of the bulk of poor freemen, headed and led on by some ambitious deserter from the aristocratic ranks. The history of ancient Greece consists for the most part, in the mutual struggle of these two parties. In general, the aristocratic party had the ascendency; when the opposite faction came into power, it was only by a sort of accident commonly of very limited duration.

This serves to explain a curious part of ancient history, to which we have no parallel in modern times, namely, the frequent projects for an artificial distribution of property, and of laws for the remission of debts. It was clearly perceived by many politicians of antiquity, that a certain equality of wealth was absolutely essential to political equality. They saw that the nominal equality of all the citizens amounted to but little, so long as all the wealth of the state was possessed by a few, and the great bulk of the citizens not only had nothing, but were even deeply in debt to the few rich. Hence the various projects for abolishing debts, prohibiting usury, limiting the amount of property which any individual might possess, and making new and equal distributions of existing wealth.

But these schemes did not touch the root of the evil. So long as slavery existed, it was a natural and inevitable consequence that all property, however equally it might at first be divided, should presently concentrate in the hands of a few, leaving the mass, idle and poor,—poor, because idle.

The operation of the same cause is very evident in the history of the Roman Republic. A few patricians were possessed of enormous wealth, counting their slaves by tens of thousands, and owning almost entire provinces, while the great bulk of the citizens were in a state of the most deplorable poverty, depending for their support upon distributions of corn from the public granaries, upon gratuities bestowed upon the commonality by the ambitious rich, and on the pay and plunder of the military service.

Such are some of the instances which history affords, of the natural effect of slavery in concentrating wealth in a few hands, and in reducing the mass of the free to poverty and political degradation. History also furnishes instances of the contrary process, by which liberty has given a spring to industry, and has thus operated to disseminate wealth, and to create an intermediate body between the rich and the poor, a body which with the increase of civilization and knowledge, is destined perhaps to embrace the great mass of mankind. About the tenth century of the christian era the greater part of Europe was reduced by a combination of causes, to a most barbarous condition. A few great lords, who were in fact little better than so many Tartar or African chiefs of the present day, possessed all the land, the only sort of property which remained in existence. This land was cultivated by slaves. The mass of the free population depended for its support upon the bounty of the feudal chiefs, which bounty was repaid by the constant attendance and warlike services of those who received it. The sole occupation of the free was, hunting and war.

In this state of things we can discover no element

9*

of social improvement. What then has changed the
condition of Europe to the state of comparative advancement in which we now see it? A few serfs
flying from the tyranny of their lords, founded here
and there, a little settlement. They built walls to
protect themselves from feudal aggression. In many
cases they resorted to some ancient city, a remnant of
former times, dwindled to a ruin, but which their industry helped to repair, and their courage to defend.
They applied themselves to the mechanic arts and to
trade. Gradually they amassed wealth. In these
cities slavery was not tolerated, and the serfs of the
neighborhood found first protection, and presently
citizenship. These cities thus founded and thus built
up, are the origin of that great class of merchants,
manufacturers, and industrious men, to whom Europe
is indebted for its present advancement, and on whom
its future hopes depend.

The same tendency of servitude to produce great
inequalities of condition among the free is as visible
in the history of America as of Europe. The insurrection of the slaves of St. Domingo had for its immediate occasion a violent quarrel between the white
and the mulatto slave-holders of the island. While
these two factions of the free were engaged in a bloody
contest on the question of political equality, the slaves
seized the opportunity to reclaim their liberties.

Slavery produces the same effects in the southern
states of the American union, which it ever has produced in all the world beside. Several cases have
hitherto operated to retard, or to disguise these effects,
but they are becoming every day more and more
visible.

The poor whites of the old slave states have hitherto
found a resource in emigration. All of them who had
any spirit of enterprise and industry have quitted a
home where labor was disgraceful, and in the wide
regions beyond the mountains have attained a comfortable livelihood, and have amassed wealth by means
which however innocent or laudable, they could not

employ in the places where they were born, without a certain degree of self-abasement. But by a fatal oversight, a most disastrous ignorance, they omitted to exclude that great source of evil, the bitter effects of which they had experienced in their own persons; and that same train of causes is now in full operation in Kentucky and Tennessee, Missouri and Arkansas, which drove the original settlers of those states from Maryland, Virginia, and North Carolina.

As to the southwestern states, they offer no resources to the poor whites. The cultivation of cotton has attracted thither, and still continues to attract, a host of slave-masters, and whole gangs of slaves. No man can emigrate to those states who expects to live by the labor of his hands, unless he is prepared to brave that very ignominy, and to plunge anew into that very social condition which makes him uneasy, and cuts him off from all chance of advancement at home.

Political parties in the slave-holding states, within a few years past, have begun to assume an aspect entirely new, and one which gives fearful omen that these slave-holding republics are about to follow in the career of those ancient states, whose policy was founded, like theirs, upon a system of slavery. There is already, throughout most or all of the slave-holding states, an aristocratic party, and a party which calls itself democratic. The aristocratic party is composed of the rich planters, and of those whom their wealth enables them to influence and control. The democratic party, so called, is composed in a great measure of the *poor white folks*, with a sprinkling of ambitious aristocrats for leaders. This miscalled democratic party,—for it is in fact only a faction of the white aristocracy,—by the natural operation of the slave-holding system, is rapidly increasing in numbers, and with the increase of its numbers, the social degradation and the destitution of its members will also increase. Measures of enlightened policy are hardly to be expected from such a party, even if it could obtain power and keep it, which indeed is hardly to be ex-

pected. Such is the force of habit, the power of prejudice, the invincible stupidity of ignorance that these
people seem incapable of perceiving the real cause
of their own degradation. They are apparently as
much attached to slavery and are as ardent in its
support as is the aristocratic party, thus regarding
with a blind and fatal reverence those very institutions which crush them to the dust. The influence,
however, of such a party, composed of men, poor,
degraded, ignorant and ferocious, and headed by some
desperate Catiline of the aristocracy, may at times,
prove extremely disastrous, not to the southern states
alone, but to the whole union.

SECTION V.

Education in the Slave-holding States.

That the state ought to provide for all its citizens
the means of at least that primary education which
consists in the knowledge of reading and writing, has
come to be a political maxim generally acted upon in
all civilized communities. Even such despotic governments as Austria and Prussia have admitted this
most important article into their political code ; and
primary instruction is provided by those governments
for all the people at the public expense. This shows
the progress which the idea of equality has lately
made ; for *equality of knowledge* is a most essential
part of political and social equality.

The despotisms existing in the southern states of
the American Union, are almost wholly regardless of
this important political duty of general education.
We have already seen that so far as regards the unprivileged class, the attempt to impart any instruction
to them, so far from being considered a duty, is de-

nounced as a crime. There are also obvious reasons
why no general public provision for the education of
the privileged class has ever been established.

The privileged class consists, as we have seen, of
an oligarchy of rich planters, and a comparatively
large body of persons with little or no property. The
rich planters know the value of education, and their
wealth enables them to secure it for their own children
by the employment of private tutors, or by sending
them to schools and colleges at the North. The poor
whites, bred up in ignorance, have no adequate idea
of the value of knowledge, or of the importance of its
diffusion. The rich planters have no inclination to
tax themselves for the benefit of their poor neighbors.
Their wealth, education and influence, enables them
to control the legislation of their respective states;
and perhaps they imagine that they shall best secure
their own importance and political power, by keeping
the mass of the free population in ignorance. The
same stroke of policy which they play off against their
slaves, they play off also against their poorer fellow
citizens.

What has been done in a public way for the advancement of education in the southern states, has
consisted almost entirely in the establishment of colleges,—institutions of but little use to the mass of the
population, and which are almost exclusively fre-
quented by the sons of the rich planters. For this
purpose money has been liberally appropriated.

It is true that in Virginia, South Carolina, and perhaps in some other of the slave-holding states, a trifling
sum is annually appropriated expressly for the education of *poor children*. But the very form of this appropriation, which extorts from those who wish to
avail themselves of it, a humiliating confession of
poverty, is an insult to those for whose benefit it is
intended. That aid which might be justly demanded
as a right, is made to assume the character of a charity.
Besides, the amount of these appropriations is so small,
and their management is so miserable, that little or no
benefit results.

The facts of the case then, appear to be these. Not one of the slave-holding states possesses any thing like a regular system of common schools, or has made any provision at all worthy of notice, for disseminating the rudiments of education among its citizens. Inequality of wealth has produced, as a natural consequence, inequality of knowledge.

This condition of things tends greatly to aggravate the social and political inequalities which prevail throughout the southern states. It is in vain that people who cannot read, boast of their political rights. There is no power more easily abused for the promotion of private ends, than the power conferred by superior knowledge. A man who cannot read, may be said to be politically blind. Those who see may miss the way, but the blind have hardly a chance to find it. Nothing is more easy than leading them into the pit, and thus making them the instruments of their own destruction. It is the extreme ignorance of those who compose what is called the democratic party at the South, which incapacitates that party from projecting and carrying through any real and useful reforms in the social polity of those states, and which converts it into the mere tool and stepping-stone of artful and ambitious men, who insinuate themselves into its confidence, and then employ that confidence for the accomplishment of their merely private ends. In the nature of things, the aristocracy of rich planters, as they possess all the wealth and all the knowledge, will succeed, in the long run, in usurping the whole political power. As might be expected, South Carolina, the state in which slavery is most predominant, is also the state in which the aristocracy of rich planters domineers without control. Already the doctrine, sanctioned by the constitution of that state, that every freeman is entitled to vote at elections, is violently assailed by the leaders of the aristocratic faction. They insist upon a property qualification. It is easy to see whither this doctrine will lead. By the concentration of wealth in few hands, which is the natural result of slavery, the number of those who possess the requisite qualifications will continue to diminish, till at last the whole political power concentrates in form, as it now does in fact, in the hands of a little oligarchy of rich slave-holders.

But though the equality secured to all freemen by the constitutions of the slave-holding states, is little more than nominal, though the few wealthy and well informed generally succeed in obtaining the political control, and then employ it to promote their own private ends, it is not, therefore, to be hastily concluded that the constitutional rights of the poor freemen are valueless, or that the loss of those rights with which they are threatened, is not a thing to be most seriously deprecated. Having a vote at elections, every freeman, however humble his condition, is sure of being treated with a certain degree of respect. If the mass of the people are cajoled out of their votes, they still receive for them a sort of equivalent, in kind words and fair speeches. Let them be deprived of this title to consideration, and the native insolence of power would soon display itself, and they would be trampled under foot with the same remorseless violence now exercised upon the free blacks and the slaves.

SECTION VI.

The military strength of the Slave-holding States.

The military strength of states has ever been esteemed of the highest importance in a political point of view; since it is upon their military strength that states are often obliged to depend for their defence against internal, as well as external foes. In this particular the slave-holding states of the South present an aspect of extreme weakness.

When all the inhabitants of a country have arms in their hands, and are ready and zealous to meet and repulse any invader, the military strength of a country may be said to be at the highest point, for experience has abundantly demonstrated how easy it is to transform citizens into soldiers. But those citizens who are capable of being transformed into soldiers must be principally drafted from the laborious classes of society. The hardy cultivators of the soil, when driven to the dire necessity of beating their plough shares into swords, have ever furnished the best and most patriotic soldiers,—soldiers, who after repulsing the hostile invader, have willingly resumed again the useful labors of their former calling. Men of this class composed those armies of the revolution to whose courage, fortitude and patient spirit of endurance, we are indebted for our national independence.

But in the slave states, these cultivators of the earth, these very men upon whom reliance ought to be principally placed in the hour of danger, would in that hour, be regarded with more dread and terror even than the invaders themselves. In case of a threatened invasion, so far from aiding in the defence of the country, they would create a powerful diversion in favor of the enemy.

When the French, in the first years of the revolution, marched into the neighboring countries proclaiming "liberty and equality," they were received with such good-will on the part of the inhabitants as ensured a speedy triumph, notwithstanding the superior force arrayed to resist their progress. The events of those wars placed in a strong light, the fact obvious enough in itself, but which had not then attracted sufficient attention, that the inclination of the inhabitants of a country is much more apt to decide its fate, than the strength of armies in the field. When half the inhabitants of a country wish success to invaders, it is not easy to resist them.

Considering the odious light in which slavery is now regarded by all civilized nations, it is not likely, in case the United States became involved in war with any people of Europe, that any repugnance would be felt on the part of the hostile state, in seeking aid at the hands of the slaves. A lodgement being effected upon some part of the Southern coast, by an army of respectable strength, and emancipation being promised to all such slaves as would join the invaders, a force would soon be accumulated which the unassisted efforts of the slave-holding states would find it impossible to resist. If the invaders were expelled it would only be by troops marched from the North. In such a crisis the fear of outbreaks on their own plantations would keep the planters at home; or if they assembled in force to resist the invaders, their absence would be likely to produce such outbreaks. When a servile was added to a foreign war, between the rage of the masters and the hatred of the slaves, it would assume a most savage aspect.

There exist, indeed, sufficient reasons for entertaining the belief that an experiment of this sort was projected during the war of 1812, and that nothing but the fact that Great Britain at that time had slave colonies of her own, prevented it from being carried into effect.

The difficulty of raising troops in the slave-holding states is obvious from the fact, that Massachusetts alone furnished more soldiers to the revolutionary armies, than all the slave-holding states united. The obstacles in the way of raising troops in those states, have greatly increased since that time.

The military weakness of a slave-holding community was strikingly illustrated in the capture of the city of Washington by the British in 1814. Could such an army have marched such a distance, and effected such destruction in any of the free states? To that question let Concord and Lexington reply. Had the slaves of those counties through which the British army marched, been free citizens, had not Washington itself been a slave market, the British troops would never have arrived within sight of the capitol.

Should the slave-holding states become involved in a war, which it would be necessary for them to prosecute from their own resources, they would be obliged to depend upon a standing army levied from among the dregs of the population. Such an army would be likely to become quite as much an object of terror to those for whose defence it would be levied, as to those against whom it would be raised. It would not be easy to disband an army composed of men destitute of every other resource, but who had found in military service a means of living at the expense of others. It would be insisted, and with some show of justice too, that the country was bound to maintain and provide for those to whom it was indebted for defence and even existence.

One other observation will place the military weakness of the slave-holding states in a clear point of view. They are dependent for all manufactured articles upon foreign supply. Even the very tools with which the plantations are cultivated, are furnished from abroad. Every article of equipment necessary to enable an army to take the field, must be imported, and unless their agricultural productions can be freely exported in return, they have no means whereby to purchase, or to pay. The coast of the slave-holding states is but scantily furnished with harbors; all the trade of export and import, centres at a few points. These points may be easily blockaded by a small naval force. The slave states have no facilities for equipping or manning a fleet. In a naval warfare, half a dozen of the fishing towns of New England might compete with the whole of them, and a strict blockade of their harbors for three or four years, would reduce the whole of the Southern States to a condition of the greatest distress.

In point of military strength the slave-holding states are not by any means all to be placed upon the same level. Such states as Kentucky and Tennessee where the proportion of slaves is small, are very strong in comparison with Carolina and Louisiana, where the unprivileged class form a majority of the population.

CHAPTER THIRD.

ECONOMICAL RESULTS OF THE SLAVE-HOLDING SYSTEM.

SECTION I.

Effect of Slavery upon the Sources of Wealth.

The public wealth consists in the sum total of the wealth possessed by all the individual members of the community. Generally speaking a community is wealthy in proportion to the relative number of its members who are possessors of property. A few very rich men may make a great show, and create a false impression as to the wealth of a community; but a large number of small properties added together will far outrun the sum total of a few large ones. The pay of the officers of an army is very large compared with that of the rank and file; but the sum total of the pay of the rank and file, far exceeds in amount the sum total of the pay of the officers.

That the slave states of the American Union are excessively poor compared with the free states, is conceded on all hands. The slaves, forming in some of the states, the majority of the population, are incapable of holding property. They are not the owners even of their own labor, and of course they can contribute nothing to the sum total of the public wealth. The class of poor whites, including a large proportion of the free population, are possessed of a very trifling property. Almost the entire capital of the country is in the hands of a comparatively small number of slave-holders; and of the property which they possess, a great portion consists in the minds and muscles of the unprivileged class. In free communities, every man is the proprietor of his own muscles and intellect; but as these commodities however valuable, are not the subject of bargain and sale in the market, they are not usually reckoned as property. Compare the tax valuations of the slave-holding states with that of the free states, and it will be discovered, that almost the only kind of property, in the usual acceptation of that word, which exists at the South, is, the land, and the buildings upon it. Exclude the slaves, and the amount of what is called personal property existing in those states, is exceedingly small; and upon examination it will be found to fall greatly short of the amount of debt always due to the North and to Europe.

In estimating the actual wealth of the slave-holding states, the amount of this debt ought always to be taken into account. A great part of the banking capital of those states is borrowed; and so of the money invested in rail-roads and other public works. A large proportion of the planters have beside great private debts of their own, secured by mortgage upon their plantations and slaves, many of them being little better than tenants at will to some northern capitalist, to whom all their property in fact belongs.

As the Southern States possess advantages of soil and climate peculiar to themselves, it becomes an interesting inquiry, what is the cause of this comparative poverty?

1. Political economists have generally agreed that *labor* is the sole source of wealth. Whether this doctrine be literally and absolutely true, may perhaps be doubted; it is however beyond all doubt, that labor is a very principal source of value.

The great motive to labor, the great inducement to exertion, that motive, that inducement which has raised man from the primitive barbarism of the woods to such degrees of refinement and civilization as have yet been attained, has been, *expectation of reward*. There is in this motive a sort of creative power, which seems to give new strength and alacrity. It even possesses the capacity of making labor delightful. The only other motive powerful enough to overcome the natural indolence of man, is the *fear of punishment;* but that is a melancholy and miserable motive which seems to add a new distastefulness to labor, and to wither up the energies of those whom it influences.

Now with respect to the whole unprivileged class, that is to say the principal laboring class in the slave-holding states, their only motive to industry, is this second, this enfeebling motive, the fear of punishment. Their labor is compulsive and reluctant, and its results are proportionably small.

With respect to the other laboring class at the south, to wit, the poor whites, their industry is paralyzed by a fatal prejudice which regards manual labor as the badge of a servile condition, and therefore as disgraceful,—a prejudice which not even the expectation of reward is strong enough to overcome. It is a prejudice similar to this which has operated in no small degree to keep Spain in a stationary state, two centuries behind the civilization of the rest of Europe. But even Spain in this respect, is more fortunate than the American slave holding states. It is the mechanic arts which the Spaniards regard as derogatory, whereas agriculture is comparatively respectable. In the slave holding states of America, agricultural labor is the most derogatory of all, because the labor of the field most assimilates the condition of a freeman to that of a slave. Whenever such notions prevail, they are fatal to public prosperity. Poverty keeps pace with pride.

Take the slave-holding states together, and the free inhabitants are about twice as numerous as the slaves. Yet all the great articles of production in which the wealth of the slave-holding states consists, cotton, tobacco, rice, sugar and flour, are produced almost exclusively by slave labor.

What then is the occupation of the free? One class, the larger slave-masters, contribute absolutely nothing to the public stock. They hardly bestow a thought

10*

even upon the management of their own estates. Their sole business is, to receive the income and to spend it. Another class of the free population obtain a livelihood by acting as overseers or viceroys for their richer neighbors. They are thus saved from the degradation of manual labor ; but it is a hard service by which they earn their bread. So hard, that it is very seldom performed to the satisfaction of their employers. The planters give a terrible character of the overseers as a class. According to their account, the overseers as a general rule, are ignorant, stupid, obstinate, negligent, drunken and dishonest. For their ignorance they are hardly to blame, considering what scanty means of education this class enjoy. Stupidity and obstinacy are the natural fruits of ignorance. Negligence and drunkenness they learn from their employers; and if overseers are dishonest it is little to be wondered at, considering the temptations and opportunities by which they are surrounded, and the total confusion of all ideas of right and wrong, justice and injustice, which the nature of their employment is likely to produce.

The third and largest division of the privileged class, compelled by absolute want to the disgraceful necessity of manual labor, work with an unwillingness as great as that of the slaves, and with still less of efficiency. The produce of their labor is very small. In general it is hardly sufficient to support them in that rude and semi-barbarous condition to which they have been accustomed.

The disastrous effects of slave-holding upon free industry, are particularly obvious in the families of the small planters, and of those farmers who possess but five or six slaves. These slaves suffice to perform the labors of the farm, and when the land is fertile the owner of it lives in a rustic plenty. A family of sons grows up around him. He has no occasion for their assistance on the farm, and if he had, they would regard the labor as an intolerable disgrace. The boys grow up in idleness, with little or no education, because there is no system of public instruction, and the father cannot afford to send them to a distance in pursuit of schools. They arrive at man's estate without having been bred to any regular employment. Each has his horse, his dog and his gun; and while the father lives the sons have a home; they spend their time in hunting, or in riding about the country, or at horse-races, frolics, barbecues, or political meetings. There are thousands of young men in Kentucky and Tennessee in this unhappy predicament. Full of spirit and ambition, active, capable, eager for some honorable employment; but condemned by the social system of which they form a part, and by the unhappy prejudices against useful industry which that system engenders, to an idleness which presently becomes as irksome to themselves, as it is fatal to the public prosperity. When habit has made indolence inveterate, and when they are too old to apply themselves with zeal or success to a new course of life, the death of the father cuts off the support they have hitherto enjoyed. His property divided among a numerous family, gives but a pittance to each. That pittance is soon spent. Want stares the unhappy sufferers in the face. They lose by degrees their standing and respectability. The weaker spirited among them sink down to the lowest depths of poverty and vice. Those of more energy emigrate to the new states of the far west, and having escaped the charmed circle in which they were so long bound up, they develop a new character, and like their fathers before them, by means of their own personal industry, they bring a farm into cultivation and gradually acquire wealth. But if they have settled in a slave state, that wealth is generally invested in slaves; and their own children are bred up in that same style of helpless indolence of which they themselves were so near becoming the victims, and which their children perhaps will not so fortunately escape.

Thus it appears that one plain and obvious effect of the slave-holding system is, to deaden in every class of society that *spirit of industry* essential to the increase of public wealth.

2. The spirit of industry is not however alone sufficient for the accumulation of property. Industry quickens production; but to accumulate, it is necessary not only to produce but to save. *Economy* then, may justly be regarded as the second great source of public wealth.

But to expect any thing like economy from the unprivileged class, would be extremely ridiculous. Economy is like industry, it is like every other virtue,—it never will be exercised unless there is a motive constantly operating to produce it. Now in the condition of servitude no such motive exists. In fact, the motives are all the other way. The slave receives from his master a certain weekly allowance of food. Any attempt to lay by a part of it, would be absurd, for as soon as a store was accumulated, the master, if he discovered it, would stop the allowance till that store was consumed; or at all events, he would immediately diminish an allowance which experience had shown to be more than sufficient. It would be the same with respect to clothing. But why dwell upon this topic? Is it not plain that he who is incapable of possessing property is alike destitute of motives to produce or to save?

If slaves are improvident with respect to themselves, it is not remarkable that they are still more so with respect to their owners. No matter what occurs; if the cotton house is on fire; if the fences are down, and the cattle destroy the corn; if the horses stray away; if the tools are lost or broken; it there happens one or all the thousand accidents which are always liable to diminish the value of their master's property, and which a little care or foresight might have prevented,—any or all of these occurrences are a matter of perfect unconcern to the slave, nor will he voluntarily lift a finger to prevent them. If indeed he has any feeling about the matter, it is rather an inclination to destroy than to save. He experiences a secret delight, in the losses and sorrows of a master whom he hates.

Nor is economy likely to be practised to any considerable extent by the hireling overseers to whom the management of the great plantations is intrusted. These overseers are frequently changed, and they have little or no interest in the economical management of the property intrusted to their charge.

As little can we look to the conduct of the slave-masters for any exhibition of the virtue now under consideration. It is an old observation that what comes easy goes easy. This saying is verified by the conduct of brigands, pirates, and robbers, and all that class of men who live upon plunder. It applies with equal force and for the same reason, to slave-masters, who generally contrive to spend all they get and to run into debt all they can.

We have thus seen that with respect to the slaves and their owners, idleness and improvidence keep close company. The same is the fact with respect to the poorer class of freemen. Though their resources be next to nothing, they still contrive to imitate in their small way, the careless extravagance of their richer neighbors.

It thus appears that there is a great deficiency of the second principal source of public wealth, to wit, economy, among all classes of the population of the slave-holding states of America.

3. A third great source of public wealth consists in *invention*, by which is meant, the discovery of new and more productive applications of industry. But to call this great means of increasing the productive power of a community into action, industry must be honorable. That ingenuity which busies itself in observations and experiments for the discovery of means to produce the same effect with less labor, seldom displays itself except in communities in which the useful arts are held in high esteem. Even inventions made elsewhere, are for the most part brought into use with great difficulty, in those societies in which

men of education and reflection, if such there are, despise useful industry, and in which the great business of production is intrusted to ignorant and stupid slaves, and to overseers equally ignorant and stupid. Under these circumstances every thing proceeds in the same dull round, without change or attempt at improvement. The more men know, and the more they reflect, the more convinced they are how limited is the actual extent of their progress. Ignorance is arrogant, dogmatical, certain that it knows every thing already. The idea of improvement does not enter into all its thoughts. Hence it is that the early progress of a people from barbarism to civilization takes place by such hardly perceptible steps, and is subjected to so many hindrances and interruptions, as almost to discourage the most sanguine believers in human perfectibility, and to have given rise to the common opinion that savage nations are incapable of being civilized; while on the other hand, the history of our own age serves to show, how civilization, once set fairly in motion, advances with an impulse continually accelerated, and which not even the most serious obstacles can long retard.

The southern states derive no inconsiderable advantage from their close and intimate connection with the free states of the north, of which the social system is so essentially different. By this means the natural effect of the institutions of the south, are to a certain extent counteracted, especially in those newly settled states into which there has been a considerable influx of northern population.

SECTION II.

Slavery as it affects the amount of capital required for industrious undertakings.

All enterprises of industry, whether agricultural, mechanical or mercantile, require a certain amount of capital for their successful prosecution. Every thing which enables these enterprises to be carried on with a less amount of capital, contributes to the increase of national wealth; and on the other hand, every thing which causes a greater amount of capital to be required, is an obstacle in the way of all new undertakings.

In free communities, where the laborers have their own labor at their own disposal, and where in consequence, they are ready to sell it, either by the day, the year, or the hour, in any quantities, that is, in which it may be needed, beside the fixed capital invested in lands, workshops, tools, ships, steamboats, &c., there are required two separate portions of floating capital, one to be invested in the stock to be operated upon, and the other to be employed in paying the wages of labor. But no more labor need be paid for than is actually employed. Whenever a smaller quantity will answer, a portion of the laborers may be dismissed; whenever more is needed, more laborers may be employed.

But in a slave-holding community, in addition to these three portions of capital, another and a very large portion is required, in order to commence any industrious enterprise whatever; for though in such a community there is no payment of wages, yet a corresponding quantity of capital is necessary to furnish food, clothing, and medicines for the slaves. A fourth and additional portion of capital is also required, to be invested in *the purchase of the laborers themselves,*—a necessity which constitutes a great obstacle in the way of all industrious enterprises.

Take the business of agriculture for example. In the new cotton-growing states, a very small sum of money will suffice to purchase a plantation of several hundred acres; but a very large sum of money is needed to purchase the laborers necessary to carry on the cultivation of it. Could laborers be hired by the month or the day, as in free communities, a moderate capital would enable the planter to command the labor he would need, whereas, under existing circumstances, no person can start a new plantation in Alabama or Mississippi, who is not already possessed of a large capital, or able to command it in the shape of loans.

We shall fall, probably, much under the mark, if we assume that a capital of five thousand dollars invested in hired labor, would enable as many acres to be cultivated, as a capital of fifty thousand dollars invested in slave labor. The consequence of this state of things is obvious. It gives a monopoly of the command of labor to those who are already possessed of large means, either in the shape of property or of credit. Persons of small capital have no chance to compete with persons of large capital, because by this system, a large capital is rendered absolutely necessary to obtain that command of labor without which no industrious enterprise can be carried on. This single fact is sufficient to explain that tendency of the wealth of a slave community to concentrate in a few hands, which has been stated in a preceding chapter.

This system not only gives a monopoly of the command of labor to those who are already rich, but it is also a very wasteful and extravagant system. It compels the operator to purchase and to support a much larger number of laborers than he ordinarily has occasion for. He is obliged constantly to own and to feed the largest number ever necessary in his business, or else to submit, occasionally, to severe loss, for want of a sufficiency of labor. In the cotton planting business, for instance, a given number of slaves can cultivate a considerably larger quantity of cotton than they can gather in; so that the planter is either obliged to submit to an annual loss of a portion of the crop which he has brought to maturity, or else to cultivate less than he otherwise might, for the sake of gathering all.

The cotton crop, however, as it extends the labor of cultivation and gathering in, through almost the entire year, is less surely attended with this sort of loss, than are the grain crops and farm cultivation of the more northern slave-holding states. In those states, during the winter, there is comparatively little occasion for labor on the farms. During all that time, the capital invested in the ownership of slaves, is unproductive, and the slave-master is saddled in addition with the expense of supporting laborers, for whose services he has no occasion.

What a great discouragement to the poor, that is, to the great mass of the free population, this system presents, will be evident from a few considerations. In those parts of the slave states in which slavery predominates, it is impossible to hire free laborers. To work at all, even on one's own little tract of land, is considered a sufficient degradation; but to work for another person, to put one's self under his direction, seems to approach too near to the condition of slavery, to be at all endurable. If a person, therefore, wishes to employ any other labor than his own, he must have recourse to slave labor. But the employment of the labor of other people is in general absolutely essential to the accumulation of wealth. Where a man merely hoards up the profits of his own labor, his wealth increases only as money does when placed at simple interest, and the industry and economy of a long life will accumulate but a moderate sum. But if those profits are invested in the employment of the labor of other people, his wealth then increases like money at compound interest.

But when to employ other labor than one's own, it is necessary to buy the laborers, a considerable sum must be first accumulated, before it can be employed at all; and as has been shown in another place, so long as the number of slaves which a person possesses, is small, the investment is exceedingly precarious.

The necessity of a great capital, and the wastefulness with which that capital is employed, sufficiently explain the fact, why in all those occupations in which the industry of the free states has come into competition with the labor of slaves, the free states have been able to undersell their rivals. Slave labor is only profitably employed in those kinds of business, such as the cultivation of cotton, rice, and sugar, in which the climate and soil of the northern states prevent the people of those states from engaging. In the cultivation of grain, the raising of stock, and all the operations of farming agriculture, the profits of the slave-holding cultivators are notoriously small, and many a large slave-holder grows poor in that same pursuit, which enriches the farmer of Ohio, Pennsylvania and New York, who begins life with no other resource than his own capacity to labor. Hence that heavy drain of emigration, hence that fatal domestic slave trade, which aggravates the poverty of the older of the slave states, by carrying off that labor, which constitutes the principal means of economical prosperity.

This same necessity for a great capital, in order to undertake any industrious enterprise, and the same necessary wastefulness in the employment of that capital, afford also one reason among many others, why it has been found unprofitable to set up manufacturing establishments at the south. It is not only necessary to build your factory, and to buy your machinery and stock, but before you can commence operations, you must expend a still larger sum in the purchase of laborers. Apart from everything else, a sufficient reason for the non-establishment of manufactures at the South, is to be found in the fact, that at the North, the same annual quantity of manufactured products can be turned out, with the employment of much less than half the amount of capital, which would be necessary for the same purpose at the South.

SECTION III.

Agriculture in the Slave-holding States.

If we may believe John Taylor of Caroline, the author of *Arator*, or Mr. Ruffin, the ingenious editor of the *Virginia Farmers' Register*, the best agricultural periodical ever published in the United States, agriculture at the South does not consist so much in cultivating land, as in *killing* it. The process is as follows.

A quantity of virgin soil, in those of the slave states in which any such soil is yet to be found, is cleared up every winter. The trees are cut down and burnt, or merely girdled, and left to decay and fall with the lapse of time. When tobacco is the crop, this fresh land is planted with tobacco each successive year till its fertility is exhausted. When it will no longer produce tobacco, it is planted with corn or wheat, till it will not afford a crop worth gathering. It is then *turned out*, that is, left unfenced and uncultivated, to grow up with thickets of sassafras or persimmon bushes, or with forests of the short-leaved pine,—a majestic tree in appearance, but the timber of which is subject to so rapid a decay, as to be of little or no value.

In the cotton-growing states, corn and cotton are planted alternately, till the land is completely worn out. When its original fertility is exhausted, no further attempt is made at its cultivation. It is turned out, and the labor of the plantation is applied to new fields, which presently undergo a similar fate. Thus, every year, a certain quantity of land is given over as worthless, and new inroads are made upon the original forest. Agriculture becomes a continual process of opening new fields, and abandoning the old.

This brief account of southern agriculture, will serve to explain the remarkable fact, that what we should call improved lands, that is, lands which have been brought into cultivation, are generally of inferior value and price to the adjoining wild lands which must be cleared up before they can be planted. Every crop taken from a field diminishes its value; and as the number of successive crops which can be taken without reducing the land to a state of barrenness, is not great, the diminution in its value, is sufficiently rapid. This is one cause of the sparseness of population at the south. No planter ever thinks he has land enough. Knowing that he destroys a quantity every year, he is anxious still to enlarge his domain so as to be certain of having a supply sufficient to meet the consumption.

Almost the only wealth in the southern states consists in lands and slaves. But slaves are only valuable as cultivators of the soil; and as the productive power of the soil diminishes, the value of slaves must decline with the decreasing amount which they are able to produce. The inevitable consequences to which this system of agriculture must finally lead, are sufficiently obvious. The soil in its whole extent, being at length exhausted, the slaves will hardly be able to produce enough for their own support. They will cease to possess any marketable value; and the entire mass of the population will sink down into a state of miserable poverty, from which they can emerge only by a complete change of manners and habits, and a thorough revolution in the social system.

Nor is this period by any means so distant as may at first appear. For though the superficial extent of the slave holding states is very great, the quantity of land which they afford of sufficient natural fertility to admit of being cultivated according to the southern method, is not great. Deduct the mountains, the morasses and the vast pine barrens, and but a moderate extent of land will remain, a part of which has already been exhausted and deserted, and all of which, with the exception of some alluvial tracks, along the water courses, is of a description not fitted long to withstand the destructive processes of southern agriculture.

This progress of pauperism, presents itself under very different aspects, in different states of the union, according to the antiquity of their settlement, and the density of their population. In the newer states, in which the proportion of virgin land is still very great, to a superficial view it is altogether non-apparent. Its early operation suggests nothing but ideas of public prosperity and increasing wealth. But there is a certain point where the tide turns. The spendthrift, so long as his money holds out, has the appearance and enjoys the reputation of abundant riches. It is only when his resources begin to fail, that the reality of his condition, and the true nature of his conduct become apparent.

Virginia is the oldest of the slave states. All the rest are treading in her footsteps. From her unfortunate condition at the present moment it is easy to portend what theirs must presently become. Eastern Virginia, including all that portion of the state east of the Blue Ridge, presented to the original colonists, a most inviting country. Washed on one side by a spacious bay, into which poured numerous rivers, broad, deep and navigable, all the lower part of the state had received from the hand of nature such unusual facilities of water communication, that hardly a point could be found twenty miles distant from navigable waters; and for the most part, every plantation had its landing place. These numerous rivers were stored and still continue to be stored with such an abundance of fish, fowl and oysters as might alone suffice to support a numerous population. Above the falls of the rivers was a hilly diversified country, generally rich, and if it had some barren tracts, affording spots of the most exuberant fertility.

When Eastern Virginia first began to be settled, it afforded beyond all question, the richest and most desirable country any where to be found along the Atlantic coast of the union.

The cultivation of tobacco soon became so profitable, that the more industrious of the colonists grew

11*

rich by it. Most unfortunately they invested these profits in the purchase of slaves from Africa. The introduction of slave labor presently proved fatal to the industry of the free. But this circumstance was little thought of or regarded, so long as the tobacco cultivation continued to increase, and to bring in rich returns. The wealthier planters rose to the condition of nabobs. They extended their plantations, increased the number of their slaves, and spent freely the large incomes which their estates produced. The apparent wealth and prosperity of the country was very great.

By degrees, the entire surface in the older portions of the state had been cleared, planted and exhausted. Tobacco requires a rich soil, and the impoverished land would no longer produce it. It became necessary to abandon this species of cultivation, first in the tide-water districts, and afterwards in all that portion of the state north of the James River. The culture of tobacco in Virginia is now confined, for the most part, to a few of the southern counties, in the vicinity of the Blue Ridge, in which some virgin land is still to be found.

The cultivation of grain succeeded to that of tobacco. These crops were far less profitable; but even these, when taken in constant succession from the same soil, are scarcely less exhausting. The lands have continued to deteriorate till large tracts have been abandoned as absolutely worthless. Meantime, a constant stream of emigration has been pouring out of Virginia. It was first directed to Kentucky, and the states north-west of the Ohio. It then consisted of the poorer portions of the white population, who were the first to suffer from the general decline. This emigration is now directed towards the cotton growing states of the south-west. It is greater than ever, and embraces the wealthiest men and the largest slave-holders, who find that slave property, which is valueless in Virginia, except as an article of exportation, can be put to profitable use in the cultivation of cotton. The domestic slave-trade produces another equally serious drain upon the population of Eastern Virginia. In default of crops, the planters have no other means to meet their expenses, except selling their slaves. This affords a momentary relief, but it is fatal to the permanent prosperity of the country, which in losing its laboring men, in losing its cultivators, loses the only means whereby it can recover from its present decline.

That part of Virginia which lies upon tide waters, presents an aspect of universal decay. Its population diminishes, and it sinks day by day, into a lower depth of exhaustion and poverty. The country between tide waters and the Blue Ridge is fast passing into the same condition. Mount Vernon is a desert waste; Monticello is little better; and the same circumstances which have desolated the lands of Washington and Jefferson, have impoverished every planter in the state. Hardly any have escaped save the owners of the rich bottom lands along James River, the fertility of which it seems difficult utterly to destroy.

This thriftless system of cultivation, which consists in exhausting a field and then abandoning it, prevailed originally in the more northern states as well as in Virginia. So long as the quantity of new land appeared inexhaustible, this method of culture was a natural and profitable operation, and it was continued by habit long after its bad policy became apparent. Soon after the close of the revolutionary war the same symptoms of exhausted fertility which begun to show themselves in Virginia, made their appearance also in the more northern states. The farmers presently became fully sensible of the ruinous course they were pursuing, and the more intelligent began to turn their attention towards an improved method of cultivation. The custom of manuring, introduced by degrees, is now considered in all the older parts of the country, an essential part of husbandry. A proper rotation of crops is very generally attended to, and at present it is well understood, that lands under a proper system of cultivation ought to increase rather than decline in fertility. In fact, within the last twenty years so great has been the improvement in agriculture in the older portions of the northern states, that the face of the country has assumed a new aspect, and large tracts which were formerly considered as naturally barren, and worthless, have been transformed into fertile and productive farms. Improvements in culture keep pace with increase of population, and the soil, instead of being constantly deteriorated, is constantly increasing in productiveness and value.

Some patriotic citizens of Virginia have from time to time made great exertions to promote in their own state, an emulation of these northern improvements. But their well-intended efforts have utterly failed. Indeed they are opposed by irresistible obstacles. In the free states the land is portioned out into small farms, tilled by the hands of the owners, whose attention is exclusively bestowed upon the business of agriculture. There is a certain portion of intellect devoted to the improvement of every hundred acres. In Virginia the land is held for the most part in portions ten or twenty times larger, and even were the owners zealous for improvement, on farms so large that same careful oversight and attention could not be bestowed on every part. But then the owners of the land will not give their attention to the matter. It is contrary to the whole tenor of their habits, taste and education. They have slaves, and can hire an overseer. Why should they plague themselves with the details of a business which they do not like, and do not understand?

From the overseer and the slaves, as they have no interest in improvement, of course nothing is to be expected. In fact it is the obvious interest of the overseer to scourge as much out of the plantation as possible, without the slightest regard to future consequences, especially if he is paid, as overseers often are, by a portion of the crop.

But there are obstacles, to be encountered still more serious than these. Improvements cannot be made except by the expenditure of a certain portion of capital upon the land. Either additional slaves must be purchased, or else a certain portion of the labor now employed in producing a small crop, must be diverted from immediate production, and employed in operations undertaken with a view to distant returns. But this is an expenditure which the greater number of planters cannot afford. As it is, with all their slaves employed in scourging out of the land the greatest immediate produce, their expenses exceed their incomes, and they are running into debt every year. They are in no condition to risk the loss or curtailment of a single crop by changing the established method of cultivation, and attempting the introduction of improvements.

More yet, it is positively bad economy for a Virginia planter to undertake the improvement of his estate. Labor is the only means of resuscitating the exhausted lands of Virginia. Slave labor is the only kind of labor which in the present condition of things can be employed for that purpose. But in the slave market, the Virginia planter, even though he has money at command—which is a case sufficiently unusual,—cannot afford to compete with the slave traders from the South west. The profits which he can possibly derive from slave labor will not warrant him in paying so high a price. Of course he does not purchase; the slaves are driven off to be employed upon cotton plantations, while the lands of Virginia are left unimproved, and still declining in value. Even as regards the labor of slaves already in the planter's possession, it is a much more profitable operation to emigrate with these slaves to Mississippi or Louisiana, and there to employ their labor in raising cotton, and *killing* land, than to attempt the improvement of the worn out lands at home.

That high price of slaves in the south western market, which the Virginians regard as a fortunate addition to their diminishing resources, is likely to prove in its ultimate results, the greatest curse with which the state could be visited. If it were not for the do-

mestic slave trade, slaves would scarcely have an ex-
changeable value in Virginia; the great cheapness of
labor would facilitate agricultural improvements, and
the total impossibility of going on any longer in the
old way, would lead to important changes in the existing system.   As it is, the laboring population of the
country, that population upon which all its wealth
and consequence depends, is daily drained away. The
state is bleeding at every pore, and a fatal lethargy
must be the consequence.   The richest soil, the most
exuberant fertility without labor is unproductive and
worthless.   What will be the condition of a state
which has sold to the slave traders, the only laborious
part of her population, whose most enterprising citizens have deserted their homes, and whose exhausted lands hold out no temptation to emigrants from
abroad ?

In addition to the obstacles already pointed out in
the way of agricultural improvement at the South,
there is one yet to be mentioned, of a still more permanent and decisive nature. It is a well established
doctrine, that a rotation of crops, a variety and a very
considerable variety in the articles cultivated, is essential to a highly improved state of agriculture. But
such a rotation and variety is impossible in a country
which is exclusively agricultural, and which must
necessarily confine itself to some crops that will pay
the expense of distant transportation. The number
of these crops is exceedingly few, and they are all of a
very exhausting character. The greater number of
vegetable productions are only of use to be consumed
on the spot; and such a consumption cannot take
place to any considerable extent, except there be in
the neighborhood a manufacturing population to take
off the extra supply. Agricultural improvements have
ever kept pace with the extension of manufacturing
industry. The reasons have been already given why
the creation of a manufacturing population under
existing circumstances, is impossible at the south, and
that subject will be further considered in the following section.

The condition of agriculture in Eastern Virginia, is in a greater or less degree its condition in Maryland, in North Carolina, in South Carolina, and in the older parts of Georgia. In the two latter states the cultivation of cotton has been attended by consequences exactly similar to those produced in Virginia, by the culture of tobacco. After pouring in upon those states a momentary flood of wealth, which glittered and disappeared, it has left the soil in a state of exhaustion and barrenness, for which no present remedy appears.

The south-western states, Alabama, Mississippi and Louisiana are now the El Dorado of the slave-holders. In those states, cotton at present prices is a very profitable crop. The demand for slaves is brisk. Good field hands sell for nine hundred, or ten hundred dollars. The slaves of Maryland, Virginia and North Carolina are purchased up in droves for this market, and numbers equally large are moved off to the south-west by emigrating planters. But these slaves, if they are lucratively employed in cultivating cotton, are employed at the same time, in killing land. Slavery will presently visit the south-west with the same blight of exhaustion and barrenness, which has already alighted upon Virginia and the Carolinas. In proportion to the rapidity with which the apparent immediate prosperity of the south-western states is now advancing, will be hastened the era of their decay.

In the free states of the Union, the wealth of the west promotes the wealth of the east. The more prosperous are the new states, the more prosperous are the old. At the south it is not so. The new states are aggrandized at the expense of the old ones. But this aggrandizement has nothing in it, solid or permanent. For a short time a great annual income is obtained; but it is obtained only by the annual consumption of a portion of that natural fertility, in which consists the only real capital of those communities, and this capital being presently exhausted, their short lived prosperity vanishes like a shadow.

SECTION IV.

Manufactures and Commerce in the Slave-holding States.

No merely agricultural nation ever yet attained a high degree of prosperity, or civilization. To attain that result it is necessary that manufacturing and commercial industry should combine with agriculture. All these three branches of industry are so sympathetically connected, that neither of them alone can be carried to any great degree of perfection.

There have already been suggested several reasons why manufactures cannot prosper in the slave-holding states. It is necessary here to recapitulate them and to bring them together in a single point of view.

1. Skill in the greater part of the mechanic and manufacturing arts, is not consistent with the state of total ignorance and barbarism in which it is judged the best policy that the unprivileged class should be kept. Skilled laborers are and must be, more intelligent and better informed, than those of an ordinary kind.

2. Such skill is still less consistent with that social condition which deprives those subjected to it, of all motive to acquire that degree of expertness, on which the success of most mechanical operations so essentially depends.

3. With respect to the laboring part of the free population, the acquisition of manufacturing skill is little to be expected from the state of ignorance, indolence and depression which are to them the natural results of the existence of slavery in the community of which they form a part.

These three reasons go to cut off the supply of that kind of labor essential to the prosecution of manufacturing operations. But besides labor, there is needed knowledge, tact, skill and judgment in the oversight and direction of labor, and capital to set it in operation.

1. With regard to the oversight and direction of manufacturing operations, persons are very rarely to be found among the native population of the southern states, possessed of the necessary qualifications. The whole course of their education and habits is averse to that system of order, economy, and minute and exact attention, which such a business requires.

2. As regards capital, it has been shown in a previous section, under what disadvantages all industrious operations labor at the south, from the comparatively large amount of it, necessary to set them in operation. In any manufacturing business for example, it is necessary to have capital enough over and above all that is required for the fixtures and stock, to *purchase* the laborers who are to carry it on.

From the combined operation of these several causes it results, both in theory and in fact, that manufacturing processes, on any large scale, are almost unknown at the south, and that even the commonest mechanical arts are at a very low ebb.

It is obvious at once, when the condition of the various classes of the population at the south is considered, and when regard is had to the state of manufactures, that trade cannot greatly flourish. The unprivileged class have nothing to sell except what they steal, and of course they have but little to buy. The laboring freemen, produce but little, and of course are able to purchase but little. The class of wealthy slave-holders is very limited in number, and a large part of their income is often spent at a distance from home. The principal mercantile operations consist in the purchase and shipment of the great agricultural staples, a business which is carried on for the most part by means of English or northern capital, and at the same time by English or northern agents, and English or northern shipping.

Neither manufactures nor commerce can be regarded as adding any thing considerable to the wealth of the slave-holding states.

SECTION V.

Instability and uncertainty of values in the Slave-Holding States.

The necessity which the southern planters are under of confining themselves to the production of a few great staple crops, has been already stated and explained. Slave labor in the United States, was first applied to the cultivation of *tobacco*. But the foreign demand for that article has been stationary ever since the revolutionary war, while the domestic demand increases only in proportion to the increase of the population. Since the facilities of transportation between the western states and the Atlantic seaboard have been so much increased by the construction of canals and railroads, the farmers of Ohio have gone extensively into the cultivation of tobacco. They produce it by free labor, and the quantity of slave labor which can be profitably employed in this culture is more likely to increase than to diminish.

The second application of slave labor in the United States, was to the cultivation of *rice*. That cultivation however is and always has been, confined to a narrow tract of country along the sea coast of South Carolina and Georgia; and as the demand for the article is nearly stationary, any considerable increase of the production would so diminish the price as to make it an unprofitable business.

Sugar is produced chiefly in the southern districts of Louisiana. This culture has been fostered by a protective duty, but the climate is too cold and unsteady for its extensive prosecution. A few favorable seasons created a very false idea of the profits of this cultivation. A series of cold seasons has corrected these hasty impressions. Even including Texas and Florida, the production of cane sugar in the United States must always be restricted to a limited area.

The cultivation of *cotton*, an article of which the

consumption has so remarkably increased within the last fifty years, has alone prevented the entire depreciation of southern property. There has been thus furnished a crop, to the production of which the labor of slaves could be profitably applied, and which has prevented such a competition in the other limited applications of slave labor above enumerated, as would have rendered them utterly ruinous.

The cotton cultivated in the United States is of two distinct kinds, known in commerce, as Sea island, and upland or short staple. The Sea island cotton has a long silky fibre which adheres so slightly to the seed, as to be easily removed by means of two wooden rollers turning upon each other, which suffer the cotton wool to pass between them, but which exclude and separate the seed. This kind of cotton is employed only in the finest manufactures, and its consumption is very limited. It bears a much higher value than the other description but it is less productive, and requires great care and labor in its preparation for market. The sea air seems essential to it, and its cultivation is limited to an alluvial tract along the sea coast of South Carolina and Georgia. The cultivation of this kind of cotton was introduced about the conclusion of the revolutionary war; but it has always been of so limited an extent as to hold out no relief to the great body of the slave-holders.

The upland or short staple cotton, has a short fibre adhering with such tenacity to the seed, as to require the saw gin, an invention of the ingenious Whitney, for its separation. This kind of cotton succeeds as well in the interior as near the sea, and it is this kind, the consumption of which has so rapidly increased. It first began to be cultivated as a crop about the beginning of the present century. For the first twenty years its production was principally confined to Georgia and the Carolinas. Since that time it has spread into the new states of the south-west, which now produce more than three fourths of the entire crop, which in the period since the peace with Great Britain in

1815, has risen from two hundred thousand bales, to upwards of three millions, per annum.

The cultivation of cotton is the only employment of slave labor which admits of profitable extension. The price of cotton regulates the price of slaves, and incidentally, the value of all kinds of property at the south. When all values are thus made dependent upon a single pursuit, they are necessarily subject to great fluctuations. When there is a great variety of employments, there is established in consequence, a sort of average permanency of profits. Agriculture may be flourishing, though manufactures and commerce are suffering a temporary depression; and some branches of agriculture may be profitable, though others fail. At the south, every thing is staked upon the cast of a single die; and as is apt to happen in all such cases, the planters are either in a state of high prosperity which leads to great speculations and the creation of great debts, or else in a state of depression, ruinous both to northern lenders, and to southern borrowers.

The commercial fluctuations of the United States generally take their origin at the south. A high price of cotton creates at the south a feeling of wealth and a strong disposition to contract debts, while it produces at the north, a strong disposition to give credit. Even though the price of cotton continues high, the expectation of the planters runs so far beyond the reality, that they presently become unable to fulfil their engagements; and if a decline in the price of cotton should follow, their inability becomes total, and the severe losses experienced in consequence by the merchants and manufacturers of the north, throw their business also into a temporary confusion.

There is much reason to expect that these violent fluctuations in the value of southern property will presently terminate in a general and permanent depreciation. Whether lands and slaves, ten years hence, shall have any considerable value in any of the southern states, seems to depend very much upon the fact, whether or not the consumption of cotton shall keep pace with its production. If production should overrun consumption, the market will be glutted, the price will fall, the business will become unprofitable, and unless some new, extensive and profitable application of slave labor should unexpectedly be discovered,—an event which is highly improbable— land and labor throughout the south, must undergo a great decline in value.

There are weighty reasons for anticipating this result within a moderate period. Twice already within the last twenty years the production of cotton has so overrun consumption as to reduce the profits of the business to the lowest ebb. The price has since rallied, but this rise of profits has produced a new rush into the business, and a vast emigration from the more northern of the slave-holding states, which must result in a great increase of the production. On the other hand the consumption of cotton goods has already reached a point, which makes its extension continually more difficult. There is no reason to suppose that it can go on increasing for twenty years to come, as it has for twenty years past. That increase has been principally caused by cotton fabrics superseding for certain purposes, the use of linen and woollen cloths. That is a process which has a certain limit and which cannot be repeated. The consumption of cotton goods will doubtless continue to increase; but this increase of consumption will be more upon a par than heretofore, with the increased consumption of other manufactures.

Whatever the increased demand for cotton may be, the slave-holding states of the Union, are liable to encounter a severe competition in supplying it. All that portion of the American continent south of the United States is well fitted for the production of this article. Cotton of a very superior quality is produced to a large amount, in Brazil, and all Spanish America will presently be entering the market as a rival.

Great exertions are now making in India, by British cultivators, to improve the quality of Indian cotton, and not without success. The quantity of this article worked up by the British manufacturers is steadily increasing; and when we recollect how completely the British indigo planters in India, succeeded in destroying the cultivation of indigo in the United States, which was once a very considerable business, by producing a superior article at a less price, the competition of the Indian cotton planters, however some ignorant persons may ridicule it, is by no means to be despised.

Additional competition is to be expected from Africa. The Egyptian cottons are already well known as of very superior quality; and it seems highly probable that the French will presently introduce the same sort of cultivation into their Algerine possessions.

On the whole it must be confessed that the single prop of the cultivation of cotton, forms a most slender, fragile and uncertain support, on which to rest the prosperity of an extensive and increasing population.

SECTION VI.

Comparative Progress and Prosperity of the Free and of the Slave-holding States.

It is a fact too obvious to be denied even by the most prejudiced observers, that the slave-holding states of the Union are far inferior to the free states, in every thing that constitutes civilization,—in wealth, in education, in the useful and ornamental arts, in public institutions, in public spirit, in literature, in science, in density of population, in facility of intercourse, in the splendor of cities, the neatness of towns, the comforts and conveniency of individual dwellings.

Of the thirteen states which originally composed the Union, slavery still prevails in six. It has been abolished in the others, where indeed it never existed to any considerable extent. These old free states, by the separation of Maine from Massachusetts and the admission of Vermont, increased to nine in number, include an area of about one hundred and fifty thousand square miles; the extent of the six old slave states is upwards of two hundred thousand square miles. By the first census in 1790, the former contained a population of 1,908,000 souls; the population of the latter amounted to 1,848,000. Fifty years after, by the census of 1840, the population of the old free states amounted to 6,760,880, while the population of the six old slave states was only 3,826,323. The census of 1850 shows the continued operation of the same causes, the free section having gained upon the population of 1840 to the extent of 1,553,834, while the increase in the slave section is but 713,312, or less than half as much.

Density of population, and the existence of towns and cities, are essential to any great degree of social progress. Brought thus into contact, mind acts upon mind; what is discovered by one soon becomes known to all; emulation leads to new discoveries and enterprises; competition constantly exerts its beneficial influence; the division of labor, that essential means of improvement, is not practicable among a scattered population; cities are the central points from which knowledge, enterprise, and civilization stream out upon the surrounding country.

In the eight free States above referred to, we find three large cities, New York, Philadelphia, and Boston, the first of which is generally regarded as the commercial metropolis of the Union. There are not less than twenty other considerable towns which are growing with rapidity, and several of which promise to rise to the first importance. Villages containing five or six thousand inhabitants, are quite numerous; new ones are springing up every day, and others are passing from the class of villages into that of towns.

How different a picture is presented by the old slave States! They contain but one city deserving the name, and that one, be it observed, is situated upon

the verge of the free States, and owes the principal
part of its importance to that very circumstance. In
wealth, trade and public institutions, in literature,
science and general refinement, Baltimore is far inferior to either of the great cities of the north. Charleston is a little more than a place of deposite for the produce of the surrounding country, and a retreat for the
neighboring planters from the unhealthiness of their
plantations. It has been about stationary for this last
thirty years, and the same is true of Alexandria, Nor-
folk, Savannah, and other ancient towns. Jamestown,
the original capital of Virginia, has ceased to exist, the
ruins of an old church steeple are its only memorial.
Williamsburg the second capital of Virginia, has long
been in decay. Such existence as it has, it owes to the
ancient college established there. Richmond, the present capital presents a more thriving appearance,—
but to judge by the depopulation and impoverishment
of the surrounding country, it must soon share a similar fate.

What are called towns in these States, would for
the most part, be esteemed at the north, as little better
than villages. In addition to the small number scattered along the sea-coast, there are a few of more recent growth, situated on the great rivers, generally at
the head of steam-boat navigation. They are points
at which the produce of the country is collected for
shipment, and whence imported goods are distributed
through the adjoining country; but so few and far between, as scarcely at all to vary the dull monotony of
a poorly peopled country which presents at the same
time, all the rudeness of a new settlement, and all the
marks of old age and decay.

If the slave holding states formed a separate and in-
sulated nation, cut off from communication and intercourse with the free states of the north, there is good
reason to suppose that they would fall rapidly behind
hand, in the career of civilization. As it is, they are
sustained and dragged along by the energy of their
northern sisters. Improvements are first started and

put into execution at the north, then slowly and faintly imitated at the south. The best educated and most accomplished men of the southern states have passed their youth at northern schools and colleges; such seminaries for education as the southern states possess, are supplied almost entirely with northern or foreign teachers. The whole trade of the south, so far as relates to transactions on the large scale, is in the hands of northern merchants who carry on this important branch of business for which the native citizens of those states, seem to lack the requisite knowledge, sagacity, perseverance and application. The learned professions, physic, divinity, and even the law, are more or less, recruited from the same source. The newspapers have northern editors; even the compositors who set the types are imported. The same is the case with all mechanics who have any considerable skill in the art they profess. Southern rail roads are built with northern capital and by northern engineers and contractors. It is hardly possible to erect a large hotel, or block of ware-houses without the aid of northern artificers. The southern states are supplied with books and periodicals from northern presses; and it seems to be only by a close and intimate union with the north, that civilization at the south is enabled to make any progress, or even to preserve itself from decline. It is worthy of special remark however, that those northern men who emigrate to the south imbibe by degrees, the feelings and the habits, the indolence, and the incapacity of the population by which they are surrounded. They are unable to transmit to their children any of those qualities which they carried with them from home. These children, bred up after the southern fashion, are thoroughly southern. It is constantly necessary that new blood should be transferred from the warm and vigorous circulation of the north, to revive and quicken the veins, palsied, and made stagnant by the poison of slavery.

CHAPTER FOURTH.

SECTION I.

Personal Effects of Slavery upon the members of the privileged class.

By personal results of the slave-holding system those results are intended, which exhibit themselves in the personal character of the members of a slave-holding community.

Slavery has already been explained to be in its nature, a protracted state of war. All its results are sufficiently conformable to such an origin.

Soldiers possess a free and self-confident air, and when among friends and not irritated or opposed, they exhibit a frank good humor, an easy, companionable disposition, which renders their society agreeable, and causes their company to be generally courted. Their military duties often leave them an abundance of leisure ; for long intervals, they often have nothing to do but to seek amusement, and they give a warm and hearty welcome to all who are disposed to join and aid them in that pursuit.

These same traits of manners are sufficiently conspicuous among the privileged class of our southern aristocracies. Though a large portion of that class is destitute of education, and of any real refinement, yet almost every member of it has more or less, a certain patrician bearing, a consciousness of his own superiority which gives him an air of manliness and dignity, but which it must be confessed, degenerates too often into rudeness and braggadocio. The wealthier and better educated, passing almost the whole of their lives in a round of social pleasures, have attained to a considerable perfection in the art of pleasing; and those who visit the southern states of the Union for the first time, are generally captivated by the politeness, the hospitality, the attentions, the good humor of the people.

Manners however are far from being any certain index of character, and they are often carried to a high pitch of refinement, in cases where all the virtues which they seem to indicate, are lamentably deficient.

The soldier nursed in blood and robbery, however mildly and gently he conducts himself, is at best only a tame tiger, not rashly to be trusted. His passions are violent and unmanageable, accustomed to indulgence, and impatient of control. It is the same with the slave-master. Habituated to play the tyrant at home, unshackled regent and despotic lord upon his own plantation, where his wish, his slightest whim is law, the love of domineering possesses all his heart. The intercourse of society has taught him the policy and the advantages of mutual concession in little things, and the trifling points of ordinary politeness he yields with the ready willingness of a well-bred man. Beyond this he is not to be trusted. Alarm his prejudices, his self-love, his jealousy, his avarice, his ambition; cross his path in any shape whatever; assume the character of a rival or a censor; presume to doubt his perfect wisdom and immaculate virtue; and from a laughing, good natured companion, he is changed at once, into a fierce, furious, raving and raging enemy. He boils and almost bursts with passion; he answers argument with invective; instead of reasons, he replies to you with insults. Not content to restrain his hate within the usual limits of civilized life, he thirsts for your blood. He murders you in a duel; assaults you in the streets with pistols and Bowie knife; or deliberately shoots you from the door of his house, with a double-barrelled gun. The fear of the law does not restrain him. In the southern states, a *gentleman* is never hung. The most cold-blooded and deliberate murderers, in the upper classes of society, escape with a fine or a short imprisonment. The gallows is reserved for abolitionists, negro-stealers, and *poor* white folks.

I. The condition of society in the southern states, even among the most refined and best educated portion of the people, exhibits frightful evidences of FEROCITY OF TEMPER, such as a state of everlasting war might be expected to produce. Thucidides remarks, that from the time the Athenians laid aside the custom of going armed, civility and refinement began to make a steady progress among them. This is a point to which the people of the southern states have not yet attained. They generally carry arms ; but the pistols, knives and dirks, their favorite weapons, are of a kind more fit for foot-pads and assassins, than for well-intentioned citizens. In several of the states it has been attempted to suppress by penal enactments, this barbarous practice of carrying deadly weapons. These laws are never enforced, and it is scarcely possible they should be. To carry arms in the state of things existing at the south, seems absolutely necessary. If his slaves resist, how else shall the master maintain his authority ? Those who have been subdued by force, must be kept under by force ; and if the armed conquerors, in moments of anger, sometimes turn their weapons against each other, that is what is liable to happen among all collections of armed men. What wonder if that inhuman and blood-thirsty spirit, which the tyrannical rule they exercise, keeps more or less alive in the bosom of all slave masters, often bursts out in full fury in their quarrels with each other ? The familiarity with which, under the influence of excited passion, they talk of murder is only to be equalled, by the savage ferocity with which, under the same influence, they often commit it. The atrocity of southern duels has long been notorious,—but what duel can be compared with those "rencontres" of which we so often read accounts in the southern papers,—accounts which among the people of those states seem to carry with them all the interest of a bull-baiting or a cock-fight,—in which two men or more, armed to the teeth, meet in the streets, at a *court-house* or a tavern, shoot at each other with pistols, then draw their knives, close, and roll upon the ground, covered with dust and blood, struggling and stabbing till death, wounds, or the submission of one of the parties, put an end to the contest? These scenes, which if they take place at the north at all, appear but once an age, and then only among the lowest and most depraved of the emigrant population, are of frequent and almost daily occurrence at the south, among those who consider themselves the most respectable people. Andrew Jackson, late president of the United States, and regarded as a most illustrious citizen, had been engaged in several such affrays.

II. IMPROVIDENCE is a vice of the most dangerous character. The ancients were so impressed with the multitudinous evils and miseries to which it gives occasion, that they raised *prudence* to the dignity of one of the four cardinal virtues. Improvidence is however a failing, which is apt to prevail to a great extent in a slave-holding community. The careless, headlong rapidity with which a planter spends his money, is proverbial. This childish profusion has even been raised among them to the rank of a virtue; it is described as the mark of a noble minded man; while economy is decried and stigmatized as mean and little. This sort of profusion may dazzle and delight the weak-minded and the thoughtless. It is very clear however that it seldom implies any of that benevolence or magnanimity which it has been supposed to indicate.

It generally originates in the desire to gratify some whim of the moment, or, what is oftener the case, in the desire to be admired as a person of wealth and liberality. It is one way of gratifying the universal de-

13

sire of social superiority. A planter will spend some
hundreds upon an entertainment, and the next morning will refuse an extra pair of shoes to a lame old
negro, who has labored for him all his life. Ask one
of these lavish spendthrifts to do an act, not of benevolence merely, but of justice, by setting a slave at
liberty, and he will laugh in your face. We hear of
many acts of profusion at the south, few acts of gen-
erosity. It is not there, that institutions are endowed
for purposes of public charity. No associations exist
there, or next to none, for charitable purposes. When
a subscription is to be raised for some object of public
benevolence, the contribution of our southern planters
is extremely scanty. They lavish thousands on their
own pleasures, and the companions of those pleasures; they bestow little or nothing upon the sufferings of strangers. Indeed it would be absurd to expect it. They who are not moved by the scene of
poverty, degradation and distress, which their own
plantations every day present, how can they be affected by the comparatively little miseries of which they
only hear, or which they but casually see?

The quantity of money that can be got is a limited
sum; the quantity that can be spent is indefinite.
Take the southern states throughout, and it is probable
that seven slave-masters out of ten, live beyond their
income. The labor, the fruits of which would have sufficed to make fifty families comfortable and happy, being engrossed, with the exception of the barest subsistence to the laborers, by a single family, does not suffice
to make that single family happy or even comfortable. Improvidence subjects to all the miseries of actual poverty. Men in the possession of large estates
are tormented all their lives by sheriffs and duns, and
at their death, leave large families brought up in all
the luxury of wealth, and the helplessness of habitual
indolence, penniless and unprovided for, a prey to the
bitterest miseries of want.

III. IDLENESS, says the copy book, is the mother
of all the vices. If any one doubt the truth of this

ancient and homely maxim, to be convinced of it, he need only spend a year or two in the south. He will find a great many idle people there. Almost all the owners of slaves have hardly any occupation except to amuse themselves. Born and bred to this occupation they become incapable of any other. One would suppose that having so much leisure time, they might turn their attention to the study of agriculture, an art upon which so wholly depends not their private income only, but the public wealth of the communities to which they belong. But no,—they have no taste for such pursuits, and they leave the management of their plantations, entirely to their overseers. This neglect however ought not to be wholly ascribed to their disinclination for regular and useful pursuits. If they go much upon their plantations, so many cruel sights come under their view, they are so harrassed by petitions and complaints, they find themselves so oppressed by the cares of authority, that they hasten to relieve themselves from the burden, and to shift it to the shoulders of some case-hardened manager. All despotisms are alike. What happens to an oriental sultan, happens to an occidental slave-master. The weight of empire presses too heavily upon their effeminate and feeble necks. Both alike spend in idle luxury all that can be spunged from the forced labor of their subjects, but both alike transfer the task of spunging to a vizier, or an overseer.

Thus freed from all the cares of business, it might be imagined that the wealthy slave-masters of the south would bestow their time and thoughts upon the pursuit of knowledge, the cultivation of literature, and the agreeable arts. We might suppose that they would push scientific investigations to their utmost limits, astonish the world with new discoveries in morals and in physics, or delight it with all the graces of poetry, the beauties and sublimities of painting, sculpture, music and architecture.

In these expectations we are totally disappointed. Books are a rare commodity at the south; literature is uncommon and science still more so. Libraries, whether public or private, are seldom to be met with. A few classics thumbed over at school, a few novels old or new, a sprinkling of political pamphlets, and some favorite newspaper, form the whole circuit of letters and learning, ordinarily trodden by the most studious of the planters. The education of the females, even among the wealthiest classes, is still more superficial. In this connection, it ought to be remembered, that a very considerable portion of the privileged class are totally destitute even of the rudiments of learning. To read is an accomplishment they have never acquired. Of course, it is not to be expected that persons so unfortunately circumstanced, can find employment for their leisure in literary pursuits.

Thus situated, with no resources for the occupation of their time, the privileged class are constantly beset by a weariness of soul, perhaps the most distressing disorder to which men are subject. "Thank God I am not a negro!" said a planter one day, as he sat beneath the shade of his porch, and watched his slaves in a neighboring field, at work beneath a burning sun. Yet it may well be doubted whether the most miserable of those slaves was half as miserable, as their unfortunate master, who lived in a lonely part of the country, and suffered from a forced idleness and solitude, the most poignant distresses.

It is a common remark among the planters that the slaves are happier than the masters. Many will reject this idea with indignation, as a mere falsehood, invented to gloss over the abominations of tyranny. No doubt the observation is generally urged with that intent. But the truth of a fact does not depend upon the use intended to be made of it, by those who assert it. The more closely a man meditates upon the state of things at the south, the more inclined he will be to admit the truth of the above remark touching the comparative happiness of the masters and the slaves. Instead however of saying that the masters and the slaves are equally happy, the idea might be more clearly and distinctly expressed by saying, that both masters and slaves are equally miserable. Slavery is an invention for dividing the goods and ills of life into two separate parcels, so as to bestow all the ills upon the slaves, and all the good upon the masters. So far as regards the slaves, this attempt is successful enough. The miseries of life are concentrated upon their heads in a terrible mass. But as respects the masters the experiment fails entirely. The coveted good, like that manna which the too greedy Israelites sought wrongfully to appropriate, corrupts, putrefies, changes its nature, and turns into evil. Occupation too long continued is destructive to happiness, but idleness is not less so; and it may well be doubted whether the compulsive labor of the slaves is any more copious a source of misery than the forced idleness of the masters. I say *forced* idleness, for in depriving themselves of the motives to labor and exertion, they force themselves to be idle.

To obtain some relief from the weariness that constantly besets them, the planters seek to divert and occupy their thoughts by social intercourse. This is the origin of that *hospitality* for which the people of the south are so famous, and which is often brought forward as a virtue ample enough to cover the acknowledged multitude of their sins. Hospitality, it is true, bears a certain relation to benevolence; but it is to benevolence no more than is the flounce to the garment. The attempt to conceal the nakedness of the land by such a rag, is as contemptible as it is futile. In truth, the visiters who arrive at a plantation confer a real benefit upon the lord of it. They give him occupation. The efforts necessary to entertain, are not less agreeable to him who makes them, than to those for whom they are made. If the visiter be a total stranger so much the better. There is the zest of novelty added to the excitement of occupation. If he come from a distant part of the country, better yet. He will probably be able to suggest a great many new and interesting ideas, likely to give an agreeable mo-

tion to the stagnant soul of his host. Hospitality has
ever been a virtue abundantly practised among all
idle and indolent races. The indian tribes of America,
are all celebrated for its exercise. The plundering
Arabs of the desert look upon it as a religious duty,—
for conscience and inclination are always apt to pull
together.

But the exercise of this virtue among the people of
the south, becomes the occasion of several practices of
the most dangerous and deleterious kind. It is not
the cause of those practices, but only the occasion for
them. In itself, it is essentially good, and displays
the character of the slave-holder in the most amiable
light it ever assumes. Hospitality is benevolence on
a small scale, and how can benevolence on any other
scale be expected, from men whose total existence is
a continued violation of its clearest and most urgent
commands?

1. The spirit of *improvidence*, above described, as
one of the evil results of the slave-holding system,
when it becomes associated with the passion for hospitality, is reenforced by two very powerful motives,
which give it new impetus; first, the desire of at-
tracting visiters, by the superior luxury and expen-
siveness of the entertainment offered; and second and
principally, the love of superiority, that spirit of emulation and rivalry, which leads each planter to outvie
his neighbor in the profusion of his hospitality. It is
astonishing what a number of southern planters have
been ruined in their pecuniary affairs by the joint operation of these means.

2. The Hospitality of the south, not only stimulates
improvidence, it is the nursing mother of the vice of
DRUNKENNESS, which prevails throughout the whole
country to a frightful extent. Dinner parties end too
often in general intoxication. What is called the
Temperance Reform, has made but trifling progress
in the slave-holding states. The obstacles in its way
are immense. To drink is absolutely necessary as a
means of killing time. Among the lower orders of the

privileged class, every social meeting ends in drunkenness. Attend an election, and by the time the polls are closed, you will find a great collection of citizens at the place of voting, all or most of them, " gloriously drunk." Stay long enough and you will see a fight. In Kentucky such occasions are apt to wind up, with what is called a free fight, that is, a general and indiscriminate knock-down, in which every body present is at liberty to participate. This is the grand finale, or concluding chorus; but before this part of the performance is reached, there are duets, trios, quartets and quintets, in all possible variety In Mississippi Tennessee, and elsewhere, laws have been enacted, prohibiting the sale of intoxicating liquors in small quantities. Some movements have also been made in Georgia and South Carolina, towards obtaining the passage of similar laws. Laws of this kind are easily enacted in those states, much more so than at the north, because in those states, the wholesale trade in liquors is almost entirely confined to a few northern merchants and traders, who have no political influence, while the retail trade is in the hands of a set of poor white shopkeepers, rendered odious and infamous by their habit of secret traffic with the slaves, and belonging to that inferior class of the privileged order, which though it exceeds in numbers, is deprived for the most part, of any political authority. But however easy it may be to enact such laws, it will be impossible to enforce them, so long as the very legislators by whose votes they are enacted, are themselves perpetually in the habit of excessive drinking. These laws will fall into the same total neglect with the statutes against wearing concealed weapons already referred to, and those against gaming, to which we shall presently refer.

3. But such is the total stagnation of intellect and sentiment at the south, that even the stimulus of intoxicating liquors is not enough to give life and zest to social intercourse. There is need of more potent means. Necessity is the mother of invention. That means is at hand. It is GAMING.

This vice, more dangerous and dreadful, if possible, even than drunkenness itself, is equally prevalent at the south. Many attempts have been made to eradicate it. There are penal laws against it, in all the slave holding states. Of late, we have seen the summary process of Lynch Law applied to the same purpose. In Vicksburgh, one of the principal towns in the state of Mississippi, the most respectable people of the place assembled in the month of July, 1835, and after pulling down several buildings used as gambling houses, proceeded to seize the persons of *five* professional gamblers and to hang them on the spot, without judge or jury. "These unfortunate men," says the *Louisiana Advertiser*, "claimed to the last the privilege of American citizens,—the trial by jury,— and professed themselves willing to submit to any thing their country would legally inflict upon them; but we are sorry to say, their petition was in vain! The black musicians were ordered to strike up, and the voices of the suppliants were drowned by the fife and drum. Mr. Riddell, the cashier of the Planter's Bank, ordered them to play Yankee Doodle, a tune which we believe has never been so prostituted before, and which we hope, and we trust will never be again. The unhappy sufferers frequently implored a drink of water, but were refused. * * * * The wife of one of them, half distracted at the cruel treatment and murder of her husband, trembling for her own safety, in tears begged permission to inter her husband's body,—but in vain. She was afterwards compelled to fly, with her orphan child, in an open skiff, for her personal security. The same fate was threatened to any person who should dare to cut down the bodies before the expiration of twenty-four hours. At eleven o'clock the next day, they were cut down and thrown together into a hole, which had been dug near the gallows, without coffins or any other preparations, except a box into which one of them was put."

Of the persons who assisted at this execution there

was not probably one, who was not himself in the constant habit of gambling. Yet is the horror of this vice so great in the southern states, and its ill effects, brought home to the public mind by constant experience are so generally acknowledged, that the actors in this tragedy were never called to account before any judicial tribunal, and their conduct, throughout the entire south, was either openly approved, or very faintly condemned. The tone of reprobation in which the *Louisiana Advertiser* speaks, found but a slight and indistinct echo from the other southern prints.

Yet notwithstanding all the horror, with which this vice of gambling is regarded, the indulgence in it, at least among the men, is next to universal. Among those who have been swept away by the prevailing current, may be reckoned some of the most able and distinguished of our southern and south-western orators and politicians, unable to withstand this any more than other popular sins. When such men lead, followers are always plenty. Every little village of the south has its race-course, its billiard room, its faro table, and its gambling house, and of the three latter, perhaps several. This grows out of the moral necessity of things. Men, in all ages, and in every country, who have had much leisure on their hands, which they knew not how else to employ, have ever sought relief in some sort of gambling. It is so always with savages, sailors and soldiers, and so it is with the idle population of the south. The habit once acquired, it becomes almost impossible to resist its seductions. To reform a gambler is much the same difficult task as to reform a drunkard. The planter who has been secluded upon his estate for a week or a month, in irksome and wretched indolence, his heart all the time devouring itself, orders his horse or his carriage in a fit of desperation, and sets out for the nearest village. The gaming table offers him the speediest and most certain means of excitement, the surest method of shaking off the listless misery which oppresses him. To the gaming table he goes. It stands always ready,—for the necessity of the case has created a peculiar class of men at the south, who are gamblers by profession. It was to this class that those men belonged who were hanged at Vicksburg. This is a profession which has sprung up naturally at the south, and as has been said necessarily, and which can boast of more talent and accomplishment among its members, than the three learned professions of law, physic and divinity united.

The institution of slavery deprives a large portion of the people of their natural occupation. But as man is essentially an active animal, to supply this deficiency it is necessary to create artificial occupations. Gambling is the employment, which under similar circumstances, has ever presented itself to men, as a means of killing time. In order that this employment may be indulged in, whenever the want of it is felt, it is necessary that a peculiar class should exist, as it were, the priesthood of the gaming table, always ready at all times, to gamble with all comers. These are the professional gamblers. They practise gaming not for amusement, but as a livelihood. If they left every thing to chance and strictly observed the laws of play, it would be impossible for them to live by their business, because, in the long run, they would be certain to lose as much as they won, and so could have nothing left whereupon to live. Hence they are compelled to play *false.* They must *cheat*, or starve. They are not merely gamblers, but swindlers. This explains the odium attached to their occupation. Merely to gamble is no imputation upon any body's character in the southern states, or at most it is an imputation of which nobody is ashamed. To be a gambler by profession is infamous, because it is well understood, that every professional gambler is a cheat.

But though the profession is infamous, still it is crowded. Its members throng the steam-boats, the hotels, the cities, and the villages of the south, and among them may be found, the most gentlemanly, agreeable, insinuating, talented, well informed men of the whole population, constantly on the watch, and always laboring to attract, to allure, to please, many of them attain a peculiar polish and elegance of manners. New recruits are always crowding in. The planter who has ruined himself by improvidence, dissipation or losses at the gaming table, the young disappointed heir, bred up in indolence and luxury by a father who dies insolvent,—these persons find scarcely any other way of gaining their daily bread, except to adopt gambling as a profession. There is no other business for which they are qualified, there is no other art, which they understand. It seems hard to hold these individuals strictly responsible for the evil they do. You cannot expect them to starve. They are the victims of a social system intolerably bad.

The professional gamblers are above described such as they are, when at the head of their profession, and in the heyday of success. In general, they soon begin to go down hill. Proverbially improvident, they are abundantly supplied with money, or wholly without it. The latter presently comes to be their habitual condition. Their fate closely resembles that of prostitutes in a great city. Drunkenness relieves their distresses for the moment, but by destroying their health and their intellect, soon precipitates them into lower depths of misery. They become at last a burden upon relatives and friends; find in an early death a refuge from despair; or are precipitated into crimes which carry them to the penitentiary or the gallows.

The vice of gambling is not confined to the superior portion of the privileged order. It pervades the lower class also. There are blacklegs and gambling houses adapted to the taste and manners of all.

To the business of gambling, the professional gamblers from time to time, add several other occupations. They become passers of counterfeit money, horse-thieves, and negro-stealers. Nothing except the extreme poverty of the country, prevents them from organizing an extensive system of plunder. Horses and slaves are almost the only thing, capable of transportation, which can be stolen. In general, to pick the pockets of the planters by the help of a faro table or a pack of cards, is not only a safe, but a surer operation than to attempt it in any other way.

Party politics, state and national, afford the only topic, to any extent of an intellectual character, in which any considerable number of the southern population, take any deep interest, or which serves to any considerable extent, to dispel the fog of wearisome idleness, by which they are constantly threatened to be enveloped. Politics at the south, are rather speculative than practical. Every slave-holding community is essentially conservative, and opposed to all change. The southern politicians puzzle and lose themselves in vain attempts to reconcile the metaphysical system of liberty acknowledged by their own state constitutions, with the actual system of despotism amid which they live. Their ablest reasoners, can boast no more than to be subtle logicians, and ingenious sophists. Statesmanship is a thing they have no idea of. Yet the study of politics, barren, empty and profitless as southern politics are, has saved many of the finest minds at the south from a total stagnation, and affords to great numbers a stimulant altogether more harmless than gambling and strong drink. Great numbers of the southern planters are as great adepts in political metaphysics, as the Scotch peasantry are or were, in calvinistic divinity. Grant their premises,—which for the most part are utterly false,—and they reason like a book.

There have been enumerated above, five capital defects in the character and conduct of the privileged class at the south, viz: ferocity of temper, improvidence, idleness, drunkenness, and gambling. It is but justice to say, that the female portion of the privileged class are in general entirely free from the two last mentioned faults, nor does ferocity of temper exhibit itself among them, to any thing the same extent as in the male sex. Idleness and improvidence are their greatest and most striking defects.

Among the men however, the whole five are palpable, obvious, undeniable. As to this matter there cannot be any dispute. It must be confessed, however unwillingly that these faults are characteristic of the southern people. It has been shown how they are all aggravated, and rendered incurable, by the existence of slavery. Any attempt to remove or palliate them, while that cause of aggravation remains, can have only a partial and limited success. It is impossible to make men virtuous or happy unless by giving them some steady employment that shall innocently engage their attention, and pleasantly occupy their time. The most essential step in the progress of civilization, is, to render useful industry, respectable. But this step can never be taken, so long as labor remains the badge of a servile condition.

SECTION II.

Personal effects of slavery upon the members of the unprivileged class.

Extremes meet. The truth of this proposition, in a physical point of view is evident from the fact that every motion upon the earth's surface describes an elliptical curve. Experience would seem to show that this proposition is almost as true in morals as in physics. At all events it is a curious fact, that the existence of slavery in a community, instead of producing such diversities as might be supposed, does in fact, in many very important particulars, operate almost exactly alike upon the masters and the slaves. Ferocity of temper, idleness, improvidence, drunkenness, gambling—these are vices for which the masters are distinguished, and these same vices are conspicuous traits in the character and conduct of slaves.

14

1. *Ferocity of Temper*. The first access of suffering softens the heart, the long continuance of suffering tends to harden it. Suffering when long continued, begins to be looked upon as a thing of course. He who constantly fears to feel the whip upon his own shoulders, ceases to weep because it falls upon another. Those who are accustomed to see authority exercised almost solely in the infliction of pain, form presently a close association between the two things. They seem to be inseparable, and a liberal use of violent means comes to be looked upon as the only method of showing one's power. Now the love of power, or to speak more correctly, that love of superiority, which the exercise of power is a means of gratifying, is one of the native, and one of the strongest impulses of the human heart. The slave feels it like other men. He indulges it, when, where, and as, he can, upon his wife, his children and the horse he drives, or upon such of his companions as superior strength, or the appointment of his master has submitted to his control. He exercises his authority in the same way in which authority has been exercised over him. In this as in many other respects, he closely copies the example of his master.

Let it be recollected also that ferocity of temper is a peculiar trait of a savage or barbarous state of society. In civilized countries, it is principally to be seen among the most ignorant and least refined. Civilization is perhaps more remarkable for its effect in softening the tempers of men than for any other single thing. Slaves are purposely kept in a state of barbarism and ignorance. That they should have little control over their tempers, and should give way to violent and sudden gusts of passion, is a matter of course.

2. *Improvidence*. Among freemen, the pleasures of accumulation are perhaps not inferior to the pleasures of consumption. The pleasure that a house keeper enjoys from knowing that he has laid by a stock of provisions sufficient to support his family through the winter, is sufficient to counterbalance a great deal of

saving and self-denial. But the pleasures of accumulation are pleasures which a slave cannot enjoy. His sole pleasure consists in consuming. It is therefore his object to consume all he possibly can. To gratify a present appetite is almost all he ever thinks of. He knows that his master will not suffer him to perish for want of absolute necessaries. Any thing he should lay by, he would be in constant danger of losing, because property is a thing which the laws do not allow him to possess. When he has consumed a thing he is sure of it, and only then—

> Be fair or foul, or rain or shine
> The joys I have possessed in spite of fate are mine,
> Nor heaven itself upon the past has power,
> But what has been, has been, and I have had my hour.

The slaves never read either Horace or Dryden, but they feel and they reason in the same way.

The spirit of improvidence has for its associate on the part of the slaves as well as on the part of the masters, a remarkable disposition for hospitality. But the hospitality of the slaves may justly be regarded as a virtue of a much higher order, than the hospitality of the masters, inasmuch as the slaves bestow out of their necessities, whereas the masters in general, give from their abundance. Sunday for the most part is allowance day, and on those plantations where meat forms a part of the allowance, it often happens, where the vigilance of masters or overseers does not prevent it, that within six hours, the portion of meat given out for the whole week, is consumed in treating friends and acquaintances from some neighboring plantations, where meat is a luxury that forms no portion of the regular allowance. The slaves are as fond of nocturnal entertainments as the masters are of dinner parties, and the profuse liberality with which, from the scanty means within their power, they contribute to get them up, shows them in point of good fellowship, to be not less free hearted than their masters.

3. *Idleness.* The natural stimulus of labor is, the hope of reward. The expectation of reward is capable of exciting the most strenuous exertions, and when properly presented, never fails of effect. Where this motive does not exist, industry is unknown. The fear of punishment cannot produce it. The most it can do is, to produce an empty appearance of it, which is in fact little better than idleness in the disguise of labor.

But it is not alone the absence of reward that makes a slave necessarily idle. In his mind labor is associated indissolubly with the lash. Pain, weariness, fear, the sense of inferiority, these are in his eyes, the natural companions of labor. What wonder if he regard it with disgust? On the other hand, idleness, to his limited view, appears to be the distinguishing badge of freedom, and with freedom he associates every idea of pleasure and content.

Idleness again, in point of fact, is in the case of a slave a real luxury, a true delight, much more so, than it ever can be in the case of a freeman, and that for three reasons. First, because rest is ever delightful to the weary, and those who labor by compulsion are always weary. Second, because being idle, as has been shown in a previous chapter, is a sort of means whereby the slave is enabled to regain, as it were, a certain portion of his liberty. Third, because idleness is a means of lessening the value of that stolen labor upon which the master has seized, and so of indulging that indignation and hatred which the slave naturally feels. Do we not commonly destroy our property, whether public or private, whenever that is the only way to save it from falling into the hands of an enemy?

To make men industrious, who have all these motives for idleness, is out of the question. The experience of the world has proved ten thousand times over, and every individual who will but consider his own motives of action, must be abundantly satisfied, that the only stimulus that can be relied upon as able to produce a life of regular industry is,—the hope of reward,—a fair prospect of being permitted to enjoy undisturbed, the fruits of our labor.

4. *Drunkenness.* The excitement which drunkenness produces is of so very pleasurable a kind, that those who have once experienced it, have need of very strong motives to enable them to resist the temptation it holds out. Especially is this the case with those who lack that steady, regular yet innocent stimulus supplied by a daily occupation in which they take pleasure. When occupation is wanting, or when instead of being pleasurable the occupation to which a man is obliged to submit, is irksome and disagreeable, there results a miserable weariness of soul, against which drunkenness offers an opiate so tempting that even the most intelligent and best educated are not always able to resist it. That the slaves as a body should greedily snatch at it, is not surprising.

5. *Gambling.* That same wearisome state of mind, which among both bond and free is the greatest temptation to drink, proves also the strongest inducement to gamble. The human mind craves excitement. It is the very vital air of the soul, as essential to it as motion is to the health of the body. If this desire cannot be gratified by innocent means, means of gratification will be devised which are not innocent. Of these means gambling is one of the most potent and pernicious; and a means as popular among the slaves as among the masters. It ought to be observed however with respect both to this vice and to that of drunkenness, that both of them prevail to a much less extent among the slaves than with the free, because the opportunities, means, and facility for these kinds of indulgences which the slaves possess, are far inferior to those possessed by the free.

It is proper also to observe that the five great defects of character and conduct common as we have seen to the privileged and the unprivileged classes at the south, all exhibit themselves among the free, in a form more aggravated, and more disgusting—

14*

at all events in a form far more pregnant with mischief than among the slaves. Slavery it would seem is but the foster-mother of vice; tyranny is the real parent,—for the privileged class at the south have not yet reached that point of refinement indicated by Burke, at which vice by losing all its grossness loses half its evil.

The ferocity of the slaves is a mild thing compared with the ferocity of the masters. It is rare to hear of a slave murdered by a slave, while the murder of white men by white men, is an every day occurrence. The instrument of vengeance which the slave most commonly employs, is his fist, or at most a club. The master uses pistols, dirks, knives, and double barrelled guns. With all the bad reputation of Spain and Italy, assassinations were never a quarter so common in those countries as they now are in the south-western states of the American Union. The chance or rather I might say, the probability of dying a violent death seems to be far greater in the states of Mississippi, Arkansas and Texas, than in any other part of the known world, not even the most barbarous countries excepted.

Idleness we must consider, presents itself to the slaves under the aspect of a pure good. In them it cannot be regarded as a vice. Is it a crime to evade as far as possible, the violence of robbery?

The privileged class on the contrary, are able to view idleness in its true light. It is not only the cause, and to the privileged class perceptibly the cause of all those evils traced to it above, but the love of idleness is in fact, the real foundation of slavery. The masters wish to enjoy without working; to reap where they have not sowed, to gather where they have not strawed. This is the whole secret of the social system of the south. This unjust desire, which in the nature of things never can be fully gratified—for the enjoyment thus obtained is poisoned and corrupted by a certain secret inherent flavor of bitterness—

—Medio de fonte leporum,
Surgit amari aliquid, quod in ipsis floribus angat,—

this unjust desire to possess without labor, may be looked upon as the fruitful source of all the evils which the system of slavery involves. Under such circumstances, idleness ceases to be merely a vice, it becomes a crime, and a crime too of the very blackest die; for it is the immediate cause of all kinds of crimes which men have agreed most to stigmatize, and those crimes too not perpetrated one by one, and in defiance of law, but perpetrated wholesale and systematically, not by individual upon individual, but by one half the community upon the other half, and that too with the sanction of legislatures and tribunals.

As regards improvidence, drunkenness and gambling, on the part of the slaves they are comparatively venal offences. The harm they can do is limited, and is confined almost entirely to the person of the offender himself. There is no danger that by giving way to them, he will precipitate a whole family into poverty and distress. There is no danger that his example will have a pernicious influence upon society at large. What is the example of a slave? Nor is there any likelihood that by giving way to these temptations he may render useless gifts which properly exercised might have redounded to the benefit of the community. The only talent proper to a slave is the talent of handling a hoe. With him, these vices terminate for the most part in themselves. The secondary evils which they produce are comparatively speaking, inconsiderable. Among the privileged class these indulgences give rise to a train of secondary evils of which the mere catalogue would fill a volume; evils, which instead of confining themselves to the person of the offender, overflow, spread abroad, sweep away whole families, and inundate society. No language is too strong to describe the dangerous and fatal character, which when practised by the privileged class, these vices assume.

SECTION III.

*Points of diversity in the character of the privileged
and the unprivileged classes.*

1. Courage is one of those chivalrous virtues much
boasted of among the freemen of the south. They
are brave beyond question. All freemen are so.
Courage is a virtue which always exists in the greatest perfection among freemen, because among freemen,
it is most esteemed and most cultivated. Courage is
essential to the maintenance of liberty. When it
happens that freemen are also tyrants, courage is cultivated and fostered for the additional reason that it
is essential also to the maintenance of tyranny.
What importance is attached to this virtue at the south,
may be conjectured from the braggadocio spirit, which
so universally prevails there. Listen to southern
conversation, or read the southern newspapers, and
one would suppose that every mother's son of the free
population, was an Orlando Furioso, or a Richard
Cœur de Lion at the least. What wonder if courage
abound where it is so highly esteemed and so greatly
encouraged.

The slaves, on the other hand, are cowards. A brave
man may be found among them here or there, but
cowardice is their general characteristic. If it were
not so, the system of slavery would be very short lived. To organize a successful insurrection, something
more than mere courage is no doubt necessary. But
courage alone is sufficient to produce a series of un-
successful insurrections, and however individually un-
successful; a series of insurrections would shortly render the masters' empire not worth preserving. If the
slaves are cowards, it is a vice to which they have
been diligently trained up from their earliest childhood.
Were a tenth part of the pains bestowed to make
them brave, which are taken to render them otherwise,
they would be as courageous as their masters. The

boldest heart very soon becomes subdued, when every indication of spirit, every disposition to stand at bay is shortly visited by the whip, irons, or a prison.

2. The CHASTITY of their women is another chivalrous virtue, much boasted of by the freemen of the south. The southern people have reason to be proud of their women. From the most disgusting vices of the men, they are, as we have mentioned already, in a great measure free, and such active virtue as is to be found at the south, at least the larger portion of it, is to be looked for among the female sex.

If however the women have escaped to a certain extent, the blighting influences of tyranny it is because they are sedulously shielded from its worst effects.

Chastity like courage is to a great extent, an artificial virtue, the existence of which principally depends upon education and public opinion. Both education and public opinion are stretched to their utmost influence to preserve the chastity of the southern women, while the free and more luxurious indulgence which the men find elsewhere, causes the seduction of free women to be a thing seldom attempted.

Among the slaves, a woman, apart from mere natural bashfulness, has no inducement to be chaste ; she has many inducements the other way. Her person is her only means of purchasing favors, indulgences, presents. To be the favorite of the master or one of his sons, of the overseer, or even of a driver, is an object of desire, and a situation of dignity. It is as much esteemed among the slaves, as an advantageous marriage would be, among the free. So far from involving disgrace, it confers honor. Besides, where marriage is only a temporary contract, dissolvable at any time, not by the will of the parties alone, but at the caprice and pleasure of the masters, what room is there for any such virtue as chastity ? Chastity consists in keeping the sexual appetite under a close restraint except when its indulgence is sanctioned by marriage. But among slaves every casual union, though but for a day, is a marriage. To persons so situated, we cannot justly apply ideas founded upon totally different circumstances. If we choose however to understand by chastity the restriction of one's self to a single partner, chastity is very far from being so rare a virtue among the women of the unprivileged class as is often asserted, and generally supposed. Though the union may be dissolved in a moment, at the slightest caprice of the parties, such separations are much more rare than might be imagined. More husbands and wives among the slaves are separated by the hammer of the auctioneer, than by the united influence of infidelity, disgust, or the desire of change.

3. FRAUD, FALSEHOOD, AND DISHONESTY are represented by the masters, as distinguishing traits in the character of the unprivileged class. This charge is unfounded. It has been shown already, that as between master and slave, from the very nature of that relation, mutual confidence, trust and reliance, are out of the question. To deceive his master is almost the only means of self-defence in the power of the slave. What ground of mutual confidence is it possible to establish between the robber and the robbed? To hold those promises binding which are extorted by force, to maintain that one is obliged to keep faith with a plunderer, is to surrender up, to the hands of violence, through the influence of a weak and cruel superstition, or a piece of miserable and empty sophistry, not the body only, but the soul; not only actions, but the will; the future as well as the present;—it is to strip weakness and suffering of their last defence, and to give omnipotence to tyranny.

In their transactions with each other the members of the unprivileged class at the south, are by no means deficient in the great and necessary virtues of truth, honesty and fidelity. The difficulty of inducing them to betray each other is proverbial, and is a matter of grievous complaint among masters and overseers. There are among the slaves, as among all bodies of men, some who set up honesty for sale, and who become instruments of tyranny in the hands of the privileged class. There are others shrewd and slippery, upon whom no dependence whatever can be placed, even by their friends and relations. Characters of this sort, are quite as common among the privileged order. Indeed more so. There has been already mentioned that great class of professional gamblers, whose sole business it is to prey upon the community, to inveigle the unwary, and entrap the ignorant. There is no such class among the slaves. There is still another great class among the privileged order, who live almost wholly upon the plunder of their richer neighbors, the receivers, namely, of stolen goods, the keepers of the petty trading stores, scattered throughout the south. They take in the corn, cotton and rice stolen by the slaves, and give in exchange whisky and other luxuries. This class of traders is very large. The severest laws have been enacted to suppress them, but without success. Lynch law is now and then administered upon them in all its severity, but the nuisance cannot be abated. These men, compared with the slaves, are wholly without excuse. They live by constant violations of laws, by constant breaches of a social compact to which they have themselves assented. This is a case in which the receiver, even in a legal point of view, is a thousand times worse than the thief. Yet to speak within bounds, for every five or six acts of theft, (or what is called so,) committed on the part of slaves, there is at least one act of reception committed on the part of some freeman. We may therefore consider it to be reduced to an arithmetical demonstration, that so far as relates to violations of property, the offences of the free are greater than those of the slaves. To this conclusion we must come, even without taking into account the appalling fact that the entire existence of a large part of the privileged class is but one constant, steady violation of all those principles upon which the very idea of property depends, and upon which the virtues of truth, honesty, justice and fidelity must rest for their only sure support. We may apply to the southern slave-holders, a *jeu d'esprit* of Talleyrand's. A certain person was complaining that every body considered him a worthless, infamous fellow, yet said the complainant, I do not know why, for I have never committed but one fault in my life. "Ah!" said Talleyrand, "but when will that one fault be ended?"

To those accustomed to look only at the outside of things, the results to which this chapter has brought us, will no doubt seem strange. It is impossible, they will say, that men whose circumstances are so contradictory, and whose whole appearance is so different, can after all, be so much alike. Such readers will do well to call to mind the lines of Shakspeare,—

> Through tatter'd clothes small vices do appear ;
> Robes and furr'd gowns, hide all. Plate sin with gold,
> And the strong lance of justice hurtless breaks
> Arm it in rags, a pigmy's straw doth pierce it.

That gold however, with which the system of southern slavery is plated, is not the true metal. 'Tis but a fairy, shadowy, imaginary gold which cannot cross the running waters of truth, without being changed back again to its original worthlessness.

CHAPTER FIFTH.

LEGAL BASIS OF THE SLAVE-HOLDING SYSTEM.

SECTION I.

Preliminary Observations.

One main pillar of domestic slavery, as it now exists in the United States, is the idea that it rests upon law. Law is regarded with veneration, and no where more so than in the United States, as the great foundation and support of the right of property, of personal rights, in a word—of social organization. Jurists, with a natural disposition to exaggerate the importance of a profession to which most of them have belonged, have been induced to overlook or to disregard the *natural* foundation of rights. Most of them represent the idea of property as resting on a merely *artificial* basis—the law; not the law of nature, but the law of convention. Upon that same artificial basis, too, they are inclined mainly to rest even the most important of personal rights. These ideas, widely spread through the community, greatly modify public opinion upon the question of slavery. In the abstract, slavery, all admit, is sheer cruelty and injustice. But slavery, as it exists in the United States, is supposed to be *legal;* and being legal, is supposed to acquire a certain character of right. To use our best efforts for the suppression of cruelty and injustice, is admitted to be a moral duty. But then it is a moral duty, and, in the opinion of many, a paramount duty, to obey the law.

Prevailing ideas on the theory of government tend precisely the same way. Those ideas, derived from Hobbes, Locke, and Rousseau, represent government as a contract. The natural state of man, the state of nature, is assumed to be a state of hostility on the part of each individual against every other, or, according to Rousseau, of total isolation. To escape out of this wretched condition, men, we are told, resorted to the artificial expedient of societies and governments founded on contract. According to this theory, the only moral principle involved in the idea of government is—Contract; and this contract, we are told, must be preserved inviolate, or government is at an end, and chaos comes again. No matter how absurd; no matter how unjust towards ourselves or others: a bargain is a bargain; and though it stipulates for the pound of flesh, it must be fulfilled. Many excellent men, ready to denounce slavery in the abstract as the sum of all iniquities, will tell us, in the same breath, that the "compromises of the constitution" guaranty its existence. It is morally wrong, they say, to attempt to evade or get over, or set aside, those compromises—an appeal to notions of mercantile honor not without a powerful influence upon the best portion of the community.

These opinions respecting law and government involve, indeed, the inconsistency and absurdity of supposing that men have power, by arrangement and convention, to make that artificially right which naturally is wrong—an inconsistency and absurdity which there have not been wanting able writers to expose. These writers have shown clearly enough, that the basis of law, the basis of property, the basis of personal rights, the basis of government, are to be sought for and found not in any artificial contracts, or arbitrary statutes or usages, but in the nature and constitution of man. They have shown clearly enough, that law, so far as it has any binding moral force, is and must be conformable to natural principles of right; indeed, that in this conformity alone its moral binding force consists; and that so far as this conformity is wanting, what is called law is mere violence and tyranny, to which a man may submit for the sake of peace, but which he has a moral right to resist passively at all times, and forcibly when he has any fair prospect of success. Such, indeed, was the principle upon which the American Revolution was justified. The acts of parliament of which the colonies complained, had all the forms of law, and Mansfield and other great lawyers said they were law. But in the view of the colonists, they lacked the substance without which law cannot exist. They subverted those fundamental rights embodied in that maxim and usage of the English constitution, which couples taxation and representation together. Taxation without representation was denounced by the colonists as mere robbery, to which, though concealed under the form of law, they were not legally obliged to, and would not, submit.

The principle of the perpetuity and inviolability of contracts, no matter what their object, character, or operation, has been attacked with no less energy and success. It has been triumphantly shown, that the very essence and substratum of contract is, mutual benefit. Contracts, whether in law or morals, have no binding force without a consideration, a good and valuable consideration. Men cannot bargain away either their own rights or the rights of others. All such pretended contracts are void from the beginning —the spawn of fraud in the one party, and ignorance in the other, or of injustice and immoral intentions in both. To say, that by committing the folly or the crime of contracting to do an immoral act, a man lays himself under a moral obligation to do that immoral act, is to overturn the very foundations of morality. Nor are these principles the mere notions of theoretical moralists. So far as relates to private contracts, they are fully acknowledged and admitted by all courts of law throughout the civilized world. They constitute, indeed, the fundamental principle upon which those courts administer the law of contracts.

But all these appeals to general principles, however able and conclusive, have, when applied to the question of slavery, but little weight with the great body of the community. Did they relate to points in which that body had a direct, obvious, personal interest, the appeal, no doubt, would be irresistible. When Andros, governor of New England, undertook to deprive people of their lands, under pretence of defective titles, "the men of Massachusetts did much quote Lord Coke;" and finding that useless, they stripped Andros of his power. When Grenville attempted to levy taxes without their consent, they were ready at once to resort to fundamental principles, and, when those principles failed, to their muskets. Then, the case touched themselves. When it only touches the unfortunate negroes of the southern states, or a few poor colored people of the north, it is quite a different matter. Appeal to principle is then denounced as wild and visionary. Always fearful of effort and responsibility, the great mass of the community intrench themselves on this question behind statutes, decisions, usage, the opinions of lawyers, and the current notions of the day. To be sure, slavery is wrong and unjust, and impolitic and wicked, but then it is—legal.

Nor, indeed, is this conduct to be wondered at, the very courts, those reverend depositories of the knowledge of the law, those vicegerents upon earth of eternal equity and justice, having themselves set the example. In mere questions of private right, the courts resort, without hesitation, to those eternal principles of right reason, that is, of true morality, which they boast to be the foundation of law; and they set aside, without hesitation, every private contract which has in it any trace or tincture of fraud or crime. But when it comes to the enforcement of so called political contracts, a sad change is observable. Individual lawyers, indeed even judges on the bench, of the highest eminence, have not hesitated to say, that an act of parliament contrary to the law of God, that is, contrary to the eternal principles of right, is void. Such opinions have been thrown out incidentally, with great apparent boldness and decision. But when has an act of legislation been set aside on that ground? No court in England or America has ever yet dared to do it. Courts have bowed submissively at the feet of the governments, their creators, ascribing to those creators an omnipotence over right and wrong greater than the philosophy of our day is willing to allow even to God himself. They hold, indeed, to the maxim *Fiat justitia, ruat cœlum*, but in this sense: "the will of the government must be done, though heaven itself be trampled under foot." It must be admitted as the settled doctrine of courts of law, that the supreme legislative authority has the power to declare to be law even that which is against right. But this has been a forced concession; and as Galileo, when obliged by the Inquisition to confess that the earth stood still, mumbled yet between his teeth, as he rose from his knees, "It moves though,"—so our courts of law, blushing and stammering at the disgraceful concession extorted from them by fear and power, have done their best to limit and to nullify that concession. If the supreme legislature chooses to say that manifest wrong shall be law, the courts submit to enforce it as such. But then they will never presuppose that the supreme legislature intends to do any thing so absurd and cruel. If the intention is plain, manifest, and clear, it must be enforced; but the courts will never resort to implication, or conjecture, or construction, to make out any such intention. This principle in the interpretation of legal enactments, perfectly well settled and established in all the courts of England and America, is thus laid down by Chief Justice Marshall, in the case of *United States* v. *Fisher*, 2 Cranch, 390. "Where rights are infringed, where fundamental principles are overthrown, where the general system of the laws is departed from, the legislative intention must be expressed with irresistible clearness, to induce a court of justice to suppose a design to effect such objects."

It is thus that, in all cases of injustice attempted under the form of legislation, courts, while admitting the power of the legislature, yet reserve to themselves a power to defeat the wicked legislative intention, by refusing to suppose the legislature capable of any such intention. But the extent to which this indirect veto power is carried out in particular cases, must evidently depend very much upon circumstances, and especially upon the character and position of the court. Where a court is exceedingly indisposed to see, and is so situated as to be able to give effect to its inclinations, "irresistible clearness" is out of the question. No possible form of words can produce it. Now the disposition on the part of the court to see or not to see a wicked intention, will depend upon two things: first, the opinion of the court as to the degree and aggravation of the wickedness; secondly, their opinion as to the amount of support likely to be found in the community, should an attempt be made to defeat that wicked intention.

Take the case of slavery for example. Suppose that in a slave-holding community the question of the legality of slavery is raised, and certain legislative acts are quoted to sustain it. If the court should happen to entertain the opinions professed by Mr. Calhoun, that slavery is not only a blessing in itself, but the essential foundation of a republican government, of course they would see, with great facility, an intention in the quoted acts to give to slavery a legal basis. Even if they entertained the more common opinion, avowed by Mr. Clay, that slavery, though an evil in itself, is yet, under existing circumstances, a necessary evil, the only means of preserving the two races of whites and blacks from a war of extermination, they would still find no great difficulty in perceiving a legislative intention to legalize slavery. But suppose the judges have the feelings proper to men enlightened and humane; suppose their eyes fully open to the enormous criminality of slavery; suppose they saw in vivid colors all its multiplied evils and miseries, both for masters and slaves—it would be very difficult for any form of words to establish, with "irresistible clearness," in the minds of such men, a legislative intention to legalize so much folly and crime. If, besides, they saw opinions hostile to slavery openly avowed and spreading around them; if they saw a certainty of being powerfully sustained in reinstating justice on her seat,—what form of words would be able to satisfy such a court that the supreme legislative authority intended to sanction a system so horribly unjust? At all events, a court so constituted and so situated, would surely never discover any such intention in a case where there were either no words at all, or but very obscure and vague ones.

It is the glory of the tribunals of the common law, that, even when trampled in the mud by the feet of power, they have never consented to lie there in quiet. They have struggled, always to a certain extent, often nobly, to rise again, to cleanse the ermine robes of justice from the mire of ignorant, weak, cruel, self-seeking legislation, to lift again on high the balance of equity, and, to the full extent of their power and their light, to weigh out again equal justice to all. But to enable them to do this, the community about them must uphold their hands. What can four or five gray-haired men do against the ferocity, the wrongheadedness, the intentional injustice of a whole community? Men formed by long experience of the world in its least amiable aspects, will not cast their pearls before swine's feet. The sort of men who occupy the judicial bench are seldom much inclined to outrun popular opinion; yet however it may be fashionable among them to affect to despise such opinion, it is none the less true that their own views are greatly influenced, if not indeed mainly determined, by the prevailing sentiment of the community about them.

In these considerations we shall find a complete reply to a taunt frequently thrown in our teeth by the advocates of the legality of slavery. What more absurd, they say, than to question a legality recognized and admitted ever since the settlement of the country!

But why absurd?

From a period long preceding the settlement of North America down to the famous decision in Somerset's case, three or four years before our declaration of independence, the legality of slavery was also recognized and admitted in England. It required the indefatigable perseverance of a Granville Sharpe, the enlightened humanity of a Mansfield, an age awake to the rights of humanity, and a community free, in a great measure, from the bias of interest, to draw up "from the deep well of the law" that "amiable and admirable secret,"

"No slave can breathe in England."

"The knowledge of the law," says my Lord Coke, "is like a deep well, out of which each man draweth according to the strength of his understanding." Is it too much to hope, that we shall yet have American judges with hearts and understandings strong enough to draw up out of that same deep well the twin secret, that there is not, and never was, any legal slavery in America? It is not strength of understanding that has failed us. Have we not had on the bench of the United States Supreme Court a Jay, a Wilson, a Marshall, a Story? What has been lacking is heart, conscience, courage; more than all, the surrounding support of an enlightened and humane public opinion, to sustain our judges in looking this lurking devil of slavery in the face. No court of justice in the United States has ever yet dared do it, lest being called upon to decide against the legality of slavery, they might be called upon, in so doing, to set at defiance a conglomeration of interests and prejudices which they have not had courage to brave, which no prudent court could be expected to brave. And what has been wanting, no less than a fearless court, a court daring enough to face, in the cause of justice and right, the ferocious prejudices of a ferocious nation—has been, a learned, independent, fearless bar. The court alone, unaided by the bar, is incapable of administering justice. Points must first be presented, before they can be decided; and how much depends on the manner and the medium of their presentation! Would the English law of treason ever have been stripped of so many of its terrors, and reduced so much within the limits of justice and moderation, but for the earnest struggles of an Erskine and a Curran? Had O'Connell been an ordinary lawyer, or an ordinary culprit, would the English House of Lords ever have seen those flaws in his indictment which the Irish judges had overlooked?

No council has ever yet been retained for the slaves; no body of influential friends has ever appeared, to impress upon the judges the necessity of serious investigation, and to assure them of support in sustaining the right. The case has gone by default; or rather, it has never yet been entered in court.

SECTION II.

Slavery as a Colonial Institution.

Servitude in the Middle Ages existed in England under two forms. *Villeins in gross* were slaves, in several respects the same as ours, transferable from master to master, like any other chattel. *Villeins regardant* were serfs, attached to the soil, inseparable from it, and transferable only with it. These same two forms of servitude, but recently abolished in Hungary, may still be seen in Russia. Villeinage was hereditary — the villeins being the descendants of the ancient Britons and Saxons, held in servitude from a time whereof the memory of man ran not to the contrary.

Previous to the discovery of America, or shortly after that period, English villeinage *in gross* had almost ceased to exist. So late as the reign of Elizabeth, only a few villeins *regardant* remained, in some obscure corners. The lawyers and the clergy, in whom the principal intelligence of that age was vested, had both greatly contributed to this result. In all questions touching villeinage, the English common law courts had made it a point to lean in favor of freedom. All men were supposed to be free, and the burden of proof lay on the claimant. To prove a man a villein, unless he confessed himself such in open court,—and the last recorded confession of this kind was in the nineteenth year of Henry VI., (1441,) —it was necessary to show title to him by proscription; that is, to show that, being born in lawful wedlock, he was descended of a stock of villeins on the father's side time out of memory. For the English common law courts refused to recognize the doctrine of the civil law—that favorite doctrine of all slaveholding communities—that the children of female slaves inherit from the mother the condition of slavery. They held, on the contrary, that the child followed the condition of the father. Bastard children, being in the eye of the law children without fathers, of course were born free—a doctrine which gave freedom to great numbers, for, in all slave-holding communities, the masters esteem it a part of their right to use the slave women as concubines.

Taking a hint apparently from the Mahometans, the clergy had denounced it as a scandalous and outrageous thing for one Christian to hold another in slavery; and their preaching on this point had been so successful, that about the time of the discovery of America it had come to be considered a settled matter, not in England only, but throughout Western

Europe, that no Christian ought to be, or lawfully could be, held as a slave.

But with the customary narrowness of that age, this immunity from slavery was not thought to extend to infidels or pagans. While the emancipation of serfs was going on, black slaves, brought by the Portuguese from the coast of Guinea, became common in the south of Europe, and a few found their way to England. The first Englishman who engaged in this business was Sir John Hawkins, who, during the reign of Elizabeth, made several voyages to the coast of Guinea for negroes, whom he disposed of to the Spaniards of the West Indies. The queen granted several patents to encourage this traffic; yet she is said to have expressed to Hawkins her hope that the negroes went voluntarily from Africa, declaring that if any force were used to enslave them, she doubted not it would bring down the vengeance of Heaven upon those guilty of such wickedness. The newly-discovered coasts of America were also visited by kidnappers. Few, if any, of the early voyagers scrupled to seize the natives, and to carry them home as slaves. Sir Ferdinando Gorges, so active and so conspicuous in the early settlement of New England, had a number of these captured natives, whom he claimed as his property, kept under restraint, and employed as guides and pilots. The Mosaic law, then recently made familiar by the English translation of the Bible, and considered high authority on all questions of right, seemed to countenance this distinction between Christians and infidels. The Jews, according to the Mosaic code, could hold their brethren as servants only for a period of seven years, or at the utmost, till the next Jubilee, (for it is not very easy to reconcile the apparently conflicting provisions on this subject in Exodus and Leviticus;) but of "the heathen round about," they might buy "bondmen, as an inheritance for ever." The practice of the early English settlers in America, and their ideas of the English law on the subject, corresponded exactly with these Jewish provisions, indeed would seem to have been regulated by them. Thus they took with them, or caused to be brought out, a large number of indented Christian servants, whose period of bondage was limited to seven years, and who, till after the Revolution, constituted a distinct class in the community. Indeed, of the white immigrants to America preceding that era, the larger portion would seem to have arrived there under this servile character. But while the servitude of Christians was thus limited, the colonists supposed themselves justified in holding negroes and Indians as slaves for life. The first English colonists arrived in Virginia in 1607. In 1620 a Dutch trading vessel entered James' River with twenty negroes on board, who were sold to the settlers. Other similar importations continued to be made from time to time; but it not being imagined that any local legislation was necessary to give to the purchasers of these black servants the right to hold them and their posterity as bondmen for ever, more than forty years elapsed before any notice was taken of slaves by the Virginia statutes, as distinct from other servants.

It was not in Virginia, but in New England, that the earliest colonial legislation on the subject of slavery occurred. The Massachusetts " Body of Liberties," or " Fundamentals," as they were called, first promulgated in 1641, contain the following provision : " There shall never be any bond slavery, villeinage, nor captivity among us, *unless it be lawful captives taken in just wars, and such strangers as willingly sell themselves, or are sold, unto us.*" But in thus giving an express sanction to negro and Indian slavery, the freemen of Massachusetts did not conceive themselves to be running at all counter to the law of England, to which, by their charter, they were bound to conform, though on ecclesiastical points somewhat inclined to deviate from it. On the contrary, they supposed themselves to be conforming as well to the law of England, as to "the law of God, established in Israel." This Massachusetts law, it will be perceived, not only sanctioned slavery, but also the slave-trade. An American historian, always too much a panegyrist or an apologist to be implicitly relied on, has indeed undertaken to claim for Massachusetts the honor of having denounced, at that early day, as "malefactors and murderers," those "who sailed to Guinea, to trade for negroes"—a claim founded upon a misapprehension of a passage in Winthrop's Journal. It appears, on the contrary, from other passages in Winthrop, that "the trade to Guinea for negroes" was recognized as a just and lawful traffic. New England vessels, after carrying cargoes of staves to Madeira, were accustomed to sail to Guinea for slaves, who generally, as there was little or no demand for them at Boston, were carried to Barbadoes, or the other English settlements in the West Indies, there to be sold. In the particular case above referred to, instead of *buying* negroes, in the regular course of the Guinea trade, the Boston crew had joined with some Londoners already on the coast, and, on pretence of some quarrel with the natives, had landed "a murderer,"—the expressive name of a small piece of cannon,—had attacked a negro village *on a Sunday*, and after killing many of the inhabitants, had made a few prisoners, of whom two boys fell to the share of the Bostonians. A violent quarrel between the master, mate, and owners, as to the mutual settlement of their accounts, brought out the whole history of this voyage before the magistrates, one of whom presented a petition to the General Court, charging the master and mate, not with having "sailed for Guinea to trade for negroes," as the case is represented, but with the threefold offence of murder, manstealing, and Sabbath-breaking,—the first two capital, by the Fundamental Laws of the colony, and all three "capital, by the laws of God." It was right enough to *purchase* slaves, but wrong to steal them, especially on a Sunday, and to commit murder in

16

doing so. The kidnapped negroes were ordered to be sent back; but no other punishment was inflicted, the court doubting their authority to punish crimes committed on the coast of Africa.

The honor of having made the first American protest against negro slavery, really belongs not to Massachusetts, but to Roger Williams and his fellow-settlers at Providence in Rhode Island, exiles and refugees from the colony of Massachusetts because they had embraced the doctrine of "soul liberty," by which they signified perfect freedom of opinion in matters of religion. The people of Providence, thinking probably that body liberty was a necessary supplement to soul liberty, enacted a law in 1652, placing "black mankind" on the same level, with regard to limitation of service, as white servants, and absolutely prohibiting perpetual slavery within their territories. Unfortunately for the honor of Rhode Island, this law, never in force except in the town of Providence, presently fell into abeyance; and within a century not only did negro slavery become common in Rhode Island, but its inhabitants engaged in the African trade, for the supply of the other colonies.

In Virginia the ratio of slaves to the white population, though for many years not large, was much greater than in New England; but it was not till cases arose for which the English common law, as the colonists understood it, made no provisions satisfactory to the slave-holders, that any distinct mention of slavery occurs in the legislation of that colony. In the course of forty years, by which time the slaves numbered two thousand in a population of forty thousand, mulatto children had been born and grown to manhood. What should be the condition of these children?

By the English law, when the fathers were free the children were free also. But this did not suit the interest of the slave-holders. The mulattoes were few, ignorant, and helpless, and the Virginia legislature, notwithstanding its acknowledged obligation to conform strictly to English law, did not hesitate to disregard a great and well-established doctrine of that law, and substituting a provision of the civil, that is, of the Roman code, to enact—that children should follow the condition of the mother; and this principle, thus unwarrantably introduced into Virginia in 1662, was ultimately adopted, by statute or usage, in all the British colonies.

Another question, not less interesting to the slave-holders, presently arose. Of the negroes brought to Virginia, some had been converted and baptized, and this was the case to a still greater extent with those born in the colony. By what right were these *Christians* held as slaves?

The law of England, even according to the colonial view of it, did not allow the slavery of Christians. It was only pagans and infidels who could be enslaved. But the Virginia assembly came to the relief of the masters; and with that audacious disregard of all law and all right except its own good pleasure, by which slave-holding legislation has ever been characterized, they enacted, in utter defiance of the English law, —even their own version of it,—that negroes convert-ed and baptized should not thereby become free. This act bears date in 1669. Another act, passed the same year, in equal defiance of the English law, provided, that killing slaves by extremity of correction should not be esteemed felony, "since it cannot be presumed that prepense malice should induce any man to destroy his own estate."

For reasons of policy or humanity, it had been pro-vided that Indians should not be held as slaves,—a provision, whatever the reason of it, which places the legislation of Virginia, on this point, in honorable contrast to that of New England, where the contrary practice prevailed. But did this prohibition extend to Indian captives taken in war, elsewhere than in Virginia, and brought to that colony for sale?

This question was settled in 1670, by enacting that

"all servants, *not being Christians*, imported by ship-ping, shall be slaves for their lives," those imported by land to serve for a limited time. Freedom had just been denied to Christian negroes converted in the col-ony, or born there; but the assembly did not venture to usurp any such jurisdiction over stranger Christians.

As a necessary pendant to the slave code, the sys-tem of subjecting the free to disabilities now also began. Thus it was enacted in 1670, that negro wo-men, though free, should be rated and taxed as "tith-ables," that is, should pay a poll tax, exacted in the case of whites only from the men. Free negroes and Indians were also disqualified to purchase or hold white servants.

These acts, the legislative basis of slavery in Vir-ginia, were enacted during the government of Sir William Berkeley, well known for his famous apos-trophe—"I thank God we have no free schools nor printing, and I hope we shall not have these hundred years; for learning has brought disobedience, and heresy, and sects into the world, and printing has divulged them; and libels against the best govern-ment. God keep us from both!"—Nor was this wish uttered in vain. The establishment of slavery secured its fulfilment. Virginia has no free schools to this day; none, at least, worthy of the name. She has, indeed, a few printing-presses; but they are muzzled, gagged, —effectually restrained from libels against "the best government"—for such in that state the oligarchy of slave-holders is held to be.

The virtuous resolution of Virginia on the subject of Indians did not last long; nor did freedom from schools and printing-presses keep out disobedience and rebellion. The immediate cause of Bacon's insur-rection, so famous in the colonial annals of Virginia, was the refusal of Berkeley to authorize expeditions against the Indians, who had lately committed some depredations. Berkeley preferred a scheme of defence by forts. The colonists alleged that his interest in the fur-trade made him too tender of the Indians;

but a law enacted in 1676, by Bacon's insurgent assembly, might seem to imply, that the eagerness of the colonists for offensive war was not altogether disinterested. Into an act for the prosecution of the Indian war a provision was inserted, that Indian prisoners might be held as slaves; and notwithstanding the repeal, after the suppression of the insurrection, of all the other of Bacon's laws, this provision was still continued in force.

In 1682, during Culpepper's administration, the slave code of Virginia received some additions. Slaves were forbidden to carry arms, offensive or defensive; or to go off their masters plantation, without a written pass; or to lift hand against a Christian, even in self-defence. Runaways, who refused to be apprehended, might be lawfully killed. Already had the internal slave-trade begun,—that trade in which Virginia still bears so unhappy a part. As yet, however, the colony was purchaser, not seller, and by a partial repeal of the existing provision in favor of stranger Christians, facilities for purchasing were extended. The assembly enacted that all servants, whether negroes, Moors, mulattoes, or Indians, (including those bought of the neighboring or other Indian tribes,) brought into the colony by sea or land, whether converted to Christianity or not, *provided they were not of Christian parentage and country,* might be held as slaves. Yet, with all this eagerness for new purchases, the evils of the slave system were already felt. The colony was suffering severely from an over-production of tobacco; to such a degree, that the poorer free people could scarcely purchase clothes for themselves;—an over-production to which, as Culpepper stated, in an official report, " the buying of blacks had exceedingly contributed."

In 1691, shortly after the breaking out of the first French and Indian war, policy or humanity, or both combined, recovered the mastery, and the slavery of Indians, sanctioned by statute since the time of Bacon's rebellion, was now finally abolished. Such

16 *

at least was the interpretation given by the courts of
Virginia, subsequently to the revolution, (see *Pallas
& al.* v. *Hill & al.*, 2 Henings' and Mumford's Reports, 149,) to an act of this date, repealing all
restraints on traffic with the Indians, and declaring
that trade thenceforth free and open with "all Indians
whatsoever." But, too ignorant or too helpless to
vindicate their rights, "multitudes of the descendants
of Indians in Virginia," so says Hening, the learned
and laborious editor of the Virginia statutes, "are
still unjustly deprived of their liberty," in spite of
this decision,—one proof, among others, how little
mere legal right, though officially declared by the
highest tribunals, avails the feeble and defenceless.

By the Virginia code, as revised in 1705, "all servants imported by sea or land, who were not Christians in their native country, (except Turks and Moors
in amity with her Majesty, and others who can make
due proof of their being free in England, or any
other Christian country, before they were shipped in
order to transportation hither,) shall be accounted and
be slaves, and as such be here bought and sold, notwithstanding a conversion to Christianity afterwards;"
"all children to be bond or free, according to the
condition of their mothers." But even in this act,
under which near half the population of Virginia are
still held as slaves, the original idea, that no Christian
could be reduced to slavery, is still sufficiently apparent. In the case of servants newly brought into
the colony, religion, not color, nor race, is made the
sole test of distinction between slavery and indented
service. Whatever may have been the practice, it
is plain enough, that under this act, which continued unaltered down to the Revolution, and which
still forms the basis of slave property in Virginia, no
negro, even, who was a Christian in his native country, could, if brought to Virginia, be held there as a
slave.

This code of 1705 also provided, that persons con-
vict in England of crimes punishable with loss of

life or member, and "all negroes, mulattoes, and Indians," should be incapacitated to hold office in the colony. White women having bastard children by negroes or mulattoes were to pay the parish fifteen pounds, or, in default of payment, to be sold for five years, the child to be bound out as a servant for thirty-one years. "And for a further prevention of that abominable mixture and spurious issue, which hereafter may increase in this her Majesty's colony and dominion, as well by English and other white men and women intermarrying with negroes and mulattoes," as by unlawful connection with them, it was enacted, that any man or woman intermarrying with a negro or mulatto, bond or free, should be imprisoned six months and fined ten pounds,—the minister celebrating the marriage to be fined also. Thus early was the bugbear cry of "amalgamation" raised in Virginia. Similar laws enacted in the other colonies operated to degrade and keep down the colored race, and to prevent the institution of slavery from assuming that patriarchal character, by which, in other countries, it is greatly softened, and sometimes has been superseded.

Nothing, indeed, is more striking than the different treatment bestowed by Anglo-American slave-holders, especially those of the United States, upon their own children by slave mothers, and the behavior of Dutch, Spanish, Portuguese, and French slave-holders towards their children similarly begotten. In the slave-holding colonies of these latter nations, that white man is regarded as unnatural, mean, and cruel, who does not, if his ability permit, secure for his colored children emancipation and some pecuniary provision. Colored children are not less numerous in the United States; but there conventional decorum forbids the white father to recognize his colored offspring at all, or to make any provision for them. They are still held and sold as slaves; and among this unfortunate class may be found the descendants of more than one signer of the Declaration of Independence, patriot of the Revolution, leading politician, and presidential candidate.

The example of the Jews in their treatment of the Canaanites, was cited as good authority in all the English colonies for prohibiting intermarriage with negroes and Indians; and for denouncing the mixture of races as unnatural and wicked. But no law could control the appetite of the planters nor prevent that intermixture which inevitably takes place, whenever two races are brought into contact, especially if one race be held in slavery. That austere morality (pretending to be religious,) for which the United States are distinguished above all nations on the face of the earth, unless indeed the palm in this respect ought to be yielded to the mother country, has been obliged, in this case, as in others, to content itself, in defect of conformity to its rules, with cruel grimace, and a lie acted out. Hypocrisy, is said to be the tribute which vice pays to virtue,—a tribute of which the religious treasuries of America are full. The virtuous man,—southern church-member, or peradventure minister of the gospel,—expiates his peccadilloes with his female slaves, by looking on his own children with cold glances, in which no recognition dwells; and as a further proof of his austere morals, opportunity offering, he sells them at auction!

Yet in Virginia, this antipathy to the mixture of races was not and is not carried so far as in some of the more southern colonies. The grand child of an Indian, the great-great grand child of a negro, all the other links being white, become themselves white in the eye of the law, and therefore presumably free.

In Maryland slavery had existed from its first settlement; but the oldest statute on the subject bears date thirty years afterwards, in 1663, when it was enacted, " that all negroes and other slaves within this province, and all negroes and other slaves to be hereafter imported, shall serve during life, and all children born of any negro or other slave, shall be slaves as their *fathers* were, for the term of their lives." In 1715, however, by which time the negroes held in bondage composed a fifth part of the population, this apparent conformity to the principles of the English law of villeinage touching the hereditary descent of servitude, was silently dropped. In that year, upon occasion of the restoration of the government to the Calvert family, the laws of Maryland were revised, and the new code provided, "that all negroes and other slaves, already imported or hereafter to be imported into this province, and all children now born or hereafter to be born of such negroes and slaves, shall be slaves during their natural lives." Upon this statute rest all the claims of the colonial slave-holding system of Maryland to a legal foundation.

The "grand model," the first proprietary constitution of Carolina, the production of the celebrated Locke, drawn up in 1670, contained the following clause: "Every freeman of Carolina shall have absolute power and authority over his negro slaves, of what opinion and religion soever." But "the grand model," in compliance with the repeated and earnest requests of the colonists, was abrogated in 1693, and for nineteen years the system of slavery in South Carolina remained without any legal basis, except that furnished by the mistaken notions of the colonists as to the English law. The assembly, however, at length thought it necessary to provide some statute authority of their own for holding two thirds of the population in servitude; and an act for that purpose, passed in 1712, provided, "that all negroes, mulattoes, mestizoes, or Indians, which at any time heretofore were sold, or now are held or taken to be, or hereafter shall be, bought and sold for slaves, are hereby declared slaves, to all intents and purposes;" with exceptions, however, in favor of those who have been or shall be, "for some particular merit, made or declared free," and also of such "as can prove that they ought not to be sold as slaves." This extraordinary piece of

legislation, reënacted in 1722, and again in 1735, was
modified by an act of 1740, as follows: "All negroes,
Indians, mulattoes, and mustazoes, (free Indians in
amity with this government, and negroes, mulattoes,
and mustazoes who are now free, excepted,) who now
are or shall hereafter be in this province, and all their
issue and offspring, born or to be born, shall be, and
they are hereby declared to be and remain for ever
hereafter, absolute slaves, and shall follow the condition of the mother, and shall be deemed in law
chattels personal." In all claims of freedom, the
burden of proof was to be on the claimant, and it
was to be always presumed that every negro, Indian,
mulatto, and mestizo is a slave, unless the contrary
appear. The word *mestizo* seems to be employed
(though sometimes used elsewhere in a different
sense) to designate the mixed Indian blood; any ad-
mixture, however slight, of negro or Indian blood
being included, according to South Carolina usage,
under the epithets *mulatto* and *mestizo*, and carrying
the presumption of slavery with them. This act,
which forms the legal basis, such as it is, of the
existing slave-holding system of South Carolina, was
preceded and followed by all the customary barbarous
enactments of slave codes, which in South Carolina
were carried to a degree of unusual ferocity both in
substance and expression. Yet the South Carolina
assembly seem to have supposed themselves to be legislating within the limits of the English law; for at
the very same session at which the slave act of 1712
was enacted, the common law of England was declared to be in force in South Carolina.

In North Carolina no colonial act seems ever to
have given a legislative basis to the authority of the
master, which rested, and still rests, upon mere custom, and the old imaginary right, under the English
common law, to reduce infidels and their descendants
to servitude. So far as relates to the slavery of Indians, the Carolinians of both provinces had been from

the beginning notorious sinners. They had an irresistible propensity to kidnap the unhappy natives, and reduce them to slavery. Indeed, one chief ground of quarrel with the proprietaries of the province, grew out of efforts made by them to put a stop to this iniquity.

Georgia, it is well known, was originally intended to be a free colony; and during the eighteen years that its affairs were administered by the Trustees who had planted it, slavery was strictly prohibited. But the vagabonds from the streets of London, (for such were the English settlers in Georgia,) raised a loud outcry against this prohibition, ascribing to it the poverty and slow progress of the colony, the natural result of their own incapacity and idleness. The famous Whitefield pleaded with the Trustees in favor of slavery, under the old slave-trading pretence of propagating, by that means, the Christian religion. The German Lutherans settled in Georgia long had scruples; but they were reässured by the heads of their sect in Germany: "If you take slaves in faith, and with the intent of conducting them to Christ, the action will not be a sin, but may prove a benediction." Thus, as usual, the religious sentiment and its most disinterested votaries were made the tools of worldly selfishness, for the enslavement and plunder of mankind. One of the first acts of the new government, which succeeded to the authority of the Trustees, (1752,) was, the repeal of the prohibition of slavery. It was not, however, till thirteen years afterwards that the legislature of Georgia reinforced what they supposed to be the common law on this subject, by positive enactment. In 1765, they copied the South Carolina act of 1740; excepting, however, from the stern doom of slavery, not only such negroes, mulattoes, mestizoes, and Indians as already were free, but such also as might afterwards become free; thus acknowledging a possibility of future manumissions, which the South Carolina statutes seemed to cut off.

Such is the legislation, and all the legislation, by
which it can be pretended that slavery, as it now
exists in the United States, acquired during the
colonial times the character and the dignity of a
Legal Institution. Was this legislation valid? Could
it have the effect to legalize slavery in America?

As our state legislatures are now restricted in their
powers by constitutions, state and federal, so the
colonial legislatures were restricted in their powers
by the law of England. Contrary to the great principles of that law they could not make any acts.
This limitation was expressly declared in the colonial
charters. Thus, for instance, the charter of Maryland
provided, that all laws to be enacted by the provincial
legislature " be consonant to reason, and be not repugnant or contrary, but (so far as conveniently may
be) agreeable to the laws, statutes, customs, and
rights of this our kingdom of England." Similar
provisions are to be found in the charters of Virginia,
Carolina, and Georgia. It is true, that these charters,
except that of Maryland, were surrendered or taken
away, previous to the Revolution. But this proceeding, so far from extending the authority of the
colonial legislatures, operated the other way; conformity to the law of England being still more strictly
demanded in the royal than in the chartered provinces.
The very commissions of the governors, under the
authority of which alone the legislative assemblies
of the crown (or uncharted) colonies had any existence, expressly restricted the enactments of those
assemblies to such acts as " were not repugnant, but
as near as may be agreeable, to the laws and statutes
of the kingdom of England." This doctrine of the
restricted powers of the colonial legislatures was
perfectly well established, and it has been repeatedly
recognized by the Supreme Court of the United
States, as well as by the state courts. No lawyer
would pretend that any colonial legislature had power, for instance, to abolish trial by jury. The limits
of colonial legislative authority may be well exem-

plified by a transaction in South Carolina. That province being violently distracted by disputes between churchmen and dissenters, in 1704 the churchmen, happening to have a majority of one in the assembly, passed an act, by the help of a good quantity of good liquor, that none but churchmen should vote. This act was approved by the proprietaries; and as the charter of Carolina reserved no negative to the crown, it thus obtained the form of law. But the dissenters, indignant at this outrage, sent an agent to England, on whose petition the House of Lords, swayed by the eloquence of Somers, pronounced this disfranchising act unreasonable and contrary to the laws of England, of which, since the revolution of 1789, the toleration of all regular Protestant sects had become an established principle; and Queen Anne, by the advice of the attorney and solicitor-general, issued a proclamation declaring the obnoxious act void, because it violated that clause in the charter which required the laws of the colony not to contradict those of England.

If the colonial legislatures could not abolish trial by jury; if, after the toleration of all Protestant sects had become the law of England, they had no power to enact laws disfranchising any Protestant—had they any legal power to establish slavery?

Certainly not, if slavery was contrary to the law of England. And that it was contrary to the law of England we now proceed to show.

And here again, as in the whole of this discussion, it becomes necessary clearly to distinguish between law and practice; between that which might legally have been done, and that which actually was done without law, or against it. It has already been mentioned, that while the last remnants of the old system of villeinage were disappearing, the nascent maritime enterprise of England had led to the occasional importation of the pagan natives of other countries, who were claimed and held as slaves. On the trial of the impeachment against the judges of the Star

17

Chamber, ordered by the Long Parliament in 1640,
and reported in *Rushworth's Collections*, a case was
cited, said to have occurred in the eleventh year of
Elizabeth, (1569,) in which "one Cartwright brought
a slave from Russia, and would scourge him; for
which he was questioned, and it was resolved that
England was too pure an air for a slave to breathe
in." But the first recorded English case, in which
the legality of holding men in slavery came in question, was that of *Butts* v. *Penny*, decided in 1677, in
the Court of King's Bench. (2 Levintz, 251; 3 Keble,
785.) Though in form an action of trover, brought
in London, to recover damages for the taking away
of ten negroes, this case in fact related to a
transaction between the parties in India, (see Har-
grave's statement on the subject, in his published
argument in the case of Somerset;) and it being
found by a special verdict "that the negroes were
infidels and subjects of an infidel prince, and are
usually bought and sold in India as merchandise,"
and that the plaintiff bought these, and was in possession of them till the defendant took them, the
court held "that being usually bought and sold among
merchants as merchandise, there might be a property
in them sufficient to maintain trover." And the same
doctrine appears also to have been held in the Common
Pleas in 1694, in the case of *Gilly* v. *Clive*, (1 Lord
Raymond, 147.) But in 1705, in the case of *Smith*
v. *Gould*, (Salkeld, 666; 2 Lord Raymond, 1774,)
which was also an action of trover for a negro, the
case of *Butts* v. *Penny* was expressly overruled. "The
common law," said Lord Holt, "takes no notice of
negroes being different from other men. By the common law, no man can have a property in another but
in special cases, as in a villein, but even in him not to
kill him; so in captives taken in war, but the taker
cannot kill them, but may sell them to ransom them.
*There is no such thing as a slave by the law of Eng-
land.*"

Nor was this the only occasion upon which Lord

Holt, one of the most illustrious names in English jurisprudence, vindicated this principle of the common law. In the case of *Smith* v. *Brown & Cooper*, (Holt, 495; Salkeld, 666,) the court over which he presided refused to sustain an action of assumpsit to recover the price of a slave, "because," said Lord Holt, "as soon as a negro comes into England he is free. One may be a villein in England, but not a slave." It was indeed suggested that the decision might have been different, had the sale been stated in the declaration to have been made in Virginia, with an averment that, by the laws of that country, negroes were saleable,—"for the laws of England," said Lord Holt, "do not extend to Virginia: *being a conquered country*, their law is what the king pleases, and we cannot take notice of it but as set forth." This, however, was a view of the relation of the mother country to the colonies, and of the rights of the inhabitants, the correctness of which (though it was held down to Lord Holt's time by the English lawyers generally) was never admitted by the colonists themselves, and which, in the course of the next half century, as to all the colonies originally planted by English emigrants, was, by the general consent of the English bench and bar, given up as untenable. Nor would even the existence in the crown of such an arbitrary power of colonial legislation have afforded any legislative basis for slavery to stand upon ; for, so far from any authority having been given by the crown to the colonial legislatures to legalize slavery, it had been expressly provided in all the American charters, and in all the instructions to the royal governors, that no local laws were to be enacted repugnant to those of England ; so that the question of the legality of slavery in the colonies would still come back to the question of its repugnancy to English jurisprudence.

Yet notwithstanding the two express decisions above cited of the Court of King's Bench, that negro slavery was a thing unknown to the English law, which

recognized no distinction between negroes and other
men, and which had never admitted slavery except
in the peculiar and now extinct form of villeinage,
negroes still continued, as before, to be brought to
England, and there to be held and treated as slaves—
a practice which, with the growth of the African
slave trade and the increase of slaves in the colonies,
became, during the first half of the 18th century,
more and more frequent.

The negroes thus imported were too ignorant and
too helpless to vindicate their own rights; nor was
there any thing in the public sentiment of that gross
age, of which Mammon was the peculiar god, to
check the growth of this new system of slavery.
Some little annoyance seems indeed to have been
occasionally given to the slave-holders, by claims of
freedom set up on the ground of baptism, or on the
common law principle of the right of all men to
liberty; but these claims were met, and to a great
extent silenced, by a legal opinion obtained in 1729,
from Sir Philip Yorke and Charles Talbot, (afterwards Lord Talbot,) in which "they pledged themselves to the merchants of London to save them
harmless from all inconvenience" growing out of such
claims;—an ex parte opinion to which a judicial sanction seemed to be given by Yorke, then become Lord
Hardwicke, and Chancellor, by his decision in 1749,
in the case of *Pearne* v. *Lisle*, (Ambler, Reports, 75.)
In that case an application was made for a writ of
ne exeat regno, a prohibition, that is, to Lisle to leave
the kingdom, till he had first paid to the plaintiff a
certain stipulated rent, due for certain negroes hired
and held as slaves in the island of Antigua, and had
also returned the negroes; which application Hardwicke declined to grant, on the ground that the plaintiff had a sufficient remedy in the ordinary course of
law. "I have no doubt," he said, "that trover will
lie for a negro slave; it is as much property as any
other thing. The case in Salkeld, 666, (*Smith* v.
Gould,) was determined on the want of a proper de-

scription. It was trover *pro uno Æthiope vocat. negro,* (for one Ethiopian called a negro,) without saying slave. The being negro did not necessarily imply slave." [Here we have a specimen of the cool assurance of eminent lawyers in explaining away cases which they do not venture to overrule, since it is abundantly apparent from the report of the case in Salkeld, and still more so from that in Lord Raymond, that so far from the decision having been grounded on this alleged defect in description, its very basis was the fact that the negro was claimed as a slave. Indeed, Lord Holt stated in so many words, as the reason of the decision, that "there is no such thing as a slave by the law of England."] "The reason said at the bar," so Lord Hardwicke proceeded, "to have been given by Chief Justice Holt as the cause of his doubt," [another specimen of bold judicial misrepresentation, since it was no *doubt* of Lord Holt's, but a solemn decision of the Court of King's Bench,] "viz., that the moment that a slave sets his foot in England he becomes free," [this reason was not given in the case of *Smith* v. *Gould,* but in the other case of *Smith* v. *Brown & Cooper,* which is found indeed on the same page in Salkeld,] "has no weight with it, nor can any reason be found why they should not be equally so when they set foot in Jamaica, or any other English plantation. All our colonies are subject to the laws of England, although, to some purposes, they have laws of their own." [On this point doubtless Hardwicke had the advantage of Holt; for the opinions of the English lawyers, since the English revolution, had gradually been brought into coincidence with that of the colonists, who had all along claimed that the common law was as much in force in the colonies as in England.] "There was once a doubt," continued the judge, "whether, if they were christened, they would not become free by that act; and there were precautions taken in the colonies to prevent them from becoming baptized, till the opinion of Lord Talbot and myself, then attorney and solicitor-general,

17 *

was taken on that point. We were both of opinion that it did not at all alter their state." [The opinion indeed went much further, but the judge perhaps did not think it decorous to mention the pledge which he had given to the London slave-holders to save them harmless from all claims of freedom.] "There were formerly villeins or slaves in England, and these of two sorts, regardant and in gross; and although tenures are taken away, there are no laws that have destroyed servitude absolutely. Trover might have been brought for a villein. If a man were to come into a court of record and confess himself villein to another, (which was one way of being a villein,) what the consequence would be I would not say, but there is no law to abolish it at this time." Such is the reasoning, and all the reasoning, upon which Lord Hardwicke, sitting as an equity judge, undertook to overturn two solemn decisions of the King's Bench on a point of common law. Villeinage, though it had died away and disappeared, had not been formally abolished; and therefore negro slavery, a relation wholly different in its origin and incidents, agreeing with villeinage only in the fact of involving personal servitude—a relation introduced within two or three centuries, quite within the time of legal memory, and without any basis or foundation, except the convenience and gain of certain London merchants—this relation, by some unexplained transfusion, had inherited all the legal character of villeinage! There was no law to prevent a man from going into court and confessing himself the villein of another, and therefore—there was no law to prevent London merchants from holding negroes in slavery against their will!

The personal character of a judge will often throw no little light upon his judicial opinions, especially those in which general principles are involved. Hardwicke, we are told by Lord Campbell, in his *Lives of the Chancellors*, was "the most consummate judge who ever sat in the Court of Chancery," the "greatest contributor to the English equity code,"—

not any very high commendation, perhaps, with those who have had much experience of chancery suits. But the character of a "consummate judge"-has too often been obtained by a ready ingenuity in giving plausible reasons to sustain power against right, or in defect of plausible reason, by a bold effrontery in trampling under foot the weak and helpless, for the benefit and convenience of the rich and powerful. That there was nothing in Lord Hardwicke's personal character to deter him from such a course, but much to prompt him to it, Lord Campbell himself shall be our witness. "His career was not checkered by any youthful indiscretions or generous errors. He ever had a keen and steady eye to his own advantage, as well as to the public good. [Is there not a little irony in this last clause?] · Amid the aristocratic connections which he formed, he forgot the companions of his youth, and his regard for the middle classes of society, from which he sprang, cooled down to indifference. He became jealous of all who could be his rivals for power, and he contracted a certain degree of selfish-ness and hardness of character which excited much envy [?] and ill will amid the flatteries which sur-rounded him." His first patron, for whom he assidu-ously worked, and by whose partial favor he was brought into notice, was the Earl of Macclesfield, that "trafficker in judicial robes, and robber of widows and orphans," who was afterwards impeached and found guilty of corruption. He then attached him-self to the Duke of Newcastle, who, in a long political career, endeavored to make up for personal imbecility by the freest use of patronage and money. "The best thing that can be remembered of the chancellor," says Horace Walpole, "is his fidelity to his patron; for let the Duke of Newcastle betray whom he would, the chancellor always stuck to him in his perfidy, and was only not false to the falsest of mankind!" Such was precisely the sort of "consummate judge" from whom might have been anticipated an attempt to give to the enslavement of man a character of legality.

What sympathy for the mere laborers could be felt by one who, engrossed by his aristocratic connections, had become coldly indifferent even to the middle classes, from whence he sprang?

But in spite of the glosses of Lord Hardwicke, and the increasing number of slaves in England, there were still those who felt and those who held that Lord Holt's version of the common law was the true one. An attempt having been made in 1762, in the case of *Shanley* v. *Hervey*, (3 Eden's Reports, 126,) before Lord Hardwicke's successor as chancellor, Lord Northington, characterized by Lord Eldon as "a great lawyer, and very firm in delivering his opinions," to appropriate to the use of a pretended master a gift or legacy to a negro, he indignantly dismissed the bill with the exclamation—"As soon as a man puts foot on English ground he is free. A negro may maintain an action against his master for ill usage, and may have a habeas corpus if restrained of his liberty." The famous Granville Sharpe embraced this opinion with so much enthusiasm as in fact to devote his life to its vindication. Many cases, through his agency, were brought before the courts; and though often foiled, he succeeded at last in obtaining for this great question a solemn rehearing and a final decision.

James Somerset, an African by birth, carried to Virginia as a slave, and purchased there by James Stewart, had been brought from Virginia to England, where he refused to serve any longer, in consequence of which Stewart seized him, and put him on board a ship to be sent to Jamaica. Being taken before Lord Mansfield (1771) on a writ of *habeas corpus*, and these facts appearing on the return, the question was referred to the full Court of King's Bench, before which it was argued at different times by five lawyers retained by Sharpe, while two of the most eminent counsel of the day (Wallace and Dunning) appeared on the other side.

Mansfield was endowed with a warmth of sentiment, a sympathy with humanity, and a philosophical spirit, which, in giving a vitality to his legal learning and abilities, has elevated him high over the heads of so many other "consummate lawyers." Yet he was not celebrated either for intrepidity of spirit, or for any special enthusiasm in behalf of personal liberty. Here was an opportunity for the establishment of a great principle; but an opportunity which he did not court, and from which indeed he strove to escape. He was not insensible to the wealth and social standing of the parties interested as slave-holders, and he attempted to get rid of this case, as he had done of several similar ones, by urging the settlement of it by an agreement between the parties. The decision seems indeed to have been once or twice postponed, to give Stewart an opportunity to act upon the hint, that if he would manumit Somerset the case might be ended in that way, without any formal decision, which Mansfield openly expressed his anxiety to avoid. If the decision went against the master, it would overturn the established practice and prevailing ideas of the last fifty years, backed by the legal opinion of "two of the greatest men"—such were the terms in which Lord Mansfield referred to Yorke and Talbot— "of this or any other time."* But on the other hand was the extreme difficulty of adopting the relation of slavery as it existed in the colonies, without adopting it in all its consequences, many of which were "absolutely contrary to the municipal law of England." "The setting fourteen or fifteen thousand men"—for that had been stated by the counsel for the claimant as the estimated number of negro slaves in England —"at once loose by a solemn opinion" was "very disagreeable in the effects it threatened." "Fifty pounds"—the estimate of Stewart's counsel—"may

---

* Yet in the course of the argument, he had spoken of their opinion above referred to with no great respect, as a case "upon a petition in Lincoln's Inn Hall, after dinner, therefore probably might not be taken with much accuracy, as he believed was not unusual at that hour." See Loff's Reports.

not be a high price. Then a loss follows to the proprietors of about £700,000 sterling. How would the
law stand in respect of their settlement, their wages?
How many actions for any slight coercion by the
master?"

But though these prudential considerations made
the timid Mansfield anxious to escape a formal judgment, they did not alter his opinion of the law.
"We cannot, in any of these points, direct the law;
the law must direct us." "If the parties will have
judgment, *fiat justicia ruat cœlum*—let justice be done
whatever be the consequence." At the same time he
suggested, as a consolation to the slave-holders, "an
application to parliament, if the merchants think the
question of great commercial concern," as "the best,
and perhaps only, method of settling the question for
the future,"—a suggestion, however, upon which, in
the existing state of public sentiment, the London
slave-holders did not venture to act.

At last, after several postponements, as Stewart
declined to terminate the case by manumitting Somerset, Mansfield proceeded to render judgment; which
he did very briefly; and yet, as his peculiar manner
was, in terms sufficiently comprehensive not only to
decide the case before him, but to establish a principle
for the decision of other cases.

"We pay all due attention," he said, "to the opinion of Sir Philip Yorke and Lord Talbot, whereby
they pledged themselves to the British planters for all
the legal consequences of slaves coming over to this
kingdom, or being baptized, recognized by Lord
Hardwicke, sitting as chancellor," in the case of
Pearne v. *Lisle*. "The only question before us is,
whether the cause on the return is sufficient. If it is,
the negro must be remanded; if it is not, he must be
discharged. The return states that the slave departed
and refused to serve, whereupon he was seized to be
sold abroad. *So high an act of dominion must be
recognized by the law of the country where it is used.
The power of a master over his slave has been exceed-*

*ingly different in different countries. The state of
slavery is of such a nature, that it is incapable of being
introduced on any reasons, moral or political, but only
by positive law, which preserves its force long after the
reasons, occasions, and time itself from whence it was
created, is erased from memory. It is so odious that
nothing can be suffered to support it but positive law.*
Whatever inconveniences, therefore, may follow from
the decision, I cannot say this case is allowed or approved by the law of England, and therefore the black
must be discharged."

It is very true that this decision is limited in its
terms to the case of persons claimed as slaves within
the realm of England, that being the particular case
before the court. It is also true that the counsel for
Somerset, conscious of the pecuniary influence weigh-
ing against their client, and anxious to limit that
influence as much as possible, were very careful not
to question the legality of slavery in the colonies.
But as all the colonial assemblies were specially restricted, either by charter or the royal commissions
under which they met and legislated, to the enactment
of laws not repugnant to those of England, how
could those assemblies be competent to legalize a
condition, many of the consequences of which were
pronounced by Lord Mansfield "absolutely contrary"
to English law?—and did it not follow, as one of the
"inconveniences" of that decision, as Hardwicke had
suggested it would, that slavery, illegal in England,
was also illegal in the English colonies?

To evade this conclusion, the omnipotence of parliament was invoked, as having, at least by way of
inference and recognition, legalized slavery in America; for which purpose several acts were cited relating to the African trade, particularly that of 9 and
10 Wil. III. ch. 26; also the act of 1732, for the
speedy recovery of debts in the colonies. The first
of these acts plainly speaks of negroes as a species
of merchandise, the export of which from the African
coast in British ships was particularly favored, by

their exemption from a duty of ten per cent., imposed, for the sustentation of the West African forts, on all exports from that coast, "negroes excepted." The great object of the other act was, to make real estate in the colonies liable to be levied upon for debts the same with personal property; and as some of the colonies, to protect the planters against their creditors, had declared negroes to be real estate, such negroes too were made by this act seizable for debt along with the lands to which they were attached. But so great an innovation upon the common law as the legalization of negro slavery, is not to be sustained by a mere statute implication; especially when the provisions relied upon do not necessarily imply any thing more than what the long-established common law had fully recognized. The importation into the colonies, and the sale there, of servants, to be held for a limited period, to be esteemed during that period the goods and chattels of the purchaser, to be sold at his pleasure, and liable to be seized for his debts, was undoubtedly permitted by the law of England. Such servants were regularly imported from England, Scotland, Ireland, and Germany, in numbers at least equal to the negroes; nor is there any thing more than this necessarily implied in the acts above cited. There is nothing to show that parliament intended to place Africans in this respect on a different ground from other men. Such, indeed, would seem to have been the view taken of these acts by Lord Mansfield. The exportation of negroes was not limited to America. In the act above referred to for regulating the African trade, England was mentioned in precisely the same terms as the colonies, as one of the places to which African merchandise, including negroes, might be brought; and the holding of negroes in slavery, so far as that act goes, was just as much authorized by it in the one country as in the other. But though these statutes were cited in Somerset's case, Lord Mansfield allowed them no weight. And in the case of *Forbes* v. *Cochrane*, (2 Barnwell & Cresswell, 443,) decided in 1824 in the Court of King's Bench, Chief Justice Best expressly stated " that he did not feel himself fettered by any thing expressed in either of these acts, [the acts, that is, in relation to the trade with Africa,] in pronouncing the same opinion on the rights growing out of slavery as if they had never passed."

There is indeed a still further distinction as to the case of those held as slaves in the colonies, apt to be overlooked in these discussions, but which cannot be disregarded, at least by those who coincide with Lords Camden and Chatham and the Continental Congresses of 1765 and 1774, in their views of colonial and metropolitan relations. Whatever the condition might legally have been of those unfortunate aliens purchased in Africa as slaves, and brought to America and sold to the planters ; suppose even that it might have been consonant to English law to hold them as servants for life, as Blackstone seems to have imagined; yet the case was very different as to their children born in the colonies, who were in every respect, according to the views above stated, natural-born subjects of the King of England, and entitled to all the rights of Englishmen, from which not even parliament itself, and much less the colonial legislatures, had any power to exclude them. Such was the ground taken by James Otis, in his famous pamphlet on *Colonial Rights*, published (1764) in anticipation of the Stamp Act, and justly regarded as the first trumpet blast of the American Revolution ; in which pamphlet he laid it down as a fundamental proposition, the basis of all his reasoning, that all the colonists, whether " black or white," born in America, were free born British subjects, entitled to all the essential rights of such.

The decision in Somerset's case is sometimes spoken of, even by judges on the bench, as having changed the law of England. But such a view of it is entirely false. Judgments of courts do not change the law. They are not the law, but only evidence of the law. The Somerset case did not make nor alter the law of England; it only freed it from the false glosses with which ignorance, avarice, violence, and the practice of two or three hundred years had obscured it. It did but repeat, and now, from the altered state of the public sentiment, in a more authoritative and effectual tone, the very declaration which Lord Holt, three quarters of a century before, had then ineffectually made,—that the law of England did not allow the reducing men to slavery, and did not regard negroes as any way different, in this respect, from other men. Such being the fact, there surely existed no power in any colonial assembly, restricted as all those assemblies were to the enactment of laws "not repugnant to those of England," to legalize a condition many of the consequences of which were, in the words of Lord Mansfield, "absolutely contrary" to English law.

But it is not by the mere declaration of what the law is—especially where there is no spirit or disposition on the part of those in authority to enforce or even to recognize it—that wrong is ever to be rectified; nor has it been in America alone that courts and lawyers have trampled law as well as justice under foot, in their zeal to gain the favor and to conform to the wishes of those possessed of wealth and of social and political influence. The American Declaration of Independence, which took place within a little more than four years after the decision in Somerset's case, removed the colonies, now become the United States, from all further control by English tribunals or English authority; but there were several other colonial dependencies of the British empire, in which, for more than sixty years after that decision, negro slavery continued in full energy, too strong, too rampant, for any English judge to dare to apply to it the principle of the Somerset case; since here it was not a question of £700,000 and fourteen thousand negroes, but of a sum and a number near a hundred times as great; the difficulty of redressing wrongs unfortunately increasing in something like geometrical proportion to the number of those whom they crush. Even such a judge as Chief Justice Best, while giving such authority to the case of Somerset as to hold, (in *Forbes* v. *Cochrane*, above referred to,) that slaves flying from a Spanish colony, and taking refuge on board a British ship on the high seas, thereby became free, was very careful to add, "There may possibly be a distinction between the situation of these persons, and that of slaves coming from our own islands, for we have unfortunately recognized the existence of slavery there, though we have never recognized it in our own country." Indeed, he specially desired that nothing he might say in that case [and he said several very fine things] "might be considered as trenching on the local rights of the West India proprietors to the services of their slaves in that country."

Nor when, at last, the question of the legality of slavery in the colonies was distinctly raised before an English court, (unfortunately not a court of common law,) did the slave-holders fail to find, in the person of Lord Stowell, another "consummate judge," not less ready than Lord Hardwicke had been, in his day, to give to a cruel and oppressive custom all the character and attributes of a solemn legislative authority. The case of *The Slave Grace*, (2 Haggard's Admiralty Reports, 106,) decided in 1827, is indeed most instructive, as showing to what extent your "consummate lawyer" will go, on behalf of the interests, or what he esteems such, of property and commerce, no matter at what expense of human agony, and disregard of the plainest principles of justice. Set aside the state of Mississippi, under the chief justiceship of the notorious Sharkey, and the circuits of Judges Grier and Curtis, of the United States Supreme Court, and it would be impossible to match that case in all the American Reports. Indeed, the main point decided in it has been ruled the other way in some half dozen American slave-holding states, in all, in fact, Mississippi excepted, in which

the point has been directly raised. For it is to be
noted, that, until quite recently, the courts even of the
slave-holding states have exhibited no little alacrity
in giving freedom to individuals, and even to families
claimed to be held as slaves, speaking out in such
cases very warmly for liberty, and exhibiting evident
gusto and satisfaction in knocking off the fetters. It
has only been in cases likely to prove too sweeping
as precedents, cases involving principles comprehensive enough to give freedom to large numbers, that
this judicial tendency in favor of liberty has been
checked. The case above referred to was that of a
girl born in slavery in the Island of Antigua. She had
been brought to England, but whether from ignorance
or want of inclination had failed to claim her liberty
there, and had returned to Antigua, where she was
still held as a slave. The circumstance, however, that
she had been in England, was presently set up as
having made her free; and since the local courts would
not recognize the claim, to give her and others in her
condition the chance of an English adjudication, without the heavy expenses of an ordinary appeal, (if
indeed it were possible, by the ordinary course of
appeal, to carry such a case to England,) she was
libelled in the Vice Admiralty Court of Antigua, as
having been introduced into that island as a slave,
contrary to the acts abolishing the slave trade; and
the local admiralty judge having decided against her,
the case came before Lord Stowell by appeal. It was
but a decent regard for appearances for an English
judge in Lord Stowell's position, and especially one
about to make such a decision as he did, to indulge
in some flourishes on the subject of liberty, which his
lordship did very cheaply, and with a sort of judicial
demagoguism sufficiently common both in England
and America, by breaking out into a burst of indignation that a person claiming to be free should suffer
herself to be libelled as an illegally introduced slave!
— when, without resorting to any such humiliating
method of vindicating her rights, she had nothing

to do but to claim to be free, and to act as such! As if such a claim made in Antigua, as it then was, would have availed poor Grace! As if my lord did not perfectly well know why a procedure in the Admiralty Court had been resorted to!

Stowell had gained the reputation of a "consummate judge," by a series of learned and ingenious decisions, by which, during the war between France and England, he had zealously, and, according to a common enough view of such matters, patriotically labored to secure to the merchants of England a much coveted monopoly of ocean commerce — an object which he had accomplished by giving to a few questionable old precedents, and especially to an arbitrary rule introduced by England during the war of 1756, the character of the Law of Nations, and on that ground, justifying the wholesale capture and plunder of American and other neutral vessels, trading between France and her colonies. As was natural enough for such a judge, he did not at all share in the sentiment then fast spreading in England against negro slavery; indeed, he was eager to give to that crumbling institution all the support of his professional reputation. Yet he felt obliged to admit, however good a thing slavery might be, that the practice of dragging back into it those who had once enjoyed the blessings of freedom, had been attended by lamentable consequences. "Persons, though possessed of independence and affluence, acquired in the mother country, have, upon a return to the colonies, been held and treated as slaves, and the unfortunate descendants of these persons, if born within the colony, have come slaves into the world, and, in some instances, have suffered all the consequences of real slavery." Yet in the eyes of such a man as Stowell, what were these agonies of oppressed humanity in competition with the necessity of giving to the holders of property a sentiment of security, and especially to the holders of property in men, attacked at that moment by so many wicked or thoughtless abolitionists?

18 *

— for it was in the midst of the anti-slavery agitation
in England, that this judgment was rendered.

Yet, if Grace had left England a free British subject, as the decision in Somerset's case would seem to
imply, by what process, on landing in Antigua, had
she been transformed into a slave? The case of
Somerset was directly opposed to the decision which
Stowell's antecedent and present associations and
opinions had predetermined him to make; and, therefore, it was necessary to explain that decision away.
That Somerset had been properly discharged, he did
not venture to deny, but the reasons given by Lord
Mansfield for that discharge he set aside altogether.
Putting those reasons aside, that case, according to
Lord Stowell, went no further than this: " The slave
continues a slave, though the law of England relieves from the rigor of that code while he is in England, and that is all that it does." All that had been
said about a slave not being able to breathe in England, was a mere flourish of rhetoric, and as soon as
Grace returned to Antigua, her master, freed from the
annoying interference of the English law, regained
all his rights!

But supposing that to be so, yet by what law of
Antigua was Grace held as a slave? The legislature
of Antigua had no power to make laws repugnant
to those of England; and not only had they no power,
but taking it for granted that slavery was recognized
by the common law, they had allowed it to rest on
that basis alone. Not only was there no statute of
Antigua expressly authorizing the slavery of negroes,
but by a statute passed in 1705, and never repealed,
the common law of England was declared to be the
law of that colony, except when altered by written
laws of the island, and " all customs and pretended
customs and usage, contradictory thereto," were pronounced " illegal, null, and void." Here was fresh
and urgent occasion for attacking the reasoning of
Lord Mansfield in Somerset's case; for where, so far
as Antigua was concerned, was that basis of positive

law which he had demanded as the only one upon which so "odious" an institution could be made to stand?—an institution which he had pronounced incapable of being introduced upon any reasons moral or political, but only by positive law.

Lord Hardwicke, in his attempt to legalize slavery, had seemed disposed to represent it as a mere continuation of the system of villeinage. Lord Stowell did not fail to perceive the weakness of that position; for if villeinage was too odious a system to stand against the public sentiment even of the fifteenth century, how could any mere copy or imitation of it in the shape of negro slavery be expected to be tolerated in the nineteenth? Alarmed apparently lest the same strict constructions and legal principles which had operated to abolish villeinage might be brought to bear against the enslavement of negroes, he labored to distinguish and exalt *that* "as part of a system extending into foreign countries and transmarine possessions," and therefore not to be subjected to the narrow constructions and local humanities of English jurisprudence. The English sailors have a proverb, "No Sunday off soundings," and exactly in the spirit of that proverb seem to be conceived many of the decisions of the English Admiralty Courts, and indeed much of the foreign policy of Great Britain, of which the Chinese opium war may be cited as a flagrant instance. Yet the Law of Nations, a mantle wide enough, as it proved in Lord Stowell's hands, to cover such a multitude of wrongs, could not by itself alone sustain slavery in an English colony. In the particular case of Antigua, it became necessary not only to set aside the reasons given by Lord Mansfield for his decision in the Somerset case, but to take issue on the very turning point of those reasons. Lord Stowell therefore, under the form of modestly questioning, proceeded to deny, point blank, the fundamental proposition of Lord Mansfield, that to uphold slavery some "positive law" must be shown for it. "Ancient custom," so he suggested, "is gen-

erally recognized as a just foundation of all law."
" A great part of the common law itself, in all its relations, has little other foundation than this same
custom."   " That villeinage which is said to be the
prototype of slavery, had no other origin than ancient
custom."   And on the strength of these observations,
he held slavery to be legalized in Antigua by a
usage not two hundred years old, (since Antigua was
first settled in 1632,) and though the local statutes of
the island, coinciding in this particular with the metropolitan authority, expressly denied any validity to
any usage not conformable to the law of England!

These ideas, upon which Lord Stowell thus attempted to base the legality of negro slavery in the
colonies, and which would just as well have sustained
it in England, though not unusual on both sides of
the Atlantic, involve, however, a total ignorance or
disregard of the perfectly well established doctrine of
the English courts as to the nature and origin of law.
According to that doctrine, there are only two possible sources of law; viz., 1st, enlightened reason,
equity, natural justice; and 2dly, positive legislation.   The character and force of law is never conceded to customs and usages unsustained by positive
enactments, except so far as they appear to correspond to the dictates of enlightened reason, equity,
and natural justice, and not to contradict any positive law.   When the common lawyers first began to
consider law in a systematic and scientific point of
view, they found, indeed, the institutions of the state,
and the proceedings, maxims, and methods of the
courts, to be principally based upon certain ancient
usages, as to the origin of which no record or memorial existed.   But whatever the historical fact might
have been, (as to which we have no resource beyond
probable conjecture,) the English courts of common
law never based the authority of these ancient usages,
institutions, and maxims on custom, or the mere lapse
of time during which they had prevailed, nor on the
inconvenience of disturbing them.   On the other

hand, they constantly represented these usages and institutions, including among the rest the prerogatives of the king, the authority of parliament, the jurisdiction of the courts, the privileges of the peers, the rights of the commons, and the servitude of the villeins, as being founded, in the words of Lord Mansfield, on " positive law "—that is, on formal statutes and precise enactments, of which, however, from the lapse of time and the dilapidation of records, no memorial any longer existed, except in the general usage of the realm and the memory of the courts. But thus to invest a usage or institution with the character of " positive law," (which the courts held themselves bound to carry out without stopping to inquire into its justice, expediency, or reasonableness, of which the legislature was admitted to be the sole authoritative judge,) that usage or institution must, like the peerage, villeinage, or the rights of primogeniture, be traceable back to a time beyond the period of legal memory, which period was held by the courts to commence with the reign of Richard I., A. D. 1189, very few records of an earlier date being in existence. As to customs and usages of a more modern date, the origin of which could be shown, *they* must depend exclusively for their sanction upon their reasonableness,—their conformity, that is, to natural equity and justice, and to an enlightened view of the public welfare; and it was still further necessary that they should not conflict with any rights already established by law, that is, that they should conform to the general policy of the realm.

Undoubtedly the modern common law consists to a great extent of modern customs introduced by the growing exigencies of society, and confirmed and sanctioned by the courts. Nobody ever did more, nor indeed any thing near so much, as Lord Mansfield himself, thus to amplify and enrich the common law, grafting upon it the best portions of the civil law and of the commercial codes of modern Europe. But

negro slavery being an institution neither reasonable,
just, nor tending to the good of society, nor to the
mutual benefit of the parties concerned, and being
moreover, in many of its consequences, "absolutely
contrary" to English law, it was impossible for Lord
Mansfield to hold either that the pecuniary convenience of the London merchants, or that the two
or three hundred years during which such slavery had
prevailed, could make it legal. And if negro slavery
could not be legalized by mere usage in England,
neither could it be so legalized in the colonies. That
which the colonial assemblies had no power to do directly, could not be done indirectly by the mere act
of the inhabitants. Even admitting that negro slavery, as Lord Stowell seems strongly disposed to argue,
though a bad and unreasonable custom in England,
was a good and reasonable one in the colonies,—in fact
he secretly thought that slavery was a good custom
every where ; nor on any other assumption could it
have been logically possible to render the judgment
which he did;—yet even that admission could not
alter the case ; because whether good or bad, yet
being an institution "repugnant" to the law of England, neither the legislation of the assemblies nor the
usage of the planters could give to it, in the colonies,
the character of law.

The difference between Lord Mansfield and Lord
Stowell is, it will be perceived, absolute and fundamental. According to Lord Mansfield and the common lawyers, injustice never can be clothed with the
character of law by mere usage, however long continued, nor in any way, except by some positive act
of the governing power. Some legislator must be
found on whom the responsibility of such injustice
can be fixed. Some positive law must be pointed
out by which this privileged wrong is expressly and
plainly authorized in its whole extent. Here is surely
a great check to oppression, the greatest perhaps
which existing circumstances admit of—a check which
Lord Stowell and the lawyers of his school seek to

break down. Besides the government openly legislating, and thus in the face of public opinion assuming the responsibility for whatever it enacts, the dread authority of making unjust laws is to be conferred in addition upon private interest working secretly in the dark! Whatever advantages superior force and cunning may, as in the case of negro slavery, have been able to take and to keep for a generation or two over weakness and ignorance, shall thereby become law! Surely a most alarming doctrine, tending to create the most terrible of tyrannies, infinitely more to be dreaded, infinitely more fruitful in wrong than crime and violence ever could be if compelled to show themselves and to act openly in the face of the world! No other comparison will suit such legislation but that of the snake swallowing down by imperceptible degrees his crushed and slavered victim.

This doctrine of the power of possession and usage to give legal validity to slavery is the natural consequence of confounding men with things. With respect to things, that which the peace of the community chiefly requires, that in which the interests of commerce are concerned, is, that every *thing* should have a certain definite owner; and therefore public convenience imperatively demands that the neglect, for a certain period, to vindicate one's claim to the property of a thing should be esteemed a relinquishment of that claim in favor of the person already in possession. But this doctrine can have no application whatever to the case of men, in whom the English law does not admit any power to convey away or surrender up even their own liberty, and still less that of their unborn children; and whom therefore no mere lapse of time can ever bar from claiming their personal freedom whenever they feel the impulse to do so.

In the particular case of the British slave-holding colonies, it may have been very true, as Lord Stowell suggests, (and the same idea is dropped also by Chief Justice Best in the case of *Forbes* v. *Cochrane,*) that a sovereign state like England, looking quietly on, and allowing slavery to prevail without law and against law in her colonies, was quite as guilty of the wrong as the colonies themselves, if not indeed more so. That might have been a very good reason why the act of parliament about which Lord Mansfield had spoken, (though perhaps in a somewhat different sense,) when it came at length to be enacted—and its passage was probably hastened by Lord Stowell's decision—took upon the mother country a large share of the burden of the abolition of slavery. And the same reasoning might be forcibly urged as between the slave states and the free states of our American confederacy. But the question of the relative guilt of those who trampled on the weak and of those who connived at it, and of the distribution between them of the burden of restitution, cannot in any way affect the legal status of those who, in the mean time, are deprived of their rights; nor can any distribution of the blame of it give to that deprivation any of the qualities of legality.

Overlooking this undeniable fact, the apologists for American slavery, not content with insisting that the mother country connived at, and indeed positively authorized, its original introduction, have gone still further, and have boldly asserted that slavery was forced upon the colonies by the mother country, against their will, and in spite of their efforts to prevent it. Bancroft, in his History, has labored, with his usual patriotic partiality, to give color to this charge, which originated with Jefferson, and which made its first appearance in the declamatory introduction to the first constitution of Virginia. Jefferson wished to repeat it, in a still more direct and emphatic form, in the Declaration of Independence; but it was rather too much to ask the delegates from Georgia to denounce the slave-trade as "a cruel war against human nature, violating its most sacred rights of life and liberty." Having struggled against, and finally defeated, the attempt to make her a free community, how could Georgia charge the mother country with forcing upon her that "execrable commerce," the slave-trade? Jefferson hated Britain, he hated slavery, and he wished to bring these hatreds into juxtaposition; but to do so required a very excited imagination. Had any colony ever prohibited the introduction of negroes; had any colony ever enacted that negroes should stand on the same ground as white servants, and be discharged at the end of seven years' service; and had the king vetoed such enactments—he might then have been justly charged with forcing slavery on the colonies. But no colony ever passed any such law, or thought of doing so. The vetoes on which Jefferson relied were of a very different sort. The colonies, especially those of the south, wished to raise a part of their revenue by duties on imports, with the double object of lightening the burden of direct taxation, and giving protection to domestic manufactures. Among the chief imports into the southern colonies were negroes. But in seeking to impose a tax of a few pounds on each negro imported, the colonial legislatures, as a general thing, no more intended to abolish or even to restrict slavery or the slave-trade, than Congress, when it agreed to the square yard minimum duty upon cotton goods, intended to abolish or restrict the use of muslins and calicoes. The English merchants, in whose hands the commerce of the colonies was, were then, as now, advocates of free trade; they complained of these duties, the one on negroes among the rest, as an interference with their commercial rights; and they had interest enough with the British government to procure a standing instruction to all the royal governors not to consent to such sort of taxes. Finally, however, the matter was compromised by allowing the colonial legislatures to impose such duty as they pleased on negroes imported, provided it were made payable, not by the seller, the English trader, but by the buyer, the colonist planter.

19

It seems, then, to be very plainly made out, that at the commencement of our Revolution, slavery had no *legal* basis in any of the North American colonies.* It *existed*, as many other wrongs existed, in all of them. In many of the colonies, the assemblies, under a mistaken view of the law of England or of their own powers, or through wilful disregard of acknowledged restraints, had attempted to give to it the sanction of law. But by that same law of England, which the colonists claimed as their birthright, and to which they so loudly appealed against the usurpations of the mother country, all such statutes were void. The negroes were too ignorant to know their rights, and too helpless to vindicate them. They could not appeal to England, like the South Carolina dissenters, nor had they a powerful party there to support their rights; but, legally speaking, they were all free; and this, as to all of them at least who had been born in the colonies, was fully admitted, as has been already noticed, eight years previous to the decision in Somerset's case, by James Otis, in his famous tract on the " Rights of the Colonists."

It remains, then, to inquire, whether that Revolution, which we are accustomed to extol as an outburst of liberty, a memorable vindication of the Rights of Man, did, in fact, give to slavery a legal character; whether men, entitled by British law to their freedom, because slaves under the State and Federal Constitutions; and this is the question which we propose to discuss in the following section.

---

* For further details on this subject, and an account of the particular incident upon which Jefferson's charges seem to have been chiefly based, see Hildreth's *History of the United States*, vol. ii. chap. xxvii.

SECTION III.

Slavery in the States, and under the Federal Constitution.

WE examined in the previous section the pretensions of slavery—as it existed in the British North American colonies prior to the Revolution which converted those colonies into the United States of America—to rest upon a legal basis. We found, in most of the colonies, statutes of the colonial assemblies of an earlier or later date, and in all of them, a practice assuming to legalize the slavery of negroes, Indians, and the mixed race; to make that slavery hereditary wherever the mother was a slave; and, as to all claims of freedom, to throw the burden of proof on the claimant. But we also found that this practice, and all the statutes attempting to legalize it, were in direct conflict with great and perfectly well settled principles of the law of England, which was also the supreme law of the colonies; principles which the colonial legislatures and the colonial courts had no authority to set aside or to contradict; and thence we concluded that American slavery, prior to the Revolution, had no legal basis, but existed as it had done in England for some two centuries or more prior to Somerset's case—a mere usurpation on the part of the masters, and a mere wrong as respects those alleged to be slaves.

Nor is this view of the matter by any means original, or at all of recent origin. It was taken and acted on and made the basis of emancipation in Massachusetts, while the British rule still prevailed in America. The best account, indeed, almost the only original account of the abolition of slavery in Massachusetts, is contained in a paper by Dr. Belknap, printed in the Massachusetts Historical Collections. Dr. Belknap states, that about the time of the commencement of the revolutionary disputes, several opponents of slavery "took occasion publicly to remonstrate against the inconsistency of contending for our own liberty, and at the same time depriving other people of theirs." Nathaniel Appleton and James Swan, merchants of Boston, distinguished themselves as writers on the side of liberty. "Those on the other side generally concealed their names, but their arguments were not suffered to rest long without an answer. The controversy began about the year 1766, and was renewed at various times till 1773, when it was very warmly agitated, and became the subject of forensic disputation at the public Commencement in Harvard College."

So far, at least, as concerned the further importation of negroes and others "as slaves," the subject was introduced also into the General Court; but neither Bernard, Hutchinson, nor Gage would concur in any legislation upon it. "The blacks," says Belknap, "had better success in the judicial courts. A pamphlet containing the case of a negro who had accompanied his master from the West Indies to England, and had there sued for and obtained his freedom, was reprinted" at Boston, in 1771, "and this encouraged several negroes to sue their masters for their freedom, and for recompense of their services after they had attained the age of twenty-one years." "The negroes collected money among themselves to carry on the suit, and it terminated favorably. Other suits were instituted between that time and the Revolution, and the juries invariably gave their verdict in favor of liberty." The old fundamental law of Massachusetts authorizing the slavery of Indians and negroes was no longer in force; it had fallen with the first charter. Under the second charter no such statute had been reënacted, but slavery had continued by custom, and had apparently been recognized by the statutes of the province, as a legal relation. "The pleas on the part of the masters were, that the negroes were purchased in open market, and bills of sale were produced in evidence; that the laws of the province recognized slavery as existing in it, by declaring that no person should manumit his slave without giving bond for his maintenance, &c. On the part of the blacks it was pleaded, that the royal charter expressly declared all persons born or residing in the province to be as free as the king's subjects in Great Britain; that by the law of England, no man could be deprived of his liberty but by the judgment of his peers; that the laws of the province respecting an evil existing, and attempting to mitigate or regulate it, did not authorize it; and on some occasions the plea was, that though the slavery of the parents be admitted, yet that no disability of that kind could descend to the children." "The juries invariably gave their verdict in favor of liberty;" nor does it appear that these verdicts were in any respect inconsistent with the instructions of the judges as to matter of law.

The blow thus dealt at slavery in Massachusetts might perhaps have been repeated in other colonies; but before there was time for any thing of the sort, the Revolution occurred, and new governments stepped in to take the places of the old ones. This brings us back to the question started at the close of the preceding section: Did the new governments, established at the Revolution, do any thing, or could they do any thing, to give an additional character of legality to the institution of slavery?

Let us begin with the commonwealth of Virginia. The convention of delegates and representatives from the several counties and corporations which assumed the responsibility of framing a new government for that state, very properly prefaced their labors by setting forth a Declaration of Rights, as its " basis and foundation." This Declaration of Rights, bearing date June 12, 1776, announced, among other things, "that all men are by nature equally free and independent, and have certain inherent rights, of which, when they enter into a state of society, they cannot by any compact deprive or divest their posterity; namely, the enjoyment of life and liberty, with the means of acquiring and possessing property, and pursuing and obtaining happiness and safety." Upon "the basis and foundation" of this Declaration of Rights, the convention proceeded to erect a "constitution, or form of government," in which it was provided that the "common law of England," and all statutes of parliament not local in their character, made in aid of the common law prior to the settlement of Virginia, "together with the several acts of the General Assembly of this colony *now in force*, so far as the same may consist with the several ordinances, *declarations*, and resolutions of the general convention, shall be considered as in full force until the same shall be altered by the legislative power of this colony." But this provision could give no validity to the colonial acts for the establishment of slavery; in the first place, because those acts, legally speaking, were not *in force*, and never had been, being void from the beginning, enacted in defiance of great principles of the English law, by which the powers of the colonial assembly were restricted; and in the second place, because they did not and could not consist with the above quoted "declaration," laid down by the convention itself as "the basis and foundation" of the new government.

Immediately after the adoption of this constitution, provision was made for revising the laws of Virginia, and a committee was appointed for that purpose; but nothing was done till 1785, when several bills prepared by the committee of revision were sanctioned by the assembly and enacted as laws. In one of these acts it was provided, "that no persons shall henceforth be slaves in this commonwealth, except such as were so on the first day of this present session of assembly, and the descendants of the females of them." This act, embodied into the codification of 1792, still remains in force; and through it all legal titles to slave property in Virginia must be traced. But in 1785, there were no persons legally held as slaves in Virginia. The practice on this subject, and the acts of the colonial assembly which countenanced that practice, were contradictory to the law of England, always binding on the colonial assembly, and specially adopted by the revolutionary government as the law of Virginia; and contradictory, also, to those general principles and that declaration of natural rights specially adopted as "the basis and foundation" of the new government.

The convention which framed the constitution of Virginia was far from conferring, or from claiming any power to confer, on the assembly any authority to reduce any of the inhabitants of that state to a condition of slavery. The assembly was far from claiming the possession of any such power, or from attempting to add any thing to the legal basis upon which slavery rested prior to the Revolution. It remained then what it had been in colonial times, a mere usurpation, without any legal basis; a usurpation in direct defiance of the Declaration of Rights, upheld by mere force and terror, and the overwhelming power and influence of the masters, without law and against law.

The convention of Maryland, (which upon the breaking out of hostilities with the mother country had displaced the proprietary government,) following in the footsteps of Virginia, adopted, on the 3d of November, 1776, a Declaration of Rights, the introductory part of a new constitution, in which they declared, "that all government of right originates from the people; is founded in compact only, and is constituted solely for the good of the whole;" and "that the *inhabitants* of Maryland are entitled to the common law of England; to all English statutes applicable to their situation, passed before the settlement of Maryland, and introduced and practised on in the colony; and also to all acts of the old colonial assembly "in force" on the 1st of June, 1774. But the

acts of assembly sanctioning and legalizing slavery
were not "in force" on the 1st of June, 1774, nor at
any other time. They never had been in force; they
were contrary to the law of England, to a corre-
spondency with which the colonial assembly was
specially limited by charter. Yet it is on these void
acts that the supposed legality of slavery in Maryland still continues to rest.

The constitution of North Carolina, formed Decem-
ber 17, 1776, contains not one single word respecting
slavery. That institution did not receive even the
semblance of support derived in Virginia and
Maryland from the continuation in force of the colonial acts; for no act of the colonial assembly of
North Carolina had ever attempted to define who
were or might be slaves. Nor was any such attempt
made by the newly-established assembly. Slavery
remained in the state of North Carolina what it had
been in the colony,—a mere custom, a sheer usurpation, not sustained by even the semblance of law.

Neither the first constitution of South Carolina,
adopted in March, 1776, nor the second constitution,
adopted March, 1778, contains a single word attempting to legalize slavery, nor even any clause continuing in force the old colonial acts. But in February,
1777, in the interval between the two constitutions,
an act of assembly revived and continued in force
for five years certain of those acts, among others the
act of 1740, on the subject of slavery, of which a
synopsis was given in the preceding section; and in
1783, this act was made perpetual. But the act of
1740 was void from the beginning, by reason of numerous contradictions to the law of England which
the colonial assembly of South Carolina had no
power to enact into law. If, then, the reviving acts
of 1777 and 1783 are to have any validity, they must
be considered as original acts, subjecting half the
population of South Carolina to perpetual slavery.

Had the assembly of South Carolina any authority to pass such acts? Has it any such authority at this moment? Could the South Carolina democrats, having a majority in the assembly, pass a valid act for selling all the whigs into perpetual slavery? or all inhabitants of Irish descent? or all white men not freeholders and not possessed of visible property? or all citizens of Massachusetts who might land on her hospitable coast?

We must always remember, in considering questions of this sort, that not the federal government only, but the state governments, also, are governments of limited powers. The sovereign power is in the people, or that portion of it possessed of political rights; the holders of offices created by the state constitutions possess no authority not specially conferred on them by those constitutions. Admit, for the sake of the argument, that the sovereign people of South Carolina are omnipotent, and can give the character of law to the most atrocious wrongs; yet, surely, no state legislature can exercise any such authority, unless it be expressly delegated. But the constitutions of South Carolina delegated no such power; and a power in a state legislature to reduce, at its pleasure, to the condition of perpetual servitude, any portion of the inhabitants of a state, and that not for public but for private uses, is hardly to be presumed as one of the ordinary powers of legislation, at least in a state which, in the solemn act of separation from the mother country, had united in declaring that all men are born free and equal, and that life, liberty, and the pursuit of happiness are inalienable rights.

The first constitution of Georgia, formed in February, 1777, contains no allusion to slavery. The legislative power of the assembly is restricted to "such laws and regulations as may be conducive to the good order and well being of the state." Unsupported by any new authority, the system of slavery

was left in Georgia, as in the other states, to rest on
such legal basis as it might have had during colonial
times. The rottenness of that basis was not perceived by the state legislatures nor by the state courts.
Their preconceived prejudices, their unwillingness to
look into the matter at all, kept them blind to it;
but their blindness, their ignorance, their mistakes,
could not alter the law, nor make that legal which in
fact was not so.

There was, indeed, the best of reasons why none
of the States—however several of them might be willing to leave to slavery such character of legality as
it had acquired from colonial legislation—should have
ventured upon any direct attempts, by virtue of their
newly-assumed powers, to bestow upon it a new and
original character of legality. For, however jurists
and courts of law may have admitted a legal omnipotence in governments, the people of the United States,
in rising against the mother country, and establishing
themselves as a separate nation, had expressly re-
nounced any such claims. Not to mention particular State Bills of Rights, their joint Declaration of
Independence—that public and official exhibition of
reasons for the steps they had taken in breaking up
their union with Great Britain—proceeded on the
very ground that men possess certain inherent and
unalienable Rights, including life, liberty, and the pursuit of happiness—rights which no government has
authority to take away, unless, indeed, in the way of
punishment for crimes—and any deliberate and continuous attempt to invade which, justifies resistance
even unto death. With what face could governments
which had just made such a declaration of principles
proceed to enact laws subjecting to perpetual and hereditary servitude one half or more of their inhabitants? How paltry, how trifling, side by side with
such a terrible assumption, must have appeared the
parliamentary claim to tax the colonies, out of which
the Revolution grew!

Nor was the renunciation thus made without a more direct and positive influence in many of the states; for the Supreme Court of Massachusetts decided, in 1784, that the natural freedom and political equality of all men, proclaimed in the Declaration of Independence, and in the Bill of Rights prefixed to the Constitution adopted in that state in 1780, were totally inconsistent with the existence of involuntary servitude, and that slavery under that Bill of Rights could not be legal. A similar clause in the second constitution of New Hampshire was held to guarantee personal freedom to all persons born in that state after the adoption of that constitution. In Pennsylvania, Connecticut, and Rhode Island, personal liberty was secured by statute to all future natives of those states; and, to complete this scheme of abolition in these three states, as well as in New Hampshire, the further introduction of persons claimed as slaves, or the exportation of such persons from those states, was prohibited.

In five of the eight remaining states, New York, New Jersey, Delaware, Maryland, and Virginia, slavery was regarded, by the more intelligent and enlightened citizens, including all those distinguished men who had taken a conspicuous part in the late Revolution, as an evil and a wrong inconsistent with the principles on which that Revolution was founded. Its termination was anxiously looked for, and confidently hoped. All those five states had taken the first step in that direction by prohibiting the further introduction of persons claimed as slaves; while Virginia and Maryland, by repealing the old colonial acts which forbade manumissions, except by the allowance of the governor and council, had opened a door for the action of individual sentiment in favor of liberty which came soon into active exercise.

Such was the state of things in the ten northern states when the Federal convention came together; and, pending the session of that convention, the famous ordinance of 1787 was passed by the Congress of the confederation, by which involuntary servitude, except for crime, was forever prohibited in the territory north-west of the Ohio, the only territory to which, as yet, the confederacy had any title.

Yet this rising sentiment in favor of impartial liberty encountered a formidable opposition. The abolition of slavery had been carried, indeed, in five of the states, but in only one of those five had it been thorough, sweeping, and complete. Four had provided for the future, but had not thought it expedient to interfere with the present. In five other states, a commencement only had been made. The mass of the slave-holders in those five states clung with tenacity to their prey; and the friends of emancipation, though their influence was apparent, did not yet venture to propose any very decisive measures. In the Carolinas and Georgia the case was much worse. The Quakers of North Carolina had indeed commenced the emancipation of their slaves, but the assembly of that state put a stop to that "dangerous practice," as they pronounced it, by forbidding emancipations, except by allowance of the County Courts, and directing all slaves hitherto emancipated without that allowance to be seized and resold into slavery. Since the peace, the importation of slaves from the coast of Africa into the three southern states had been recommenced, and was vigorously carried on. In those states there was little thought of foregoing a system from which great gains were hoped; though the legislature of North Carolina, in a recent act imposing a duty on future importations, expressly admitted the further introduction of slaves to be of "evil consequence, and highly impolitic."

Let it be remembered, however,—and this consideration, though frequently overlooked or disregarded, is absolutely essential to a correct understanding of the case,—that the Federal convention did not assemble to revise the laws or institutions of the states; nor to determine or enforce the political or social rights appertaining to the inhabitants of the states, as such. That had been done already by the state constitutions. The states existed as bodies politic; they had their laws defining the rights of their citizens and inhabitants, and their courts for enforcing those rights; and with none of those arrangements, either by way of enforcement or alteration, was it any part of the business of the Federal convention to interfere, unless in cases where these arrangements had or might have an injurious bearing upon the citizens of other states, or upon the foreign relations of the confederacy. The business of the Federal convention was, so to amend the articles of confederation as to carry into effect the objects at which that confederation aimed; namely, the enabling the states to act as one nation in their foreign affairs, and securing the several states and their individual inhabitants against injustice, oppression, or injury, on the part of other states or their individual inhabitants.

It might indeed become necessary, for the accomplishment of these objects, to interfere to some extent with some of the existing laws and institutions of the states, or at least to reserve to the authorities, to be created by the new constitution, the power of doing so; and under the plan adopted of submitting that constitution to be separately ratified by each of the states, any alterations so made or authorized would rest on the same basis of popular consent with the state constitutions themselves. But this interference with state constitutions or state laws, any interference in any shape with the internal affairs of the states, was a power to be very daintily exercised, especially in its application to particular cases, as, otherwise, any constitution which the convention might form would be sure of being rejected.

Thus the Federal convention had chiefly to do with the people of America, not in their character as individuals about to enter into a primary political organization, but in their character as inhabitants of certain states already constituted and organized. Their rights as inhabitants of each particular state it belonged to the state governments to settle : the Federal constitution had only to declare what should be their additional and supplementary rights as citizens and inhabitants of the confederacy.

It was from this view of the work before them that the convention omitted to prefix to the Federal Constitution any general Bill of Rights—an omission much complained of by those who opposed its adoption. Slavery in the states, under this view of the subject, was a matter with which the convention was not called upon directly to interfere, and which, indeed, could not be directly interfered with without exposing the proposed constitution to certain rejection. It did, however, come before the convention incidentally; and the question which we now have to consider is, Whether, in dealing with it thus incidentally, the Federal constitution has acknowledged the *legal* existence of slavery in any such way as to bind the confederacy.

The first article in the Federal constitution relied upon by those who maintain the affirmative on this point is that which determines the ratio of representation in the House of Representatives. That article, indeed, is frequently spoken of as though it were the great compromise ; the fundamental concession upon which the constitution was based. But this was not by any means the case. The great difficulty that occurred at the outset was, to reconcile the pretensions of the larger and the smaller states. The smaller states insisted upon that political equality which they already possessed under the articles of confederation ; the larger states maintained that representation in the national legislature ought to be based on " wealth and numbers." A resolution to that effect, as to both branches of the legislature, having been carried by the larger states, the smaller states threatened to quit the convention ; and this result was only prevented by a concession—recommended by a committee of one from each state, to whom the subject was referred, and which was finally adopted by the convention—yielding to the small states an equal representation in one branch of the national legislature, namely, in the Senate, in which each state, large or small, was to have two delegates.

This was the great compromise : the particular ratio of representation to be adopted in the other branch was quite a subordinate matter. Yet, though subordinate, it was interesting and important. One party, headed by Gouverneur Morris, wished to leave the ratio of representation in the lower house entirely to the discretion of Congress, with the avowed object of enabling the existing states to retain a political ascendency over such new states as might be admitted into the Union. But this was objected to as unjust, and it became necessary to fix upon some precise rule of distribution. There was a general agreement that this distribution should be regulated by " wealth and numbers ; " numbers might easily be ascertained by a census ; but how was wealth to be measured ?

This was a point upon which, under the existing confederation, difficulties had already occurred. In framing the articles of confederation it had been proposed—on the ground that population, on the whole, was the best practicable test of wealth, and ability to pay taxes—to distribute the charges of the war, and other common expenses, among the states in proportion to their population. But the southern states had strongly objected to that arrangement, alleging that the labor of their slaves was far less productive than the labor of the same number of northern freemen ; and the value of buildings and cultivated lands, to be ascertained by an appraisement made by the authorities of each state, was finally adopted as the basis of taxation and pecuniary liability. But such an appraisement was found liable to great difficulties, expenses, delays, and objections ; very few states had made it ; and Congress, since the peace, by a concession to the slave-holders, and an admission of the wealth-producing inefficiency of slaves as compared with freemen, had proposed to amend the articles of confederation by substituting as the basis of taxation, and of the distribution among the states of the expenses of the Revolutionary war, "the whole number of white and other free citizens and inhabitants of every age, sex, and condition, including those bound to *servitude* for a term of years, and *three fifths of all other persons not comprehended in the foregoing description;*" and this proposed amendment, agreed to in Congress after a good deal of higgling between the northern and southern members as to the relative productiveness of free and slave labor, had been already acceded to by eleven out of the thirteen states.   The question of the measure of wealth as the basis of representation being now raised in the convention, the same compromise was suggested there; and, having first agreed that representation and direct taxation should go together, it was finally arranged, and so it now stands in the Federal constitution, that the number of representatives from each state shall be determined "by adding to the whole number of free persons, including those bound to *service* for a term of years, and excluding Indians not taxed, *three fifths of all other persons.*"

The question then is, whether the phrase *three fifths of all other persons* recognizes the validity of the slave laws of any particular state, and affords a sufficient basis for those laws to stand upon, notwithstanding their original defects already pointed out. Let us observe, in the first place, that the validity of those laws was not of the least consequence in settling the point under consideration, to wit, the productiveness of the industry—in other words, the relative wealth—of the several states. Whether the negroes of Virginia, for instance, were held in slavery by law or against law, made, in that point of view, no difference. Suppose, for example, (as we hold,) that they were illegally deprived of their liberty; the illegality of their servitude would not increase their industry, nor the wealth of the state, so as to entitle her whole population to be counted in determining her representation. What the constitution had to deal with, in settling this distribution of representation, was a question of external fact, not a question of law or right. The question of the individual rights of the inhabitants of the states was one over which this article required the assumption of no control. Their condition in fact, not their condition in law, was the real point according to which the distribution was to be regulated.

But even in referring to the matter of fact great caution was used. "The question of slavery in the states," said Gerry, in reference to another point to be presently considered, "ought not to be touched, but we ought to be careful not to give it any sanction." Madison thought it wrong to admit into the constitution "the idea that there could be property in men;" and in his report of the doings of that convention, to which we are mainly indebted for what we know of it, he represents the whole phraseology of the instrument to have been carefully settled in accordance with that view. Thus, in the original draft of the clause above cited, instead of *bound to service*, the phrase *bound to servitude* had been used, following in this respect the proposed amendment to the articles of confederation from which the idea of the Federal ratio was derived; but *servitude* was struck out, and *service* substituted, as Madison informs us, because *servitude* seemed to be only appropriate to express the condition of slavery.

It is fair enough to conclude that the " other persons," referred to in this article, were those held as slaves in the several states. But the constitution takes care not to commit itself by calling them slaves, nor by using any term that would seem to pass a judgment on the legal character or particular legal incidents of their condition. That remained what it was; this article did not affect it in any way; and if the laws of the states fail, as we maintain, to give any

20 *

legal authority to those who claim to be masters, they
will surely look for it in vain in this article of the Federal constitution.

When the Federal convention, in the course of its
labors, arrived at the clauses investing Congress with
the power to regulate navigation and foreign commerce, a new occasion for compromise arose. Ten
states out of the thirteen had already prohibited the
importation of slaves from abroad, and if the Federal
government were invested with unlimited control over
the intercourse with foreign countries, it was plain
enough that one of its first acts would be the prohibition of the African slave trade.

For this Georgia and the Carolinas were not prepared ; and the opinion was very warmly and confidently expressed by their delegates, that such an unlimited power conferred upon Congress would insure
in those states the rejection of the constitution. To
avoid this result, and to induce, also, the southernmost
states to concede this power over commerce, to which
in common with all the merely agricultural states, they
had several other objections, a provision was inserted,
" that the emigration or importation of such persons
as any of the states now existing shall think proper
to admit, shall not be prohibited by Congress prior to
the year 1808 ; but a tax or duty may be imposed on
such importation not exceeding ten dollars for each
person."

Observe in this clause the same cautious phraseology as in that already discussed. As to the legal
character or condition of the persons so to be admitted, nothing is said. There is not the slightest implication that the constitution assented in any way that
any of the persons so introduced into the states should
be held in slavery. If that was done, it could only
be on the responsibility of those who did it, and of the
states that allowed it. The constitution did not as-
sent to it, and by the power which it reserved to Congress,—all the power which was possible under the

circumstances,—it secured the right, after the lapse of twenty years, of preventing the possibility of such an occurrence. But for this right, thus reserved to the Federal government, there is every reason to believe that in all the states south of Virginia the foreign slave trade would be now vigorously prosecuted. The concession made to Georgia and the Carolinas was temporary and limited; the point carried was of a permanent character.

There still remains one other clause of the constitution relied upon as sanctioning slavery in the states. "No person held to service or labor in one state, under the laws thereof, escaping into another, shall, in consequence of any law or regulation therein, be discharged from such service or labor; but shall be delivered up on claim of the party to whom such service or labor may be due." It may be worth while to notice that in the article now under consideration, the term *service* is employed—"no person held to service or labor;" whereas, according to the distinction above quoted from Madison, the term *servitude* would have been the proper one, had the clause been expressly intended for the case of refugee slaves. But, without dwelling on this distinction, it is sufficient for our purpose to refer to the pointed difference between this and the apportionment clause, in the express reference which this clause makes to law. Practice, usage, fact merely, is not sufficient, but law is required. "No person held to service or labor in one state, *under the laws thereof*," &c. The question, then, whether this clause stipulates for the return of fugitive slaves, is entirely dependent on the previous question whether there is any lawful slavery in any of the states—a question upon which this clause expresses no opinion, and throws not the slightest light whatsoever. If there be any such slavery, it must exist by virtue of state laws, laws complete and authoritative in themselves; for whatever might have been the intention, or whatever may be the legal effect of this clause, it surely neither intended to give, nor can it have any effect to give, a legal or rightful character to any claims of service not previously rightful and legal.

From numerous recent speeches, published opinions, and other apologies for the fugitive slave act of 1850, one might be led to imagine that the surrender of fugitive slaves had been one of the great questions on which the Federal convention had divided, and which, as an indispensable condition of union, it had become necessary to settle by a solemn compromise embodied in the article here under consideration. To show how utterly fabulous these statements, so derogatory to the convention and to the nation, are, we subjoin, from Madison's Report of the Debates of the Convention, all that is known of the history of this clause; merely premising, what seems to be sometimes forgotten, that the Union did not originate with the convention, but had been established by the Articles of Confederation ratified by all the states some years before—articles which the convention had met to amplify and amend so as to give greater efficiency to the central administration.

After warm and protracted debates, and the compromise, as already briefly mentioned, of two very exciting questions—one, that of the relative political weight in the general government to be allowed to the great and small states, which, by the articles of confederation, possessed an equal voice; the other as to ratio of representation in the lower House,—for the third of the three great compromises, that relating to the importation for twenty years of such persons as any of the states might see fit to allow, did not take place till a subsequent stage of proceedings,—the convention came at length to certain resolutions embodying the result of its previous discussions and compromises, and supplying the rough material of the constitution as subsequently adopted. These resolutions, which did not embrace any more than the articles of confederation, any thing on the subject of fugitives, whether from justice or labor, were referred to a committee of detail, whose report, among other specific provisions, now first suggested, contained an article giving to the citizens of each state all the privileges of citizens in the several states, and another, providing for the mutual surrender by the states of fugitives from other states charged with treason, felony, or high misdemeanor. The first of these articles coming up for debate, General Charles C. Pinckney, of South Carolina, expressed himself not satisfied with it. " He seemed to wish that some provision should be inserted in it in favor of property in slaves." Very likely he had in his head a provision as to the states similar to the pretension lately set up by the slave-holders as to the territories, giving the right to hold slaves into whatever state the holder might choose to carry them. But if so, he did not venture upon any such barefaced proposition ; and the article, as it now stands in the constitution, was adopted by the votes of all the states present except South Carolina in the negative, and Georgia divided. The proposed article on the subject of fugitives from justice coming up immediately after, Butler, another South Carolina member, moved " to require fugitive slaves and servants to be delivered up like criminals." To this, Wilson, of Pennsylvania, objected " that it would require the executive of the state to do it at the public expense." Sherman, of Connecticut, added that " he saw no more propriety in the public seizing and surrendering a slave or servant than a horse." With a view to some separate provision, Butler withdrew his proposition ; but the next day offered the draft of a clause, the idea of which was evidently derived from a similar provision in an ordinance just passed by the Continental Congress, which, in prohibiting forever slavery and involuntary servitude, except in punishment of crimes, in the territory north-west of the Ohio, (lately ceded to the Union by the states of Vir-

ginia, New York, Massachusetts, and Connecticut,)
had also provided "that every person escaping into
the same, from whom labor or service is lawfully
claimed in any one of the original states, such fugitive may be lawfully returned, and conveyed to
the person claiming his or her labor as aforesaid."
Guided evidently by this precedent, Butler proposed,
and the convention—in compliance, as we may reasonably conjecture, with an understanding come to
out of doors—adopted without debate or dissent an
independent proposition in the following terms : " If
any person bound to service or labor in any of the
United States shall escape into another state, he or
she shall not be discharged from such service or
labor in consequence of any regulations subsisting in
. the state to which they escape, but shall be delivered
up to the person justly claiming their service or
labor."   The committee on style, appointed to revise
and arrange all the articles agreed on, proposed to
amend this one as follows : " No person *legally*
held to service or labor in one state, escaping into
another, shall, in consequence of regulations subsisting therein, be discharged from such service or labor ;
but shall be delivered up on claim of the party to
whom such service or labor may be due ;" but, before its final adoption, the phraseology was still further altered, and it was brought into the shape in
which it now stands—in compliance, as Madison tells
us, with the wish of some who thought the word
legally equivocal, and favoring the idea that slavery
was legal in a moral point of view.

Wholly apart from any application of this clause
to the case of runaway slaves, there was ample matter for it to operate upon, not only in apprentices and
minor children to whose labor the father has a legal
right, but in those indented servants who had constituted, during the whole of the colonial times, so considerable a part of the population, especially in the
Middle States, and whom, as their importation, in-
terrupted by the war, was again beginning to be

resumed, the convention might reasonably have expected soon to become as numerous as ever. As applying to apprentices, children, and indented servants, the article in question confers a right in which the citizens of all the states may share; viewed as a provision for the surrender of runaway slaves, it assumes an unequal and exclusive character, conferring a very invidious power on the citizens of a part only of the states—a character not to be found in any other article of the Federal constitution, and wholly incompatible with its whole spirit.

The simple state of the fact seems then to be this. A clause was inserted into the constitution perfectly appropriate though there had not been a slave in the Union, and which may very properly stand there after slavery shall be completely abolished, as it was the general expectation in the convention that it soon would be. But in framing this clause, terms were used sufficiently comprehensive to enable the courts, if so disposed, constructively to include under it, during the temporary existence of slavery, the case of runaway slaves—provided, the courts should be of opinion that in the states whence the fugitives had fled, slavery existed not merely as a fact, but "under the laws thereof." In this clause, so much vaunted as a Federal recognition and indorsement of the legality of slavery, not the slightest reference even to the mere fact of its existence can be found, except by first taking for granted the very point which it is so often cited to prove, viz., that slavery did and does exist in the states by virtue of law. (See *Appendix*.)

The three clauses of the Federal constitution above considered are the only portions of that instrument which have ever been set up as giving any sanction to slavery. But, so far from finding in these clauses any such sanction, we find, on the contrary, evidence of a fixed determination in the constitution not to yield it. They contain no indorsement of the slave laws of the states; no recognition of slavery as a state institution; no express recognition even of the bare fact of the existence of slavery, and much less of its existence as an institution entitled to the favorable regard and protecting care of the Federal government. General Pinckney, of South Carolina, in the course of the debates of the convention, more than once asked for such guaranty for slave property; but, so far from yielding to this demand, the greatest care was taken not to admit into the constitution " the idea that there could be property in men;" that is to say, the very fundamental idea upon which the whole slave system rests. It was impossible for the Federal constitution, by its own proper vigor, to abolish slavery, or to make its abolition one of the conditions of the Federal compact—for on such conditions no constitution could be formed. It was even necessary to take into account, in several of its provisions, the actual, but, as it was hoped and expected, temporary, existence of slavery. Yet, on the other hand, the greatest care was had not to give any sanction to a practice so inconsistent with those natural rights upon which all the American constitutions professed to be founded, nor indeed even to recognize, except by remote and obscure implication, its bare existence as a fact. The utmost length to which the members of the convention would go, was a silent toleration of slavery as it existed; leaving it to be disposed of—and, as the convention expected, to be speedily abolished— by the states themselves. They were not anti-slavery men in that sense which makes hostility to slavery paramount to all other considerations; but, so far as an extreme dislike of that system, and a hearty wish for its speedy extinction, could go, the majority of them were decidedly anti-slavery men; and the constitution, and especially the amendments to it subsequently adopted, contain many provisions very inconsistent with the existence of slavery.

This view of the Federal constitution corresponds very nearly with the view taken of it, both north and south, for many years subsequent to its adoption. It is only within a recent period that the idea has been set up, that the "compromises of the constitution" include the recognition of slavery as an institution of the states, or some of them, entitled to protection and support. Still more recent is the doctrine that the distinguishing trait of "nationality" among us is the recognition and support of the system of slavery, and zeal for the return of fugitive slaves. Not only does the Federal constitution, so far from recognizing slavery in any such character, take the greatest pains to avoid doing so, but in point of fact, as we maintain, slavery is not even a state institution, legally speaking, but a mere usurpation, unsupported by law, and in that character certainly not entitled to support or countenance from the Federal government or any other.

But if the Federal constitution, though cautiously avoiding to commit the Union to the support of slavery, has yet left the determination of the rights of the inhabitants of the states to the state authorities, —even allowing that slavery exists by usurpation and not by law,—has the Federal government any warrant to interfere, in any way, to set this matter right? Is it not bound to wait patiently till the state authorities shall themselves do it?

Besides the specific and particular powers conferred upon Congress by the Federal constitution, that body, by a clause of a very extensive and comprehensive character, is authorized "to provide for the common defence and general welfare of the United States;" at least in all the cases in which that end can be accomplished by the expenditure of money. Now, suppose the opinion to be adopted, by the majority of the people, that the "common defence and general welfare of the United States;" their defence against invasion from abroad, and insurrection at home; their welfare, moral, social, and economical, demand the termination of the system of slavery;—and, in this point of view, it seems to matter but little whether we consider that system an illegal usurpation or a legal institution of those states in which it exists;— suppose the conclusion to be arrived at, that the continued existence of slavery, whether legal or not, will be fatal to the success of that great democratic experiment which the American people are now making;—looking at the matter in this point of view, has not the Federal government a right to interfere, and to adopt such measures as seem best calculated to stop the increase of this evil, and to bring it to an end? If, under the clause above cited, Congress had power to buy Louisiana, to buy Florida, to annex Texas, to buy California, has it not power, under the same clause, to vote money towards the liberation of some millions of native-born inhabitants from most cruel servitude?

It is true that, heretofore, Congress has not legislated with this intention. It is also true, that, on a petition signed by Franklin and others, and presented to the first Congress, praying that body to take measures for the abolition of slavery, the conclusion was arrived at, after a warm debate, that Congress had no jurisdiction over the subject of slavery within the states. But this decision, binding only on the Congress that made it, though very generally acquiesced in since, still remains open to revision; and a change of circumstances, changing the light in which the question presents itself, cannot fail to have a serious influence on the decision to be made upon it.

When the first Congress met, slavery was a crime and disgrace in which the whole of Christendom was more or less involved; and in the wars which the nations of Europe carried on with each other, their practices in this matter were mutually respected. When France, England, Spain, and Holland invaded each other's colonies, they never thought of putting arms into the hands of the slaves. Early in our Revolutionary war, some suggestion was thrown out in the British House of Commons, that the slaves in the southern states might be liberated, armed, and employed to keep those colonies in subjection ; but the opposition, headed by Burke and Fox, denounced the idea as barbarous, atrocious, and infamous, and the suggestion, never seriously entertained, remained, to a great extent, unacted upon. Mason, of Virginia, feelingly acknowledged in the Federal convention, that if the British had availed themselves, as they might have done, of the aid of the negroes, the war in the southern states might have had a very different termination.

During the last war with England, a plan, it is said, was formed for occupying the peninsula between the Chesapeake and the Delaware with a British army, turning it into an asylum for the slaves of Virginia and Maryland, to whom liberty was to be proclaimed ; organizing and training a black army, under English officers, and marching with it to the conquest of the South. But Britain had slaves of her own ; it would not do to set an example of insurrection and of liberty won at the point of the bayonet ; and this brilliant scheme was consequently abandoned. Had it been energetically undertaken, something more might have happened than the burning of the Capitol.

Since that period opinions have greatly changed. England has abolished slavery throughout her wide-spread dominions. France has also abolished it in her colonies. All Christendom cries out against it. Should we become involved in war with France or England, especially with England,—and war with England is one of the commonplaces of our politics, —no matter what the cause or origin of the war, a proclamation of freedom to the enslaved would sanctify it in the eyes of the world. It would become the cause of humanity against despotism—a despotism the more hateful from its attempt to cloak itself with the name of democracy, and from its audacious efforts to trample out the doctrine of the rights of man in the very states by which that doctrine was first proclaimed as the basis of political organization. The enemy would strike us in our vital parts, and Christendom would honor and applaud the blow. Under these circumstances, will not due regard to the "common defence" justify Congress in adopting a course of legislative policy such as may narrow, limit, restrict, and tend to the extinction of a source of weakness which no provision of forts and steam frigates can guard against?

The "welfare of the United States," their internal well-being, apart from any dangers from without, and more especially the welfare of the slave states themselves, seem to call still louder for Congressional interference. The perception of the evils of slavery has, till recently, been confined to a speculative few —a class of persons more inclined to think than to act, and disabled, by the smallness of their number, from any effectual political action. But sensibility to those evils, especially to the obstacles which the existence of slavery opposes to the further extension of the principles of equality and justice even in their application to the free,—thanks to the efforts and labors of those known as *Abolitionists*,—is now beginning to penetrate the mass, and to find representatives and an expression in the legislatures of the free states, and even in Congress. When a majority in Congress come to be thoroughly impregnated with these ideas; when they come to look upon slavery, not merely as an evil, a calamity, a thing to be lamented and regretted, but as a fatal obstacle to the progress of our free institutions, a consuming cancer eating into the heart of our liberties, and threatening the extinction of those principles upon which our constitutions are founded; —perceiving that the "welfare of the United States" is seriously compromised,—can they hesitate to come to the rescue? Will they not feel themselves called upon, not alone by humanity, by patriotism, but by the very letter of the constitution itself, to come to the rescue?

But even grant that Congress might not rightfully assume to legislate upon the subject of slavery independently of and adverse to the states to be directly affected by such legislation, yet their consent and co-operation would certainly go far to remove this obstacle. Nor is it to be supposed that such a feeling as we have above referred to can become predominant in Congress without penetrating, also, to a greater or less extent, into the slave states themselves. But the evil of slavery is so immense, and in most of our slave states it has become so firmly rooted,—swallowing up, as it were, the state and the church, and enlisting in its support the wealth, the talent, the intelligence, the education, the ignorance, the prejudices, and the passions of the people,—that to wait for those states to take the leadership in the abolition movement would be absurd. The effects of such waiting have been long since manifest. The abolition of slavery in Maryland and Virginia, so confidently expected and so devoutly wished for by Henry, Washington, Jefferson, Mason, Madison, did not take place. The slave-holders of those states have, on the contrary, added to the injustice of slave-holding the cruelty and turpitude of slave-breeding and slave-exporting; and, in diffusing this evil over the new regions of the south-west, they have found new inducements for continuing it among themselves. For the purpose of extending this slave market, they do not hesitate to involve the Union in disgraceful wars of conquest. Not content with the seizure of Texas, the annexation of Cuba is already suggested —to which Virginia might serve as a new Africa, the slave trade to that coast having been mainly cut off by the vigilance of the English cruisers. This let-alone policy, this waiting for the parties most immediately interested to take the lead, came near proving fatal even to Congress itself. The right of petition, even freedom of debate, seemed about to be extinguished in that body. The Federal government has put itself forward as the champion and defender of slavery; the antagonist, on this point, of all Christendom. What a change, even on the question of the African slave trade!—that very government, which

had itself once proposed a mutual right of search on
the coast of Africa, exerting all its efforts, and not
without success, to defeat a treaty of that sort into
which Britain had induced the great powers of Europe to enter! The thraldom, thank God, into which
Congress was fast sinking, has, by the steady efforts
of a few noble men, at last been partially shaken off.
The attention of the people has been aroused to the
question—Shall the Federal government be a slave-
holding or an anti-slave-holding government? Experience seems to show that any middle ground,
practically speaking, is out of the question. If the
Federal government is not the one, it must be the
other.

But supposing the Federal government to have
power, to have a constitutional right to act in this
matter, how is it to act? Shall Congress employ
force? Shall a law be passed declaring the right of the
southern negroes to freedom, and an army be marched
into the southern states to enforce such law? Such
rude and violent methods of effecting political changes
correspond neither to the principles of our institutions
nor to the enlightened philosophy of the present age.
It is not the office of the Federal government to abolish slavery by a mere act of its own authority imposed upon the slave-holding states—an act which
might justly be denounced as arbitrary, and which
the whole white population of the South would unite
to resist. Great evils are not thus to be got rid of by
a single blow. To be effectually and peacefully abolished, slavery must be abolished by the legislatures
of the slave states themselves. There exist in all the
slave-states ample materials for a party ready to undertake that great and illustrious task. Some mov-
ing of the dry bones has been of late discernible; but,
for the most part, the anti-slavery party of the South,
strong, morally and intellectually, and by no means
contemptible in point of numbers, lies at this moment
prostrate, completely paralyzed by terror, and pre-

vented thereby from any movement or organization; held down in as pitiable a state of fear and helplessness as can well be imagined. The great excitement of 1834—the alarm then raised among the slave-holders by the symptoms of an anti-slavery movement at the North—caused the extemporaneous introduction into the southern states of a suppressive system, based apparently on the Spanish inquisition—but with the democratic improvements of turning every slave-holder into an inquisitor, and the miserable, uneducated mob of the southern villages and hamlets into spies and officers—the proceedings, without any troublesome or tedious formalities, being regulated by the code of Lynch law, the same parties acting in the fourfold capacity of accusers, witnesses, judges, and executioners. That same despotic spirit, indeed, which holds the slaves in subjection without law and against law, does not hesitate a moment to set aside all the most sacred principles of law, all our much-vaunted safeguards of personal security, for the sake of speedy vengeance upon those inclined in any way to question its authority. Such, indeed, is the just retribution of nature. Establish despotism over one class of the community, and it will soon extend itself over all the others. Give your neighbor a right to tyrannize over slaves, and he will soon assume a right to tyrannize over you.

Yet it is to this down-trodden party, this humbled and silenced party, this party existing, indeed, as yet only in embryo, without organization or self-consciousness, these southern anti-slavery men, that we must look for the abolition of slavery. The spirit of despotism must be encountered in the slave states themselves, by a power potent enough to awe it down, and keep it under; and this power can only be a mass of citizens combined together, acting in concert, and having such weight of social, and especially of political influence, that it shall become necessary to respect their feelings, their opinions, and their rights. Such a combination must be formed in all the slave states before the first effectual steps can be taken, we do not say towards the abolition of slavery merely, but even towards the enforcement of the rights of those nominally free; those great rights of free discussion and a free press which no despotism, or would-be despotism, willingly tolerates.

Congress, however, or the friends of freedom in Congress, are not to wait till such a party rises up. It is their business to help it up, to reach out a hand to it, on every possible occasion. Could the immense patronage of the Federal government once be directed to that point, we may judge of the result likely to follow by the effect which that same patronage has produced at the North, in a counter direction. It is by calling upon the Federal government, on every possible occasion that occurs, or can be made to occur, to abjure all responsibility for slavery and all countenance of it; it is by finding and making perpetual occasions to point out the evils of slavery in particular instances, its incompatibility with the "general welfare," and the obstacles which it opposes to the "common defence;"—it is by imitating the example of steadfast old Cato, and repeating at every opportunity, in season and out of season, "I think also that slavery ought to be abolished;"—such are the means by which even a very few members of Congress may effect great things; not indeed by way of direct legislation,—for direct legislation constitutes, after all, but a small part of the influence which Congress exerts,—but by keeping this subject constantly before the public mind; enabling and compelling the slave-holders to see what they have hitherto so obstinately shut their eyes to; and what is of more importance yet, giving the non-slave-holding freemen of the South an opportunity to see what the slave-holders hitherto have so dexterously kept out of their sight.

Just in proportion as the anti-slavery party increases in Congress; just in proportion as that body shall evince symptoms of a settled, firm, and steady opposition to slavery; just in the same proportion will the southern anti-slavery men be encouraged to confess themselves, first to themselves, then to one another, and then to the world. Only through the medium of Congress, and the Federal government, can the anti-slavery sentiment of the North be brought into any active coöperation with the anti-slavery sentiment of the South; and surely, until northern representatives of non-slave-holding constituencies can stand up on the floor of Congress and boldly speak their minds upon the subject, and secure a hearing too, it is quite too much to expect any such boldness, or any such hearing, in the legislature of any slave-holding state.

It needs, as we believe, only this free discussion to show that even the technical legality behind which slavery claims to entrench itself cannot be maintained. This point has hitherto been conceded to the slave-holders, hastily, without examination, and, as we believe, without reason. The truth seems to be that, although the people of the southern states were willing, and a large majority of them desirous, to allow slavery to continue among them as a matter of fact, they left its legality to rest upon the enactments and practice of the colonial times, without undertaking by any fundamental act of sovereignty on their part to confer any new or additional legality upon it. The legality of American slavery rests, then, upon a colonial usage—a usage not only unsustained by the English law, but, in several most important points, directly contradictory to it; a usage totally incapable of furnishing any legal foundation for any claim of right; a usage upon which neither the state constitutions nor the Federal constitution undertake to confer a legal character; and upon which, indeed, taking into account the very fundamental principles of the American government, they could not confer a legal character.

When the colonists set forth in their Declaration of Independence, as the justification and basis of the stand they had taken, the natural Right of all men to life, liberty, and the pursuit of happiness, they must be esteemed as pledging themselves to the world, and to each other, for the recognition and maintenance of that right. Nor was this declaration the mere act of the Continental Congress, whose power might be disputed; for it was distinctly and solemnly ratified, adopted, and confirmed by every individual state in the Union. From that moment, then, it was a solemn pledge on the part of all the states, and a tacit condition of the Union, that slavery should be done away with as soon as possible. By adopting, two years before, the non-importation agreement, known as the American Association, the states had already pledged themselves to import no more slaves; a pledge from which they were never released, though the Carolinas and Georgia chose afterwards to violate it, and to insist on a constitutional permission to continue that violation for twenty years. The same understanding as to the abolition of slavery prevailed when the Federal constitution was adopted. Slavery was regarded as a transitory evil, to be speedily removed, and the greatest care was taken not to mention it by name, nor to recognize in that instrument any such idea as that of property in man.

The northern states have waited a great while, patiently, for their southern neighbors to carry out their agreement. If the conclusion should be arrived at, that the southern states are unable or unwilling to redeem their pledge, certainly the least we of the North can do is, to proclaim, every where, our conviction of the utter illegality of this accursed institution, and of the bad faith of the South in prolonging its existence.

Nor, indeed, can it reasonably be expected that the men of the North will stop there. The abolition of slavery, not to mention how essential it is to the preservation of the rights and liberties of the free, is a debt due from the United States to the memory and honor of our Revolutionary fathers, to the principles of democracy, to human nature itself; and just in proportion as our southern brethren shall fail to take the lead in this inevitable enterprise, that leadership must of necessity devolve on us of the North. It has only been by professions of ultra democracy, of exceeding respect for the natural rights of men, and of opposition to all arbitrary and unnecessary authority, that the slave-holding body have been enabled to exercise so long-continued and so decided an influence over our national politics. The time has now come—the ascendency of democratic ideas having, under southern patronage, been firmly established at the North, and the domination of the old aristocratical cliques completely put down—that the northern democracy can return the favor by aiding the southern states in the substitution of a democracy like that of the North, in place of those slave-holding oligarchies by which the entire laboring population of the South, white as well as black, has hitherto been held in such entire subjection. And, in adopting such a course, the northern democracy will consult not more the spirit of their own policy than the true intent of the framers of the Federal constitution. For whatever disputes may be raised as to the precise intent of the framers of that instrument in particular clauses, one thing at least is certain,—whatever monstrous assumptions to the contrary may have lately been countenanced in quarters where more knowledge and better feelings might naturally have been expected;—the framers of the constitution never intended, the people who ratified the constitution never intended, to found a slave-breeding and a slavery-propagating republic. The barest suspicion that the constitution could operate to perpetuate the institution of slavery would have caused its indignant rejection by all the northern and by a part of the southern states. The general intent of the framers of the constitution is clearly and comprehensively expressed in its preamble, by which its objects are declared to be, " To form a more perfect union, establish justice, insure domestic tranquillity, provide for the common defence, promote the general welfare, and secure the blessings of liberty to ourselves and our posterity." Now, to which of these great objects has not the existence among us of domestic slavery proved a stumbling-block from the day the first Continental Congress met down to the current moment? So long as slavery continues, the union of the states never can be perfected; justice is but an empty name; our domestic tranquillity will always be in danger—and that even less from the slaves, reluctantly held in bondage, and watching an opportunity to throw off the yoke, than from the idle, turbulent, hot-headed, and insolent among their masters, who, not content with lynching private individuals, and even sovereign states of the Union in the persons of their representatives, threaten separation and civil war whenever thwarted in any of their pretensions. What aid does the institution of slavery afford to the common defence? Officers, perhaps, but neither men nor money. As to securing the blessings of liberty to ourselves and our posterity, the slave-holders, backed by the mercantile interest of the North, in which they have found a humble but zealous ally, have, within the last fifteen years, made not less than two desperate attempts entirely to suppress all freedom of speech and of the press, and to make universal that reign of terror so vigorously enforced during that entire period throughout the southern part of the Union!

And yet those who labor to eradicate this lasting and inevitable source of discord, this eating cancer of our liberties and peace, are accused of hostility to the union of the states—and that, too, by a set of political pharisees, who, in parading their anxiety to carry out the alleged implied intentions of the framers of the constitution as to the return of runaway negroes, do at best but pay tithe of mint and cumin, while they wholly neglect those weightier matters, those great overruling intentions, not implied, alleged, made out by construction, or discovered by a resort to contemporaneous history, but proclaimed in the preamble to the constitution, and throughout the whole text of the instrument—the growth of the United States into a great, united, FREE republic!

That which the fathers planned, and of which they laid the foundations, building upon them according to the measure of their means and enlightenment, it becomes us of this generation, with the advantage of far superior means, and greater experience, to carry out and perfect.

That the abolition of slavery is by no means so impracticable a thing as many represent, and that even the slave-holders themselves may, by a reasonable regard to their claims to pecuniary indemnity, be induced heartily to concur in it, an attempt will be made to show in a subsequent treatise.

SECTION IV.

The Fugitive Act of 1850.

It is upon the clause of the constitution of the United States for the delivery up of " persons held to service or labor under the laws " of any state escaping into another, that the fugitive slave act (commonly so called) of 1850 is founded. That act, however, it is to be observed, notwithstanding its popular title, and the avowed purpose of its enactment, says nothing, any more than the constitution itself, in direct terms, about *slaves* or *slavery*. Its application to the case of fugitive slaves proceeds entirely on the assumption that slavery exists in certain of the states not merely in fact but by law, so that under the description of persons bound to service and labor under state laws slaves are included—an assumption which judges and commissioners may declare too plain to be argued about, or to require to be sustained

22

by any reasons, but which, for all that, may be entirely groundless and gratuitous, as we have already attempted to show.

Wholly independently, however, of the argument upon that point, or of the particular application of the act of 1850 to the case of runaway slaves, two distinct sets of objections have been taken to the constitutionality of that act, besides many others to its arbitrary spirit, and its grossly evident disposition (so abundantly illustrated as well by several of its provisions as by many of the proceedings which have taken place under it) to sacrifice the rights of persons claimed to the convenience and even to the rascality of persons claimant.

I. The ground is taken, in the first place, that this return of fugitives from labor is a matter which belongs, at least in its initiative, wholly and exclusively to the authorities and tribunals of the states, and with which Congress has no right to interfere, nor to authorize any body else to interfere, until the proceeding shall have resulted in a suit cognizable by the Federal tribunals. The intention and effect of the clause in the Federal constitution respecting fugitives from labor seems to be, that no right to service under the laws of any state shall be defeated, notwithstanding any differences of local law, by any escape into another state; but to the extent of recapturing such fugitive,—and if the services to which he is bound be of such a nature that the exaction of them is not permitted under the laws of the state in which he is found, still, of holding him for a period sufficient for his removal,—that right shall be recognized and enforced by the tribunals of the state in which the fugitive is found; the proceedings of such state tribunals of course being liable, should the procedure take the form of a judicial contest to be transferred to or reviewed by the Federal courts, under the general jurisdiction given to them in all cases arising under the Federal constitution and laws, there to be proceeded with according to the general methods prescribed in the judiciary acts. To give thus to a South Carolinian, for instance, claiming service or labor from a fugitive found in Massachusetts as due to him under South Carolina law, precisely the same right and the same means, neither more nor less, to reclaim that fugitive, which a Massachusetts man has in Massachusetts in the case of his runaway child or apprentice, would seem to be quite as much as any reasonable slave-holder could ask; at all events quite as much as the Federal constitution ever intended to allow.

According to this view of the matter, no special legislation, whether state or Federal, respecting fugitives from one state into another, is necessary, nor even allowable. The constitution of the United States being the supreme law of the land, and recognized as such by all the State courts and authorities, its provision respecting fugitives is quite sufficient to give, in each state of the Union, through the agency of the state tribunals and state authorities in the first place, or if they fail of their duty, then through the agency of the Federal courts, the same protection and the same justice alike to all claimants and to all fugitives, to whatsoever state they may belong, or upon the laws of whatsoever state their respective rights may be based.

Nor is this view of the case, so reasonable and satisfactory in itself, and so free from the multifarious difficulties and objections to which any other interpretation of the clause in question is exposed,* wanting in support from the most respectable quarters. That Congress has no power to legislate for the return of fugitives from labor, and that the act of 1793 on that subject (and of course the act of 1850) is unconstitutional, was elaborately maintained by Chancellor Walworth, of New York, by his opinion given in the New York Court of Errors in the case of *Jack*

---

* "If, as seems to be admitted, legislation is necessary to carry into effect the object of the constitution, what becomes of the right when there is no law on the subject?" Opinion of Judge Thompson in *Prigg* v. *Pennsylvania*, 16 Peters 631.

v. *Martin*, (14 Wendall, 507) ; and even Mr. Webster, in his famous 7th of March speech, emphatically declared himself to entertain the same view. " I have always thought," such are his words, " that the constitution addressed itself to the legislatures of the states, or to the states themselves. It says that those persons escaping to other states 'shall be delivered up,' and I confess I have always been of the opinion that it was an injunction upon the states themselves. When it is said that a person escaping into another state, and coming, therefore, within the jurisdiction of that state, shall be delivered up, it seems to me the import of the clause is, that the state itself, in obedience to the constitution, shall cause him to be delivered up. That is my judgment. I have always entertained that opinion, and I entertain it now. But when the subject, some years ago, was before the Supreme Court, the majority of the judges held that the power to cause fugitives from service to be delivered up was a power to be exercised under the authority of this (i. e., the Federal) government." The case here alluded to is that of *Prigg* v. *Pennsylvania*, (16 Peters, 539,) of which we shall presently have occasion to speak.

The necessity failing, of any legislation, and especially of any Federal legislation, to carry into effect the clause for the delivering up of fugitives from labor, the only other ground on which any such Federal legislation can be or has been attempted to be sustained, is the mere ground of precedent—the notion so great a favorite with a certain class of lawyers, more learned than profound, that usage makes law, or rather, that the law is to be determined by usage. It is said that the right of Congress to legislate on this subject cannot now be questioned, because that right was exercised by the second Congress, some sixty years ago, and has ever since been acquiesced in ; an argument that seems to count for nothing the adverse opinions of such lawyers as Walworth, Webster, and others to be presently mentioned.

The advocates of this estoppel have a great deal to say (see Nelson's opinion in *Jack* v. *Martin*, in the Supreme Court of New York, 12 Wendall, 311) about the large number of members of the Federal convention who sat also in the Congress of 1793, and of the great and special knowledge which they, and the other members of that Congress, must be supposed to have had of the intimate intentions of the framers of the Federal constitution, and of the true meaning and proper interpretation of that instrument. But to all this there are two very sufficient answers. Whatever knowledge there might have been in the Congress of 1793 of the secret history of the Federal constitution, and of the expectations, hopes, wishes, or intentions of the individuals concerned in framing it, or procuring its ratification, we of the present day—since we have, besides the text of the constitution, the labors of more than sixty years bestowed by the courts and the bar upon its interpretation and exposition—are in a vastly better position for apprehending its real legal purview and effect than the men of 1793, or even than the very men that made it, who, in all the questions that speedily arose as to its interpretation, were even less unanimous than the expositors of to-day. In point of fact, the members of the Federal convention, of whom many subsequently sat in the early Congresses, seem in general to have had but a very imperfect and confused idea of the real nature of the national government which they had created, and of its true relations to the governments of the states. The idea of two, or rather of sixteen coördinate governments so intimately intertwined, and yet each, in its own sphere, sovereign and independent, was at first very difficult to be apprehended, at least in its consequences; and no inconsiderable part of the legislation of the early Congresses—and the fugitive act of 1793 affords an instance of it—proceeded upon the false idea that in the execution of its own powers, Congress and the Federal executive had a right not

22 *

only to employ but to command the officers of the states.

But, in the second place, quite apart from the errors into which a body no better suited for such purposes than Congress would be likely to fall, especially at first, as to the extent of its authority,—the whole theory of the scope of Federal legislation, upon which those who had the control of the early Congresses proceeded, was subsequently greatly modified. The Federalists, as they called themselves, the consolidationists, as they were considered by their opponents, who controlled the early Congresses, and who, like the present Union men, so called, professed a special attachment to the constitution and the Union, proceeded upon the idea of making a strong national government; indeed, of drawing within the range of Federal legislation every thing that might be most conveniently so dealt with—that is to say, about every thing. The Democratic or State Rights party held, on the other hand, that the legislation of Congress ought to be strictly limited to cases expressly authorized by the constitution. Such was the doctrine so emphatically set forth in the famous Resolutions of '98; and such, at this moment, is the doctrine not only ostentatiously professed by those at the head of the Federal government, but which, in a certain modified form at least, has obtained—upon all questions not involving the convenience of slave-holders—pretty entire possession even of the United States tribunals. But surely it cannot be expected, without counting more fully than facts would seem yet to warrant upon the stupidity and patience of the North, that a liberal interpretation of the powers of Congress, rejected in all cases in which the industrial and pecuniary interests of the North have been thought to be concerned, will be tolerated for the sole purpose of propping up the crumbling system of southern despotism. It was natural enough for Mr. Webster, both as an ancient Federalist and as a modern Union man, to yield up as he did, in his 7th of March speech, his own deliberate opinion, long held, and still unaltered, to the formal judgment even of a mere majority of the judges of the Supreme Court of the United States,—for it was the policy of the old Federal, as it now is of our modern, self-styled Union party, (more commonly known as Silver-Grays, or Old Fogies,) to exalt that Supreme Court into a final arbiter, if not indeed an infallible judge, not in private controversies only, but in all political questions also, involving the interpretation—as what political question does not?—of the Federal constitution and laws. But to see Franklin Pierce, who, during his six years' service in the Senate, sat a silent, humble, admiring disciple at the feet of Calhoun; who, as presidential candidate, was the choice, because the submissive catechumen, of the Democratic State Rights party, whose doctrines he took speedy occasion, after his election, to glorify and endorse; and who, as president, professes to walk in the footsteps of Andrew Jackson, he who boldly claimed for himself, and for all the coördinate branches of the government, the right to act under the constitution as they understood it, even in spite of decisions of the Supreme Court; to see this Democratic State Rights president inconsistently striking in with that consistent old Federalist, Mr. Webster, and running in his company, on behalf of slavery, into the most ultra Federal extremes—this is a spectacle rather trying to those who wish to regard the rising leaders of the young democracy of the North as at least tolerably true and sincere men, and not, as their political opponents so indiscriminately represent them, mere unprincipled scamps in pursuit of office, ready to profess and to do every thing tending thereto.

II. But even admitting that the surrender of fugitives from labor is a matter exclusively within the scope of Federal authority, and not only a proper subject for the legislation of Congress, but one upon which Congress is imperatively bound to legislate, (as was held by the majority of the Supreme Court of the United States in the case of *Prigg* v. *Pennsylvania*,) nevertheless, the act of 1850 appears to be grossly unconstitutional in not less than three important particulars.

1. It confers jurisdiction concurrent with that of the judges of the Supreme and Circuit Courts of the United States upon a set of commissioners, mere appointees of the Circuit and Territorial United States Judges; holding office at the will of those who appoint them; paid by fluctuating and uncertain fees, and, in fugitive cases, bribed to decide in favor of the claimant by a double fee in case they do so; uncommissioned by the president, and unsworn—when the constitution of the United States expressly requires that all judges, whether of the Supreme or inferior courts shall hold office during good behavior, and shall, at stated times, receive for their services a compensation which shall not be diminished during their continuance in office; shall be nominated by the president and confirmed by the senate; shall be sworn to support the constitution of the United States, and shall be commissioned by the president.

2. It deprives the alleged fugitive of the right of trial by jury.

3. It substantially denies the writ of habeas corpus by its prohibition to all courts, State or Federal, to inquire under that writ, or any other, into the grounds of the commissioner's certificate, or to correct any errors of fact or law into which he may have fallen.

Although Mr. Webster, in his 7th of March speech, announced his intention to support the bill then on the table of the senate and which subsequently became the act of 1850, " with all its provisions, to its fullest extent," " with some amendments to it," (which, however, he found no opportunity to offer) —yet he carefully avoided on that occasion the slightest allusion to its odious and questionable details. Instead of that he substituted " a solemn appeal to all the sober and sound minds at the North, as a question of morals and a question of conscience, what right they had in their legislative capacity, or any other capacity, to endeavor to get round the constitution, or to embarrass the free exercise of the rights secured by the constitution to the persons whose slaves escape from them."   A perilous appeal, in the making of which the orator seems to have forgotten that sober and sound minds, honest citizens with no political expectations or hopes of mercantile profit to warp their better judgments, might be apt, at the same time, to ask themselves, as a question of morals and a question of conscience, and with even stronger emphasis too, what right they had in their legislative capacity, or in any other capacity, to open a door to kidknapping, or to put to the slightest risk or danger the personal liberty of a single fellow-citizen, however humble his position, empty his purse, or dark his complexion.   Such persons, so appealed to, might be apt to call to mind the adjudication of " another Daniel come to judgment," a case quite as generally known and approved as any recorded in the law books.

Portia. A pound of that same merchant's flesh is thine ;
The court awards it, and the law doth give it.
 Shylock. Most rightful judge !
Portia. And you must cut this flesh from off his breast ;
The law allows it, and the court awards it.
  Shylock. Most learned judge !—A sentence : Come.   Prepare.
   Portia. Tarry a little :—there is something else.
This bond doth give thee here no jot of blood ;
The words expressly are, a pound of flesh.
Take then thy bond, take thou thy pound of flesh ;
But in the cutting it, if thou dost shed
One drop of Christian blood, thy lands and goods
Are, by the laws of Venice, confiscate
Unto the state of Venice.
   Gratiano. O upright judge !—Mark, Jew.   O learned judge !
   Shylock. Is that the law ?
   Portia.   Thyself shall see the act ;
For as thou urgest justice, be assured
Thou shalt have justice more than thou desir'st ——

Though Mr. Webster, in his 7th of March speech, —perhaps on the principle that it is hard to touch

pitch without being defiled by it,—said not a word
on behalf of the particular provisions of the bill,
which, nevertheless, he so fully endorsed; a bill
yielding up not merely the pound of flesh alleged to
be stipulated in the bond, but, along with it, the very
heart's blood of freedom; yet he was soon driven, by
the storm of indignation on the part of many of the
soberest and soundest minds of the North which that
endorsement raised against him, to attempt an apology for the misshapen monster into standing god-
father to which he had been so unfortunately whee-
dled and seduced by such busy gossips as Hangman
Foote. This he did in his letter to the citizens of
Newburyport of May 15th following the delivery of
his 7th of March speech, and containing a double
apology for the bill in question—first, a disquisition
on the nature of the process provided by it, and, secondly, an attempt to justify it by precedent.

It would appear reasonable to judge of the nature
of any proceeding by its effects, which effects in the
case under consideration are sufficiently obvious. A
man lately possessed of freedom is converted into a
chattel, and as such is delivered up to a claimant
who has the whole power of the United States to
back him in carrying off this chattelized man or woman to a slave state, where the mere fact of possession gives to the possessor the legal character and
the almost unbounded legal prerogatives and powers
of master and owner, including imprisonment at
pleasure, and the unrestricted use of the lash and of
starvation, with no liability to question for it, if death
do not immediately ensue. Yet we are gravely told
by Mr. Webster—who, in defect of other arguments,
and destitute, as usual, of all originality, has eagerly
caught at a suggestion dropped probably without
much consideration thirty years before by Chief Justice Tilghman, of Pennsylvania, in a case which we
shall presently have occasion to consider—that a
claim, an adjudication upon it, and the delivery up
of the adjudged chattel into the thus unrestricted

power of the claimant, is no judicial act, no trial, nothing but a mere executive procedure preliminary and auxiliary to a trial, a mere case of extradition, a sending back the fugitive to the state whence he came, in order that his right to freedom may there be tested.

Conscious sophistry and studied falsehood if not somewhat excusable—in a lawyer—are at least somewhat intelligible when there is an object to be answered by them. This suggestion of Tilghman's, adopted by Webster, notwithstanding an express ruling to the contrary by the majority of the Supreme Court of the United States in the case of *Prigg* v. *Pennsylvania*, (see 16 Peters, 616,) being afterwards more fully elaborated and artfully set forth in a legal opinion by an adroit lawyer, was soon followed by that lawyer's elevation to a seat on the bench of that same Supreme Court by the side of the judge of the adjoining circuit, whose previous promotion had a similar antecedent. But so far as concerns the vindication of the Fugitive Act of 1850, this elaborated lie is perfectly gratuitous, because even if it were the truth, it would not help the matter in the least. The framers of the Federal constitution were neither so foolish nor so cruel as to hold out a temptation to kidnappers by giving to every mere private volunteer claimant from any slave state, or pretending to be from some slave state, the right to carry off, on his mere claim, supported wholly by his own oath and other *ex parte* evidence, any resident in any free state, who thus, far removed from all friends and help, might be put to prove his freedom in a country where his very complexion alone would establish a *prima facie* case against him. The constitution contains no provision for delivering up fugitives from labor to parties claimant to be conveyed elsewhere, to the end that the validity of the claim to their service may there be determined. It provides only for a delivery to the party to whom such service or labor may be "due." As to any conveyance elsewhere, not a word is said about

it in the constitution; that is only an incident to the
right to service or labor; and by the express terms of
the provision, no delivery is required, and of course
no such removal can take place till it is first established that such service or labor is due, and due to
the claimant. And, notwithstanding what he wrote
in his Newburyport letter, Mr. Webster was fully
aware of the true character, in this respect, of the
clause in question. This abundantly appears from
his own draft of a Fugitive Bill in amendment of the
act of 1793, which, by a sort of judicial blindness,
such as often betrays prevaricators into furnishing
evidence against themselves, he was led to lay before
the senate—for show, however, merely, not for use—
some three weeks after the date of his Newburyport
letter, and perhaps as a supplement to it. That draft,
he told the senate, had been prepared early in the
session—(and probably it was to go with it that the
greater part of his 7th of March speech had also been
prepared)—in conference with some of the most eminent members of the profession, and especially with
" a high judicial authority," [Judge McLean?] greatly
experienced in questions of this kind. These eminent
advisers had not, indeed, saved the great " expounder
of the constitution " from the obvious oversight of
conferring upon commissioners of the United States
courts complete judicial authority, including the determination upon evidence of " the identity of the
[alleged?] fugitive, the right of the claimant, and the
existence of slavery in the state whence the [alleged?]
fugitive [was said to have?] absconded." But while
thus, for the convenience of the slave-holders, uncer-
emoniously overriding the constitution in a point as
to which, at least, Mr. Webster's eminent *judicial*
adviser might have been expected to be specially
vigilant, some attention was still paid to that instrument in another important respect, in which the act
of 1850 entirely disregards it. Mr. Webster's draft
of a bill expressly provided " that if the [alleged?] fugitive shall deny that he owes service or labor to the

claimant under the laws of the state where he was [alleged to be ?] held, and after being duly cautioned as to the solemnities and consequences of an oath, shall swear to the same, the commissioner or judge shall forthwith summon a jury of twelve to try the right of the claimant, who shall be sworn to try the cause according to evidence, and the commissioner or judge shall preside at the trial, and determine the competency of the proof."

That the Circuit Court commissioners thus invested by this draft, as well as by the act of 1850 with high judicial powers, lacked, in several important respects already mentioned, the constitutional qualifications expressly required in judges, was too plain, when once pointed out, to be denied. Hence the attempt to convert the powers bestowed upon them by the act of 1850 into a merely extradiditory authority—an afterthought, which owes all the little plausibility it has, first, to the accidental juxtaposition, in the text of the Federal constitution, of the provision for the delivery up of fugitives from labor on " the claim of the party to whom such labor may be *due*," with another and wholly distinct provision, for delivering up, "on demand of the executive authorities of the state," fugitives " *charged*, in any state, with treason, felony, or other crimes, to be removed to the state having jurisdiction of the crime;" and secondly, to a like accidental connection of the two subjects in the old fugitive act of 1793. How the two subjects happened to be brought into juxtaposition in the text of the constitution has been shown already in the preceding section. How they happened to be also brought together in the act of 1793, we shall proceed to show,—to do which will lead us back to Mr. Webster's second apology for the bill of 1850, contained in his Newburyport letter— his allegation that the bill of 1850 in principle was but the same thing with the act of 1793.

Of the act of 1793 Mr. Webster's letter gives the following history. " The act of Congress of the 12th of February, 1793, appears to have been well considered,

and to have passed with little opposition. There is
no evidence known to me that any body, at the time,
regarded any of its provisions as repugnant to religion,
liberty, the constitution, or humanity. The two
senators of Massachusetts, at that time, were the dis-
tingnished legislator and patriot of your own county,
George Cabot, and that other citizen of Massachusetts, among the most eminent of his day for talent,
purity of character, and every virtue, Caleb Strong.
Mr. Cabot indeed was one of the committee for preparing the bill. It appears to have passed the senate
without a division. In the house of representatives
it was supported by Mr. Goodhue, Mr. Gerry,—both, I
believe, of your county of Essex, (Mr. Goodhue afterwards a senator of the United States, and Mr.
Gerry afterwards vice-president of the United States,)
Mr. Ames, Mr. Bourne, Mr. Leonard, and Mr. Sedge-
wick, members from Massachusetts, and was passed
by a vote of forty-eight to seven ; of these seven one
being from Virginia, one from Maryland, one from New
York, and four from the New England States, and of
these four one, Mr. Thacher, from Massachusetts.*

" I am not aware that there exists any published
account of the debates on the passage of this act. I
have been able to find none. I have searched the original files, however, and I find among the papers several
propositions for modifications and amendments of various kinds, but none suggesting the propriety of any
jury trial in the state where the party should be arrested."

This history of the act of 1793 is tolerably correct so
far as it goes. But it omits some details as to the
origin of that act curious in themselves, and somewhat essential to the argument, and which therefore
we proceed to supply. On the 11th of May 1788, a

---

* Mr. Thacher, it is proper to note, was, in these early Congresses, the
only consistent and uniform New England opposer of slavery and all
its pretensions. In those times, indeed for the first thirty years subsequent to the adoption of the Federal constitution, almost all the opposition to slavery came from Pennsylvania and New Jersey.

month or two before the Federal constitution became, by the ratification of nine states, an authoritative act, a negro named John was seized in the state of Pennsylvania, (probably under the allegation that he was a runaway slave,) by certain persons in disguise, who bound him and carried him off. On the 11th of November following, bills of indictment were found against one McGuire and two others, as having kidnapped John, and taken him out of the state with intent to sell him as a slave. This proceeding was brought to the notice of Governor Mifflin on the 13th of May, 1791, by a memorial of the "Pennsylvania Society for promoting the abolition of slavery, the relief of free negroes unlawfully held in bondage, and for improving the condition of the African race," in which memorial it was further stated that the indicted parties had precipitately fled from justice either into Virginia, where John was held in a state of slavery by one Nicholas Casey, residing near Romney, or else into the newly erected state of Kentucky.

Shortly after the receipt of this memorial, Mifflin addressed an official letter to Beverly Randolph, governor of Virginia, enclosing the indictment, and the memorial, and requesting him to take the proper steps to cause the fugitives from justice to be delivered up, as provided for in the constitution of the United States. This letter, with its enclosures, Governor Randolph submitted to James Innis, then attorney general of Virginia, who soon after gave an opinion to the following effect: 1st. That by the laws of Virginia the matter charged in the indictments would amount, as between the individual parties, only to a trespass, and as between the offenders and the commonwealth only to a breach of the peace; that the trespass might as well be sued for in Virginia as in Pennsylvania, and that, to an indictment for a mere breach of the peace, the defendants might appear by attorney, so that it would be soon enough to deliver them up after they were convicted. On the presumption, however, that the offence charged stood on the same ground in Pennsylvania that it did in Virginia, it was of too trifling a nature to come under the description of the term *crime*, as used in the Federal constitution. 2d. That the demand was insufficient, in not containing any proof that the persons demanded were in the state. 3d. That if the delivery and removal of the persons demanded could be effected at all, it must be under the authority of the constitution of the United States; but as neither the laws of Virginia nor those of Congress directed the mode, nor delegated any authority by which the magistracy of the state could acquire any legal control over the persons demanded, no such delivery as requested could be made.

This opinion having been transmitted to Mifflin, with Governor Randolph's regrets that no means had yet been provided for carrying into effect so important an article of the Federal constitution, it was forthwith laid before President Washington, with copies of all the other documents, enclosed in a letter from Mifflin, in which he pointed out Innis's apparent ignorance of the act of Pennsylvania under which the indictments had been found, (and which indeed had only been enacted March 29, 1788,) by which the forcibly carrying any person out of the state to be sold as a slave was subjected to a fine of a hundred pounds, and imprisonment to hard labor for not less than six nor more than twelve months.*

Washington, thus appealed to, submitted the case, and all the papers connected with it, to Edmund Randolph, late governor of Virginia, then attorney general of the United States, who, on the 20th of July, gave a very lucid opinion upon it. And here let us observe, that no contemporary authority could be greater than Edmund Randolph's as to the true interpretation of the constitution. No member of the Federal convention, not even Madison himself, had

---

* This act had been copied from one passed just before in Massachusetts, where a great excitement had been produced by the enticement, at Boston, of three colored persons on board a vessel, in which they were carried to the West Indies and sold as slaves.

taken a more active part in framing it, while, as a lawyer, he had then, and has since had, very few equals, and no superiors. Randolph's opinion embraced the following points: 1st. That an indictment found was a sufficient charge on which to base a demand, under the clause of the constitution of the United States, respecting fugitives from justice. 2d. That the matter charged in the Pennsylvania indictments was a crime within the meaning of that clause, and that Innis was mistaken in supposing that the defendants could plead to those indictments by attorney. 3d. That some proof would seem to be necessary, more than had been offered in this case, that the parties demanded had fled from justice, and had been found in the state on which the demand was made. 4th. That, these requisites being fulfilled, *no law, either state or federal, was necessary to authorize their arrest and delivery.* "To deliver up," said Randolph,—and the argument appears to be wholly unanswerable,— "to deliver up is an acknowledged federal duty; *and the law couples with it the right of using all incidental measures in order to discharge it.* I will not inquire how far these incidental means, if opposed to the constitution and laws of Virginia, ought notwithstanding to be exercised, because McGuire and his associates may be surrendered without calling upon any public officer of that state. Private persons may be employed and clothed with a special authority. The attorney general [of Virginia] agrees that a law of the United States might so ordain; *and wherein does a genuine distinction exist between a power deducible from the constitution, or incidental to a duty imposed by the constitution, and a power given by Congress as auxiliary to the execution of such a duty?*

"From these premises I must conclude that it would have been more precise in the governor of Pennsylvania to transmit to the governor of Virginia an authenticated copy of the law creating the offence; that it was essential that he should transmit sufficient evidence of McGuire and others having fled from the

23 *

justice of the former, and being found in the latter; that without that evidence the executive of Virginia ought not to have delivered them up; *that with it they ought not to refuse.* The governor of Pennsylvania, however, appears to be anxious that the matter should be laid before Congress, and perhaps such a step might content all scruples."[*]

This opinion of Randolph's was sent by Washington to Mifflin, who promised, in reply, to renew his demand, accompanied with the additional evidence pointed out by Randolph. Of the result we are not informed; but when the second Congress came together, not long after, for its first session, all the papers, agreeably to Mifflin's original request, were laid by the president before that body. These papers were suffered, in both houses, to lie on their tables undisturbed. The opinion of Randolph was decided and emphatic, that to carry out the provision of the constitution respecting fugitives from justice, no legislation was necessary; and if not necessary, why, then, not constitutional,—though that was a consideration as yet not much attended to,—since the legislative power of Congress does not extend to the satisfying of scruples, but only to cases in which authority to legislate is expressly given, or is necessary to carry out powers conferred by the constitution on the general government—to neither of which categories did this case belong. In the course, however, of the next session, a committee was appointed in the senate, consisting of Johnston, of North Carolina, Cabot, of Massachusetts, and Reed, of Delaware, " to consider the expediency of a law respecting fugitives from justice, and persons escaping from the service of their

---

[*] It is rather curious that, although several judges have referred, in their opinions, to the origin of the act of 1793, and the correspondence between Governor Mifflin and Randolph, not one of them has even hinted at the existence of Attorney General Randolph's opinion, which is republished, however, along with the other documents, in Lowrie & Franklin's great folio Collection of American State Papers, Miscellaneous Documents, vol. i. p. 39.

masters, and to report by bill, (if they think proper ;) " which committee, about a month after, did report a bill, which bill, after some modifications, passed into the fugitive act of 1793.

That act consists of four sections, the first two of which, relating to fugitives from justice, have been often vouched in to support the right of Congress to legislate respecting fugitives from labor. They are used for that purpose by Story, who, speaking on behalf of himself and seven other judges of the Supreme Court of the United States, in *Prigg* v. *Pennsylvania*, (p. 620,) triumphantly flourishes the constitutionality of those sections as never having been called in question, and their provisions as having been uniformly acted upon by all the state executives. And for the best of reasons, too. These sections require nothing which, independently of the act of 1793, the governors of the states were not bound to do by the constitution itself; and though having no authority as a law, and in that respect a work of supererogation, they may, doubtless, have been convenient as suggesting a uniform method of complying with the requisition of the constitution. As to the penalty inflicted by the second section on persons rescuing fugitives while under transportation, the constitutionality of that provision seems to rest upon the same alleged authority in Congress, under which the Federal courts sustained the constitutionality of the Sedition law, and of the act to punish counterfeiters of the bills of the Bank of the United States; and I therefore turn it over, without further comment, to be dealt with by the adherents of the Resolutions of '98, in which both those penal acts were specially and emphatically denounced as unconstitutional, for want of power in Congress to enact them. Yet, to help the better to a decision of the point, I will venture to suggest the inquiry, whether the governors of the states could be subjected, by federal legislation, to fine and imprisonment, for declining to surrender fugitives from justice ?

We come now to the two latter sections of the act of 1793,—those relating to fugitives from labor.

"For many years," so we are told by Mr. Webster in his Newburyport letter, "little or no complaint was made against this law, nor was it supposed to be guilty of the offences and enormities which have since been charged upon it. It was passed for the purpose of complying with a direct and solemn injunction of the constitution. It did no more than was believed to be necessary to accomplish that single purpose; and it did that in a cautious, mild manner, to be every where conducted according to *judicial proceedings*.

"I confess I see no more objections to the provisions of this law than was seen by Mr. Cabot, Mr. Strong, Mr. Goodhue, and Mr. Gerry; and such provisions appear to me, as they appeared to them, to be absolutely necessary, if we mean to fulfil the duties positively and peremptorily enjoined upon us by the constitution of the country." [How so, if, in Mr. Webster's judgment, as declared in his 7th of March speech, the constitutional injunction was entirely on the states?]

"But since the agitation caused by the abolition societies and abolition presses has, to such an extent, excited the public mind, these provisions have been rendered obnoxious and odious. Unwearied efforts have been made, and too successfully, to rouse the passions of the people against them, and under the cry of universal freedom, and *under that other cry, that there is a rule for the government of public men and private men which is of superior obligation to the constitution of the country*, several of the states have enacted laws to hinder, obstruct and defeat the enactments in this act of Congress to the utmost of their power."

Such are the representations of Mr. Webster; such is his attempt to hide the nakedness of the act of 1850 and his own under the skirts of the act of 1793, and of its respectable authors and supporters. Those of them mentioned by Mr. Webster were all Federalists, (with the single exception of Gerry) some of them very ultra Federalists, but not one of them disposed to erect the Federal constitution either into a Diana of Ephesus by the perpetual shouting of whose name all gainsayers were to be silenced, or into a golden calf, which priests and people were alike to fall down to and worship, to the forgetfulness of any Higher Law. It is due, therefore, to the memory of these worthy men, and no less so to the assailants of the act of 1793, to state, that although that act was complained of from the very moment of its enactment by the Pennsylvania Abolition Society and others in repeated memorials to Congress, as opening altogether too wide and dangerous a door to kidnappers, yet that the indignation against it, to the results of which Mr. Webster more particularly refers, grew mainly not so much out of any thing really contained in the act itself, or intended by those who enacted it, as out of a most ungracious, cruel, and gratuitous interpretation forced out of it by a set of " consummate lawyers " of the Scott school,—men who regard personal rights in comparison with the protection of property, at least the personal rights of the poor and helpless, as nothing ; and who, ridiculously expecting to chain up and tie down the natural sentiments of justice and equity by the dry withes of their subtle ingenuity, in attempting, like the authors of the act of 1850, to lay a rising breeze, succeeded only, as the authors of that act have done, in raising a whirlwind.

An examination of the brief Federal statute book of 1793,—for then it was brief,—will lead us to the evident model after which the fugitive act of 1793 was drawn ; which model will not a little assist us to ascertain the idea entertained by those who framed the act of 1793, and by those who passed it with so little debate, of its real meaning and practical operation.

Among the acts passed by the first Congress was one, approved July 20th, 1790, " For the government and regulation of seamen in the merchant service," chiefly modelled after the English acts of parliaments on that subject, and of which the 7th section contained the following provisions: " That if any seaman or mariner, who shall have signed a contract to perform a voyage, shall, at any port or place, desert, or shall absent himself from such ship or vessel without leave of the master, or officer commanding in the absence of the master, it shall be lawful for any justice of the peace within the United States (upon complaint of the master) to issue his warrant to apprehend such deserter, and bring him before such justice ; and if it shall then appear, by due proof, that he has signed a contract within the intent and meaning of this act, and that the voyage agreed for is not finished, altered, or the contract otherwise dissolved, and that such seaman or mariner has deserted the ship or vessel, or absented himself without leave, the said justice shall commit him to the house of correction or common jail of the city, town, or place, there to remain until the said ship or vessel shall be ready to proceed on her voyage, or till the master shall require his discharge, and then to be delivered to the said master, he paying all the costs of such commitment, and deducting the same out of the wages due to such seaman or mariner."

Now, Mr. Cabot, one of the members of the committee of three by which the act of 1793 was reported, was not only a merchant, but he had been a shipmaster ; and it was undoubtedly he who suggested to his colleagues this provision respecting fugitive seamen, as a model to be followed in the case of other fugitives from labor.   Hence the 3d section of the act of 1793, which provides, " That when a person held to labor in any of the United States, or in either of the territories on the north-west or south of the river Ohio, under the laws thereof, shall escape into any other of the said states, or territory, the person to whom such labor or service may be due, his agent or attorney, is hereby empowered to seize or arrest such fugitive from labor, and to take him or her before any judge of the Circuit or District Courts of the United States, residing or being within the state, or before any magistrate of a county, city, or town corporate, wherein such seizure or arrest shall be made; and upon proof to the satisfaction of such judge or magistrate, either by oral testimony, or affidavit taken before and certified by a magistrate of any such state or territory, that the person so seized and arrested doth, under the laws of the state or territory from which he or she fled, owe service or labor to the person claiming him or her, it shall be the duty of such judge or magistrate to give a certificate thereof to such claimant, his agent or attorney, which shall be sufficient warrant for removing the said fugitive from labor to the state or territory from which he or she fled." The fourth and last section of the act imposes a penalty of five hundred dollars, to be recovered in any court proper to try the same, for the benefit of the claimant, from any one who should obstruct him in rescuing his fugitive, or should rescue such fugitive from him, or should harbor or conceal such fugitive, after notice that he was claimed as such.

As the resemblance is sufficiently obvious between the provision for arresting fugitive seamen and that for arresting other fugitives from labor, so the difference of procedure in the two cases is easily explained. In the latter case, there being no documentary evidence like the shipping paper to go upon, no action was to be taken by the judge or magistrate till after the arrest. The whole responsibility of that, and of taking care to seize nobody to whose services he had not a legal right, was very properly thrown upon the claimant, who was thus precluded from making use of process of arrest obtained on his own bare oath or other ex parte evidence, for any fraudulent or kidnapping purposes—a particular in which there is an essential difference between the act of 1793 and that of 1850.

The intention of the act for the arrest of fugitive mariners, and that of 1793 for the arrest of fugitives from labor, seems to be clear. That intention evidently was to provide a summary process to be used in cases where there was no dispute about the facts or as to the right of the claimant, leaving open to any person against whom such summary decision might be made, all the courts, state and federal, and all the processes, whether writ of habeas corpus, writ *de homine replegiando* (or of personal replevin),—this last involving a trial by jury,—or any other commonly resorted to by persons restrained of their liberty, or seeking to get possession of the persons of others. The commitment of the justice in the one case, his warrant in the other, was to be a lawful authority for retaining the seaman, or adjudged fugitive from labor, as against any private interference; but neither of them was intended to act as a bar to full investigation into the rights of the parties by the ordinary course of law. I am not aware that any court or any lawyer has ever yet pretended that the action of a justice of the peace in committing an adjudged deserting seaman to prison, or to the custody of the master, is absolutely final and conclusive, turning the seaman over to his suit for false imprisonment, and not to be otherwise inquired into or reviewed by any court, state or federal; and it was the pretended discovery in the act of 1793, of this alarming potency, that first raised against it that loud and increasing clamor of which Mr. Webster so bitterly complains.

Constant recourse to historical facts, and an exploration of contemporaneous ideas, have been deemed essential to the true interpretation of the constitutional provisions bearing, or supposed to bear, on slavery. Nor are such external aids any the less necessary towards understanding the course of judicial decisions touching the same subject. The conclusion of the war of 1812–15 was followed by a rapid extension of the cultivation of cotton, which speedily grew, with the decline of the foreign demand for breadstuffs, to be the chief article of export. This extension of cotton cultivation, besides those constantly expand-

ing scheme of territorial aggrandizement in a southern
direction, so vigorously sketched by Mr. Webster in his
7th of March speech, also gave rise to that domestic
slave-trade—that breeding of slaves for sale—a point
too delicate for that class of preachers who " never
mention hell to ears polite," and therefore omitted by
Mr. Webster,—yet chiefly instrumental in producing
that change of opinion at the south on the subject
of slavery upon which he dwells with so much
emphasis in his 7th of March speech ; and, indeed, a
coincident change of opinion at the North, at least
among ship-owners, merchants, manufacturers, and
politicians, no less remarkable.

This domestic slave-trade was a rude shock to that
patriarchal character to which, on some of the older
plantations of Maryland, Virginia and the Carolinas,
slavery had attained some shadow of title.* By keeping constantly before the eyes of the enslaved the
gloomy prospect of the auction-block and the slave
trader's chain-gang, it greatly increased their inclination to run away. If they must quit the localities to

---

* This trade, at its first commencement, was not less loudly denounced in Maryland and Virginia than the African slave trade had
been during the revolutionary period. John Randolph stigmatized
it, in 1816, on the floor of Congress, as " heinous and abominable,"
" inhuman and illegal." Even Governor Williams, of South Carolina, spoke of it, in one of his messages to the legislature of that
state, as " a remorseless and merciless traffic," " a ceaseless dragging
along the streets and highways of a crowd of suffering victims to
minister to insatiable avarice," not only " condemned by enlightened
humanity, wise policy and the prayers of the just," but tending, by
its introduction of slaves of all descriptions, to " defile the delightful
avocations of private life by the presence of convicts and malefactors."
(See Hildreth's *History of the United States*, vol vi. pp. 613–14.)

This same traffic, however, proving the chief resource of the impoverished planters of Virginia, Maryland and the Carolinas, many
of whom now live, to use the expressive local phraseology, by eating
their negroes, it has come to be cherished and defended in those
states with as much zeal as the merchants of Bristol and Liverpool
ever exhibited on behalf of the African slave-trade, or as is exhibited
on behalf of it to-day by the petty kings who live by it on the
African coast.

For Mr. Webster's remarks on the change of sentiment at the
South, and some corrections of the exaggerations into which he has
fallen, see *Appendix*.

which habit had so strongly attached them, they greatly preferred the free air of the North to the fever-breeding swamps of the South. It produced, also, another result not less deplorable. Traders for the southern market were found ready enough to purchase " likely negroes " without any particular inquiry into the means by which the possession of them had been acquired ; and in the free states nearest the slave-holding frontier, and in which the free colored people were the most numerous, so great were the abuses by ignorant and corrupt justices of the peace and other local magistrates, of the authority vested in them by the act of 1793, and the facilities thereby afforded for kidnapping, as soon to give occasion to very loud complaints. An attempt was even made in 1817, in the senate of the United States, to amend that law, so as to guard against these abuses ; but apprehensions lest the proposed changes might diminish the facilities for recovering runaways caused that attempt to be opposed and abandoned. The border slave-holders, on the other hand, provoked at the shelter, aid and concealment often afforded in the free states, and especially in Pennsylvania, to their runaway slaves, called loudly for a still more stringent law ; and in 1818, after a pretty warm struggle, they succeeded in carrying a bill of that sort through both houses of Congress. That bill, a sort of forerunner of the act of 1850, authorized the claimant to establish his claim on ex parte evidence before some judge of his own state, having done which he was to be entitled to an executive demand upon the governor of the state in which the fugitive might be found, heavy penalties being imposed upon all who refused to aid in the arrest. The senate added a provision, that after the removal, the person removed should be proved to be the same with the person claimed by some evidence other than the oath of the claimant. This amendment, by giving the northern members time to bethink themselves, defeated the passage of the bill, which, after its return from the senate, was left, notwithstanding repeated attempts to take it up, to lie and to die on the table of the house.*

The Supreme Court of Pennsylvania had lately (1816) given high offence to the slave-holders by deciding, in the case of *The Commonwealth* v. *Holloway*, 2 Seargent & Rawle's Reports, 305, apparently on impregnable grounds, that the children of fugitive slave women born in Pennsylvania more than a year after the arrival of their mothers in the state, were born free; and that, such children being neither fugitives, nor owing service to any body as slaves, no claimant from abroad could touch them. In 1819 came before the same court the case of *Wright* v. *Deacon*, 5 Seargent & Rawle, 62, on a writ of *de homine replegiando* sued out against Deacon, keeper of the Philadelphia jail, who held in custody the plaintiff Wright, at the request, and for the temporary convenience, of a claimant who had obtained a certificate to remove Wright, as a fugitive from service. The object was to obtain a review, and a trial by jury, of the grounds on which the certificate had been granted. But the court, taking a far less lawyer-like as well as less statesman-like view than that of Edmund Randolph above cited, held, 1st. That "it required a law [of Congress] to regulate the manner in which the claim should be made and the fugitive delivered up," and, on this ground, that the act of 1793 was constitutional—the first reported judicial decision ever pronounced on that point; and 2dly. That a certificate granted under the act of 1793 was absolutely conclusive as to the rights of both parties, at least until the removal authorized by it had been completed; and that after such certificate had once been granted, no state court, nor indeed any court, had any right to interfere, or to re-examine the case, either by writ of habeas corpus, writ of personal replevin, or any other method. This opinion, in which the three judges concurred,

* For further particulars respecting this bill, see Hildreth's *History of the United States*, vol. vi. pp. 635-7.

was delivered by William Tilghman, the chief justice. It is quite short, and the following paragraph embraces the most essential part of it. " It plainly appears from the whole scope and tenor of the constitution and act of Congress, that the fugitive was to be delivered up on a summary proceeding, without the delay of a formal trial in a court of common law. But if he had really a right to freedom, that right was not impaired by that proceeding ; he was placed just in the situation in which he stood before he fled, and might prosecute the right in the state to which he belonged." Here we see the origin of Mr. Webster's idea of extradition, an idea involving a prejudgment of the case in two of its most essential points ; wholly cutting off from his most obvious rights every person certified as a fugitive, but not such in reality ; and every person actually a fugitive, but certified as owing service to a claimant having no legal title to such service. What a heartless, insolent mockery to tell a native citizen of Pennsylvania, about to be transferred to South Carolina on a certificate, purchased perhaps by a bribe of five dollars— for it is but reasonable to suppose that some state magistrates may be bought at the average price established by the act of 1850 for United States commissioners ;—what a mockery to tell such a person, about to be placed in a pestiferous South Carolina rice swamp, with an iron chain and ball of fifty pounds' weight attached to his leg, and an iron collar with four prongs to it about his neck, that his right to freedom will not be impaired by this proceeding; that he is placed in the same situation in which he stood before the certificate was granted, and that he can prosecute his right in the state to which he belongs ! Such is the enormous absurdity involved in this opinion of Tilghman's, and in that of every judge and lawyer by whom it has been followed, all growing out of the gratuitous assumption, contained also in the very phraseology of Mr. Webster's draft of a bill, that every person claimed, or at least every person certified, must be a fugitive, and a fugitive owing labor to the person who claims him. But besides this prejudgment of the case in its most essential particulars, this opinion and all its echoes totally overlook the plain distinction between cases where the right of the claimant is confessed, or not contested, — as, for instance, in the case of tenants holding over, in which cases alone summary proceedings for the enforcement of rights are ever allowed,—and contested cases, in which it is the undoubted common law right of every party to have a thorough trial, both as to facts and law; especially before so serious a step is taken as the delivering him up as a chattel into the absolute power of another. So far from infringing that right, the Federal constitution has taken care specially to guard it; and, surely, it is one from which no party, however humble or helpless, is to be ousted by any implication or construction, nor, indeed, by any thing short of the most express and positive provision in terms.

Chief Justice Tilghman was a lawyer of moderate temper and decent abilities, (and the same description will apply to his colleagues), belonging to that very large class of jurists, to make one of which requires nothing but an ordinary share of judgment, diligence, and experience,—a kind of men sufficiently well adapted to the ordinary routine of the bench, but pretty certain to make some egregious blunder the moment they attempt to step beyond it. A decided Federalist, one of John Adams's midnight judges, Tilghman had been ousted from that seat by the repeal of the act under which he held office, but shortly after had been raised to the chief-justiceship of Pennsylvania by Governor McKean, at a time when that political gamester, having quarrelled with the more radical Democrats to whom he was indebted for his original election, had found it necessary to sustain himself in office by courting the aid of the Federalists. Tilghman and his colleagues probably hoped that so peremptory a decision might help to quiet the rising excitement in Pennsylvania on the subject of the

24*

reclamation of fugitives occasioned by the growing
frequency of such claims, and of kidnappings alleged
to be perpetrated under their cover, and to which
the contemporaneous controversy as to the extension
of slavery into Missouri added no little fervor. But
if such was their expectation, they found themselves
mistaken. Their harsh and unwarrantable interpretation of the act of 1793 at once overwhelmed that
act with universal odium. Hence arose the agitation against it of which Mr. Webster so bitterly
complains; an agitation in which the legislatures
of the Middle States took the lead, by enactments
of which the object was to put some restriction upon
the despotic energy which Tilghman and his colleagues
had construed into that act; restrictions for which a
recent decision of the Supreme Court of the United
States seemed to open the way.

That court, in the celebrated and much contested
case of *Hunter* v. *Martin's Lessee*, (1 Wheaton, 330,)
decided in 1816, in maintaining their right under the
constitution to issue to the Supreme Courts of the
states writs of error, in cases involving the interpretation of the constitution and laws of the United States,
had called attention to a provision of the Federal
constitution, which, under the impulse of economizing
Federal officers and salaries, seems, on more occasions than one, to have escaped the attention of the
members of the earlier Congresses, though so many of
them had sat in the Federal convention. That provision required that " the judicial power of the United
States shall be vested in one Supreme Court, and in
such inferior courts as the Congress may from time to
time *order and establish;*" which clause was held, in the
case above cited, to prohibit Congress " to vest any
portion of the judicial power of the United States, except in courts ordained and established by itself." Upon
the strength of this doctrine, and very soon after it was
declared, occasion was found, in the case of certain
parties bound over to trial for violation of the neutrality
acts in fitting out privateers to sail under the flags of the

new South American republics, to call in question the authority conferred by the 33d section of the judiciary act of 1789, upon justices of the peace, concurrently with the judges of the United States District Courts, to arrest and commit for trial, or to release on bail, persons charged with offences against the United States. This objection was sustained by some of the district judges, and Congress, in consequence, passed an act, (March 1, 1817,) conferring these same concurrent powers of arrest, examination, commitment, and release on bail, upon certain commissioners, whom, by a previous act of February 20, 1812, the Circuit Courts had been authorized to appoint for the purpose of taking affidavits and acknowledgments of bail in civil cases. Such was the origin of judicial powers exercised by commissioners of the Circuit Courts. But though these new officers were "ordained and established" by Congress, still they were obnoxious, in common with justices of the peace, to other objections already mentioned—having neither the tenure of office nor the stated salary required by the very same section of the constitution, and being neither appointed by the president nor subject to confirmation by the senate; guarantees against partiality and corruption quite as necessary in committing officers, and especially in such officers as these commissioners have come to be, under the act of 1845 and the fugitive act of 1850, as in those whose decisions as to matters of fact require the coöperation of a jury, and whose whole procedure is checked by the solemnity and notoriety of a formal trial.

Availing themselves of the decision of the Supreme Court of the United States, in *Hunter* v. *Martin's Lessee*, that Congress had no authority to command the services of the state tribunals, the assembly of Pennsylvania, justly shocked at the new interpretation put upon the act of 1793 by their Supreme Court, passed a law, (March 22, 1820,) by which the execution of the act of 1793 was restricted, so far as the state officers of Pennsylvania were concerned, to the

judges of the County Courts, who were required,
whenever they granted a certificate, to file with the
clerk of the county a record of the whole proceedings,
containing the names of the parties and witnesses,
and a statement of the evidence upon which the cer
tificate had been granted.   Aldermen and justices of
the peace were forbidden to grant certificates at all;
and it was made a felony to carry any negro or mulatto out of the state, without process, with intent to
hold him as a slave.   Afterwards, by an act of 1826,
passed at the earnest request of the authorities of
Maryland, the law of 1820 was so far modified as,
under certain restrictions, to restore jurisdiction to
justices of the peace and aldermen; but the other
provisions of the act of 1820, and especially the
penalties for removal without process, were continued
in full force.

Nor was Pennsylvania the only state to legislate
on this subject.   Her act was subsequently (1836–7)
incorporated, with some trifling modifications, into
the statute book of New Jersey.   At a still earlier
day the legislature of New York, in preparing a
revised code for that state, (1827–30,) imposed several
similar restrictions upon the action of her magistrates
and judges under the act of 1793.   She not only prohibited, as Pennsylvania had, the carrying away
of any alleged fugitive slave without process, but all
claimants who failed to make out their claims were
subjected to heavy costs and damages.   The same act,
in defiance of Tilghman's decision, specially reserved
to all alleged fugitives for whom certificates might be
granted, a right to review that proceeding, upon
habeas corpus or writ de homine replegiando, a process which involved, as we have already mentioned,
a trial by jury; which trial by jury was also authorized
by a subsequent act in cases in which the rehearing
took place under a writ of habeas corpus.

The bench of the Supreme Court of the state of
New York has often been occupied by very able
jurists.   At that time, under a recent reorganization,

it consisted of three judges, none of them of any extraordinary reputation, and whatever might be their political professions, all of them as thoroughly Federal, at least in slave cases, as Tilghman himself. This Supreme Court, in 1834, in the case of *Jack* v. *Martin*, (12 Wendall, 311,) set aside these provisions of the state legislature by holding, 1st. That Congress had the right to legislate to give effect to the clause in the Federal constitution respecting fugitives from labor; 2dly. That the act of 1793 overrode and ousted all state legislation on the subject; and 3d. That the object of the constitutional provision evidently being the return of fugitive slaves, the act of 1793 "should receive a construction such as, consistently with its terms, would operate most effectually to secure the end"—in other words, that any protection of the citizens of New York against false or unfounded claims ought not to be thought of or provided for, when such provision might be liable to interfere with the most summary proceedings in favor of southern slave claimants!*

This opinion, a mere wire-drawing in pages of what Tilghman had expressed in paragraphs, was pronounced by Judge Nelson; and according to a very remarkable coincidence, (if, in fact, it was entirely accidental,) upon the first vacancy he was raised to a seat upon the bench of the Supreme Court of the United States, successor to Thompson, and by the side of Baldwin, both of whom, it is worthy of note, had, previously to their appointments, taken strong slave-holding ground on the question of extending slavery into Missouri. And we may add, what makes these coincidences the more remarkable, that since the date of the Missouri compromise, not a single northern

---

* This case afterwards went up to the New York Court of Errors, but was decided there (14 Wendall, 507) in favor of the claimant, on the ground that the plaintiff, by his pleas, had confessed himself the claimant's slave. Any expression of opinion by the court on the constitutionality of the act of 1793, or upon the New York statute provisions, was carefully avoided, although, Chancellor Walworth, sitting as one of the judges, took that occasion to pronounce a formal opinion, already referred to, against the constitutionality of the act of 1793.

man—with the exception of Judge McLean, who was
appointed for political convenience to get him out of
an office which it was desired to fill otherwise—has
been raised to the bench of the Supreme Court of
the United States, except under similar circumstances ;
at least the only other possible exception is Judge
Grier, the successor of Baldwin, whose reputation,
previous to his appointment,—though, like his prede-
cessor, a man of decided legal ability,—was so merely
local, that I am not at present able to specify the
particular services, if any, which he had rendered to
the slave power.   But that the man was well known,
his violence, I may even say his ferocity, on the bench,
in behalf of the law of 1850, sufficiently shows.

Prior to the elevation of these latter serviceable
judges, and while Thompson and Baldwin still sat in
the Supreme Court, the question of the constitutionality of the act of 1793, and of the true interpretation
and effect of the clause in the Federal constitution
respecting the delivering up of fugitives from service,
came before that court in the celebrated case, already
repeatedly referred to, of *Prigg* v. *Pennsylvania*.
Prigg, a citizen of Maryland, had been indicted,
under the Pennsylvania act of 1826, for carrying out
of that state, without process or warrant, a negro
woman whom he claimed as his slave, and with her
several of her children, one of which, born more than
a year after the mother's arrival in Pennsylvania, according to a decision of the Supreme Court of
Pennsylvania already cited, was born a free person.

After a great deal of controversy between the two
states, Prigg having been demanded as a fugitive
from the justice of Pennsylvania, and the governor
of Maryland, as usual in such cases, refusing to deliver
him up, by an arrangement of the state legislatures
the question of the validity of the law of Pennsylvania was brought before the Supreme Court of the
United States on an agreed statement of facts, in the
form of a special verdict, in which it was admitted,
among other things, that the woman carried off had

been Prigg's slave, and had escaped from him into Pennsylvania, and also that one of the children carried off with her had been born in Pennsylvania more than a year after her arrival there.

All the judges agreed that Prigg was entitled to be discharged from the indictment; but in the view which they took of the law of the case, they differed not a little. Story, who pronounced the judgment of the court, began by a most remarkable avowal. The court, he said, did not mean to be held to apply to any other clause whatever of the constitution, any rules which, in the present case, they might see fit to lay down for interpreting the provision respecting fugitives from labor. In fact the constitution was so peculiar an instrument, made so much in the spirit of compromise, that all general rules for its interpretation seemed out of the question. It must be interpreted in the same spirit in which it had been made, and each clause must be handled by itself, according to the good discretion of the court.

In promulgating this new rule of judicial interpretation, or rather this declaration of independence and disregard of all rules, perhaps calculated to increase the already somewhat too "glorious uncertainty of the law," but also very convenient for timid and time-serving tribunals, the learned judge appears to have forgotten—or perhaps he only intended to confirm by a striking practical application of it—the strong remark of Lord Camden, that "the discretion of a judge is the *law of tyrants*, in the best ofttimes caprice, in the worst every vice, folly, and passion of which human nature is liable." Its immediate object, no doubt, was to save his brethren, and indeed himself, from certain obvious charges of inconsistency, some of which will be presently pointed out.

After this singular preamble, Story proceeded to state a point in which all the judges except McLean agreed; namely, that the clause in the Federal constitution respecting fugitives from labor is of potency and vigor enough, independently of any special Fed-

eral or state legislation, to give to a party to whom
labor is really due, under the laws of any state, the
right, in any and every other state, to seize, without
any process, and to carry off his fugitive whenever he
can do so without any act of violence amounting to
a breach of the peace. This point was in perfect
accordance with the opinion of Edmund Randolph,
heretofore cited. It had been expressly ruled by the
Supreme Courts of New York and Massachusetts in
the cases of *Glen* v. *Hodges*, (9 Johnson, 67,) and of
Commonwealth v. *Griffith*, (2 Pickering, 11,) as well as
by the Supreme Court of Pennsylvania in the case
of *Wright* v. *Deacon*. And according to the view set
forth at the beginning of this section, such a right
of seizure, without process, and without any special
legislative provision for it, must exist in all the states
whose local laws, as is generally the case, concede a
similar right of recaption whenever the control or
custody of the person of one individual is vested, by
the law, in another. But of course all such recaptions
are subject, as in all other cases of the exercise of a
similar power, to have their grounds inquired into by
the state courts.

Yet though supported by such authorities, the rule
of constitutional interpretation here adopted seems
in direct conflict with a decision made by this same
Supreme Court of the United States only the
very year before, in a case involving the effect and
force of a provision in the constitution of the state
of Mississippi. That constitution contained the following clause: " The introduction of slaves into
this state as merchandise or for sale shall be prohibited from and after the first day of May, 1833; provided
the actual settler or settlers shall not be prohibited
from purchasing slaves in any state in this Union, and
bringing them into this state for his own individual
use till 1845,"—which clause, in the case of *Graves
& al.* v. *Slaughter*, (15 Wheaton, 449,) had been set
up as invalidating a note given for slaves brought into
Mississippi as merchandise, and sold there subsequent-

ly to May 1833. In that case, for the protection of the slave-traders, who had retained Clay and Webster as their counsel, the court held that this constitutional provision was a mere injunction on the legislature, and of no effect till first it had been complied with by the enactment of a law for enforcing it. It is, however, but justice to state, that three of the judges, Story, McKinley, and Baldwin, dissented from this decision, while a fourth, Daniel, who now concurred with the majority, was not then a member of the court. The two former had held, consistently enough with their present opinion, that the constitutional provision was efficacious in itself, and the contract therefore void. Baldwin did not deny the right of a state entirely to prohibit the introduction of slaves as a matter of internal policy, but he regarded the provision in the constitution of Mississippi as a bare attempt to regulate the internal slave-trade, and to give to residents in the state advantages over citizens of other states, and on that ground he held the provision void, as conflicting with the exclusive right of Congress to regulate trade between the states.

Such had been the rule of constitutional interpretation held by the Supreme Court of the United States in 1841. In 1842 the convenience of slave-holding seemed to require a totally opposite decision, and, true to their doctrine of being tied up by no rules, the majority of the court now ran headlong with Story into the opposite extreme. Not only did they find in the bare constitutional injunction, with respect to fugitives from labor, an indefeasible right of recapture, independent of all special legislation state or national,—they allowed Story to put forth, in their name, the extravagant statement that "the constitutional clause puts the right to the service and labor upon the same ground, *and to the same extent*, in every other state as in the state to which the slave escaped, and in which he was held to service or labor;" and that "any state law that *interrupts*, *limits*, *delays*, and *postpones* the right of the owner to the immediate possession of his slave, or the *immediate command of his services*, operating *pro tanto* as a discharge, is unconstitutional." Whence it would follow, that a Virginia slave-holder has the right, not only to recapture his runaway slave in Massachusetts, but, if he pleases, there to beat, work, imprison, or starve him, at his pleasure, short of immediate death, (even the statute against cruelty to animals being unconstitutional as to him) ; and, if the slave be a woman, of compelling her to share his bed as his concubine,—all of which are " incidents " in Virginia to the right of slave-holding ;—and to continue to enjoy these incidents for any period that he may choose to remain in Massachusetts. Some such rights have been claimed, indeed, by some of the slave-holders as appertaining to them in the territories ; but never yet, so far as I know, have any of them pretended, under any circumstances, to any such rights within the limits of a free state. Even the claimants of fugitive slaves have been too modest and forbearing to attempt any thing of the sort, notwithstanding this high judicial warrant for doing so.

But not content with thus giving to the master of a fugitive slave, found within the limits of a free state, all the rights, including the right of recapture without warrant, which he would have had at home, Story, with some other judges, (McLean now supplying the place of Baldwin, who dissented,) goes on to hold, not only to the right, but to the imperative duty, of Congress to reënforce this constitutional provision by special legislation. The master " may not be able to lay his hand upon the slave. He may not be able to enforce his rights against persons who either secrete, or conceal, or withhold the slave. He may be restricted, by local legislation, as to the modes of proofs of his ownership, as to the courts in which he shall sue, and as to the actions which he may bring, or the process he may use to compel the delivery of the slave ; "—that is to say, he may be put upon precisely the same level as to his remedies with other claimants of property or personal rights, whether native or foreign. But this, according to the Supreme Court of the United States, would be a gross and intolerable violation of the peculiar and sacred rights secured by the constitution to the owners of fugitive slaves ; for the sustentation of which rights it is the duty of Congress to interfere, and, *under the judicial authority vested in the general government,* to provide, at whatever risk to free citizens of non-slave-holding states, a swift and certain method of delivery, such as will leave to fugitive slaves no possible chance of escape. The constitutionality of the act of 1793 is thus placed by the Supreme Court of the United States upon the express ground (Mr. Webster and other apologists for the act of 1850 to the contrary notwithstanding) that the surrender of a fugitive from labor is, " in the strictest sense, *a controversy between the parties,* and *a case,* under the constitution of the United States, *within the express delegation of judicial power,* given by that instrument." As to the objection that the justices of the peace and other state magistrates in whom the authority to grant certificates is concurrently vested are state officers, the court hastily pass by that, with the suggestion, that though not bound to exercise this jurisdiction, still they may do so, as long as the states do not prohibit them. But suppose this assertion to be consistent (which it hardly seems to be) with the doctrine so peremptorily laid down in *Martin* v. *Hunter's Lessee,* or supposing this new doctrine to be the better law, which must be esteemed very doubtful, still it does not touch the other and unanswerable objections of want of proper tenure and salary.

We come now to another point of the case, in which there was less unanimity. Story, Wayne, McKinley, and Catron held—and on this point they were again supported by McLean, thus still making a majority of the court—that not only was it the duty as well as right of Congress to enforce by legislation the surrender of fugitives from labor, but that the right to legislate on this subject was vested exclusively in Congress. It was this point doubtless that chiefly recommended the decision of the court to Story. Not only did it gratify his ultra Federal ideas, in which, though raised to the bench as a Jeffersonian Democrat, he far outran those eminent Federalists, Chief Justices Marshall and Taney, but it seemed to him, as he afterwards boasted in private conversation, to strike a deadly blow at the surrender of fugitive slaves, by relieving the states from all obligation to coöperate in it. Of the four judges who went with Story on this point, three were from slave-holding circuits; but as those circuits were remote from the frontier, they did not feel the immediate smart either of having lost slaves themselves, or of sympathy with friends and neighbors who had. Taney and Daniel were differently situated, and these two border judges, supported by Thompson, whom the instinct and habit of servitude naturally carried along with them, protested with all their might against the decision of the majority. They agreed, indeed, with Story and the others,—for Baldwin also went to this extent,—that the states were prohibited from passing any special laws that might in any way conflict with the most summary recovery of fugitive slaves; but they insisted also (see Taney's opinion, p. 627,) that the constitution enjoined it as a duty, no less upon the states than upon Congress, "to protect and support the owner while endeavoring to obtain the possession of his property." That is to say, while the states were prohibited by the Federal constitution from affording the least protection to their own citizens, seized by kidnappers under pretence of being fugitives from labor, at the same time they were bound to afford all possible aid to slave-owners, even at the imminent risk of facilitating kidnapping! Such is another of the absurd consequences, of which this case is so full, to which false assumptions inevitably lead, in legal no less than in mathematical reasoning. It were well that lawyers and judges were as sensible as mathematicians to the logical effects of a *reductio ad absurdum*.

Baldwin, assenting to the constitutional right

maintained by all the judges except McLean, of re-caption and removal without warrant, notwithstanding special state laws to the contrary, concurred in the judgment of the court because it was admitted that the woman carried off was Prigg's slave. He also admitted, that if any special legislation on the subject were needed, Congress alone could so legislate. But he held such legislation unnecessary, and therefore unconstitutional, thus seeming to come up very nearly, if not quite,—for we have no detailed statement of his views, —to the doctrine maintained in this section. Baldwin was a lawyer, and a very able one; nor is his authority to be set aside on the ground of any anti-slavery leanings. His antecedents have been already alluded to, as indeed they were by himself, in his opinion delivered only a year before, in the case already mentioned of *Graves* v. *Slaughter*,—an opinion in which he went far beyond any of the court in maintaining that the Federal constitution recognizes slaves as property as much as a bale of cotton; and that, as such, gangs of slaves might be driven to market through intervening free states. He had also, on the same occasion, attacked, with no little acrimony, the idea set up by McLean, and seemingly countenanced by some of the other judges, that the constitution regards slaves not as property, but only as persons, denouncing it as the first step in a career of doctrine certain to prove fatal to the whole slave-holding system.

McLean agreed with the other judges, that the act of 1793 was constitutional, and that the states had no right to legislate specially on the subject of the surrender of fugitive slaves. But he differed from them in maintaining, 1st. That Congress had a right, in certain cases, to impose duties on state officers and tribunals, and that this matter of the surrender of fugitives from labor was one of those cases; and 2d. That the states, under their acknowledged police power, had a right to preserve their own peace, and to protect the rights of their citizens, by prohibiting the removal of fugitives from justice, except under a certificate granted in conformity to the act of Congress. This view he ingeniously supported by referring to the act of 1793, which required, in express terms, that all persons arrested as fugitives from labor should be taken before a magistrate, and a certificate obtained in order to their removal; nor, indeed, would it have been possible for his colleagues to have answered him on this point, except by denouncing that portion, at least, of the act of 1793 as unconstitutional.

Three general remarks may be made upon the opinions delivered in this case. 1st. Forgetting the chariness of the constitution and of the act of 1793, as to the use of such shameful terms as *slaves* and *slavery*,—a decorum observed even by the act of 1850, —the judges, in their opinions, blurt out these obscene words, which ought to raise a blush on the cheek of every true man, at least of every judge, in a nation whose government is based upon the declaration that all men are born free, with a frequency that seems almost affected, as if, like strumpets, desirous to show how brazen they had grown. 2d. While the right of the slave-holder to his fugitive slave is urged with a vivacity which could not be exceeded, had the surrender of fugitive slaves been the sole end and aim of the constitution, not one word is dropped, except cursorily, in the opinion of McLean, about the dangers from kidnappers and false claimants, or about the duty of protecting, against the terrible fate of slavery, native citizens, and even fugitives from labor, claimed by scoundrels having no title to their services. 3d. It is not a little remarkable, that not one of the judges made the slightest allusion to the child born in Pennsylvania, and free according to the decision of the Supreme Court of that state, but carried off into slavery along with its mother. The state law might be inefficacious in the case of a person admitted to be a slave, but was it also void in its application to a native-born citizen of the state, seized and carried off into slavery without any title or legal warrant? Perhaps on the principle *de minimis non curat lex*,—the law does not concern itself with trifles,—the kidnapping a negro child was thought to be too insignificant a matter to engage the attention of so grave a tribunal. Or are we to understand the court as reversing, by silent implication, the doctrine of the Supreme Court of Pennsylvania, and holding that the children of fugitive slaves, whenever and at whatever period born, are also slaves?

There is still one other extremely important observation to be made upon this case. The point brought directly to the notice of the court was, the validity of a *special law* of Pennsylvania, in relation to fugitives from labor coming within her limits from other states. This special legislation the court held to be void, and, it would seem, soundly enough, whatever we may think of some of the grounds and reasons on which they based their decision. But, except by the sweeping, yet very nebulous and unsubstantial tails of some extravagant generalities the practical application of which the court itself, it may reasonably be supposed, would be inclined to contract within some defensible limits, the case of *Prigg* v. *Pennsylvania* does not touch, it does not even evince the least consciousness of the vastly more important questions upon which, according to the views maintained in this section, all rights and duties, existing under the constitution of the United States, in the case of fugitives from labor, must depend; the questions, namely, 1st, of the right of the states to regulate, by *general laws*, the procedure to be adopted, in all cases, for reclaiming, within their limits, actual control over the persons of others by parties who possess the legal right of control; and 2d, of the necessity that citizens of other states should be satisfied with being placed, in this respect, on a level with resident and native citizens. These are points as yet unadjudged by the Supreme Court of the United States, or by any state court, except that of Pennsylvania, in the unfortunate case of *Wright* v. *Deacon*, already sufficiently criticized.

The decision of the case of *Prigg* v. *Pennsylvania* failed to give satisfaction any where. Every where it was greeted with mingled groans and hisses; in the North, as a timid and disgraceful surrender of the rights of the free states, and of the plainest principles of common justice; in the South as not having gone half far enough. The free states very generally responded to it, not by repealing the statutes which this decision declared void, but by new laws, forbidding their officers or magistrates to act under the statute of 1793, or their jails to be employed for the detention of fugitives. Mr. Webster, in his Newburyport letter, stigmatizes this latter prohibition, as putting a serious obstacle in the way of trial by jury, in the case of alleged fugitives from labor. Lame apology for his abandonment of his own bill, since the marshals of the United States are amply authorized, by a joint resolution of both houses of Congress, to provide, in all cases where the states refuse the use of their jails to the Federal authorities, other safe places for the custody of their prisoners, under which provision, have we not seen the very court house of the city of Boston converted into a slave jail, and by the order of the city authorities, surrounded by chains, under which even the state judges were obliged to stoop, some of them, indeed, seeming even to make a merit of their alacrity in doing so? Nor is it true, as Mr. Webster seems to insinuate, that this refusal of the use of state jails was one of the devices of the treasonable abolitionists. So far from it, it was first brought into use by that good Federalist, Governor Strong, so highly eulogized by Mr. Webster in this very same Newburyport letter, in conjunction with the legislature of the Federal and patriotic state of Massachusetts, and with the full approbation, if we mistake not, of Mr. Webster himself. The occasion was the attempt of President Madison, of which the Federalists did not approve, to compel the British government, by retaliations, to relinquish their scheme of treating as deserters the natives of Ireland captured in the American ranks, by shuting up in the state jails certain British officers, prisoners of war, with the prospect of death before them, should Great Britain set the example. Afterwards, in the war, almost, which sprung up in the Western States, about the years 1820-1, against the second Bank of the United States, a like expedient was resorted to by the state of Ohio, by refusing the use of its jails for the confinement of prisoners, in all cases in which that bank was concerned; and it was upon that occasion that the joint resolution above referred to was adopted. Upon the present occasion, also, Congress attempted to meet the legislation of the states by an act, passed in 1845, extending the jurisdiction of the Circuit Court commissioners, as well to the cases of fugitives from labor, as to the closely related one of deserting seamen. But for all this, fugitives from servitude rapidly increased, and reclamations of them were attended with more and more difficulty. Every where in the free states they received aid and comfort, at least to the extent of a cup of cold water, a crust of bread, and a barn to sleep in. Many of them turned lecturers, and, travelling from village to village, revealed the secrets of the prison-house in artless and homely appeals to the natural sympathies of the human heart, which washed away, in trickling tears, all the studied and specious sophistries of the most learned and eloquent advocates of despotism. The South became more exasperated than ever. Those who had lived and grown famous by defending and expounding the constitution, hoping, at least, to levy new contributions, if not to mount to high office in the midst of the panic, raised anew the cry of " The Union in danger; " and never did the old English Tory cry of " The church in danger " drive both clergymen and laymen into greater follies. Such were the circumstances under which, by the aid of half a dozen or more congressional northern candidates for the presidency, the

act of 1850 was passed; an act which adopts, in express
terms, all the judicial extravagances, based on the
constitutional clause respecting fugitives from labor
and the act of 1793, adding, besides, others of its own ;
an act breathing, in every line, that disregard of all
right, except the right of the strongest, upon which
the system of slavery is founded, and most character-
istically forced through the House of Representatives,
without the allowance of any debate upon it.   Omit-
ting the numerous other objections which have made
that despotic enactment of a professedly democratic
legislature a finger-post for the scorn of all the world,
it has been enough for the present purpose to point
out the particulars in which it directly conflicts with
the constitution of the United States.   The opinions
of some Federal judges, confidently pronounced, and
even ostentatiously volunteered, may affect to make
light of these objections.   They may even be slurred
over and evaded by some state courts from whom
better things might have been expected.   But they
have not been answered, nor obviated ; and, like the
drops of blood on the hands of the murderer, however
muffled and hidden, for the present, under the judicial
ermine, they still bear that silent but indestructible
testimony which will one day bring the guilty to
due punishment.

There is no more admirable chapter in Gibbon than
that in which he has given a condensed but comprehensive sketch of the Roman jurisprudence,—a chapter which goes far to show, that an historian, accustomed to generalize, and to view things in the whole
as well as by piecemeal, may have clearer apprehensions of a system of laws than were unitedly possessed by scores and hundreds of laborious and erudite
jurists, who had made those same laws the sole study
of their lives, but who had still no conception of them,
except in detail.
After a humorous description of some of the formalities, the knowledge of which was confined to the early

Roman lawyers, and which continued to be observed long after their origin and meaning were forgotten, and even after the lawyers themselves had learned to laugh at them, Gibbon proceeds as follows:— " A more liberal art was cultivated, however, by the sages of Rome, who, in a stricter sense, may be considered as the authors of the civil law. The alteration of the idiom and manners of the Romans rendered the style of the Twelve Tables less familiar to each rising generation, and the doubtful passages were imperfectly explained by the study of legal antiquarians. To define the ambiguities, to circumscribe the latitude, to apply the principles, to extend the consequences, to reconcile the real or apparent contradictions, was a much nobler and more important task, and the province of legislation was silently invaded by the expounders of ancient statutes. Their subtle interpretations concurred with the equity of the prætor to reform the tyranny of the darker ages : however strange or intricate the means, it was the aim of artificial jurisprudence to restore the simple dictates of nature and reason, and the skill of private citizens was usefully employed to undermine the public institutions of their country."

The precise and simple truth can seldom be expressed in epigrams. The last clause of this instructive quotation is liable to a criticism which Gibbon's sparkling phraseology somewhat too frequently extorts,—that of sacrificing to rhetorical point. To remove the rotten materials which ignorance, thoughtlessness, or the prevailing interest of the moment had incorporated, substituting for them " the simple dictates of nature and reason," can hardly, with any justice, be said to be an undermining of the institutions of one's country, since institutions thus piously repaired, may stand forever, instead of being left, by the failure of rotten supports, to fall by their own weight. But whatever may be thought of the justice of this criticism, the leading American lawyers and courts of this present generation seem determined

that no future Gibbon shall bring any similar charge
against them.   Assuming and conscientiously believ-
ing, as no doubt all of them who have consciences
do,—though conscience is not commonly regarded
as indispensable to a " consummate lawyer,"—that
slavery is one of " the public institutions of their
country," guaranteed and endorsed by the Federal
constitution, so far from imitating the example of the
Roman lawyers, all their skill and subtlety is employed, not in reforming the tyranny of darker ages,
but in twisting new whips and forging new fetters, to
perpetuate that tyranny to the latest times, and to
diffuse it over the whole face of the country.   What
I have written on the subject of the legal basis of
slavery, I have not written with the least expectation
of producing any effect upon lawyers or judges already
committed to different views ; or, indeed, upon any
lawyer more than forty years of age.   Harvey did
not convert a single physician above that age to his
view of the circulation of the blood ; and as to new
views, whether true or false, lawyers and doctors, for
obvious reasons, are very much alike.

At the present day, however, especially in America,
the current of public opinion sets strongly in favor
of personal freedom ; and to attempt, whether by
legislative or juridical devices, to dam up and stop
short any current of public opinion, is a very hazardous
thing.   The experiment may seem to succeed for a
moment.   It may answer sufficiently well where only
a temporary object is to be accomplished.   The rushing waters of refreshment and fertility may be stayed.
The black and sharp rocks may be laid bare, and
industrious political fishermen may take much fish in
the pools.   But presently, when least expected, and
without a moment's warning, the obstruction gives
way before the still and silently rising water, which
sweeps off dam, fishermen, every thing in the way to
inevitable destruction ; a destruction which over-
whelms, also, many innocent dwellers on the river's
bank, who, though they foresaw and remonstrated,

had not been able to prevent the disaster. Such indeed is the catastrophe, as inevitable as it is formidable, with which we are threatened at the present moment. The dam has been building this twenty years or more. The accumulating waters must and will come down. To discover the means so to guide them that the evil of slavery may be swept away without leaving others behind it hardly less deplorable, is a problem to which all men of sense and judgment, whether slave-holders or non-slave-holders, ought forthwith to apply themselves. It is a question that interests all alike—for, much as we may quarrel among ourselves, and loudly as, like Adam and Eve over the tasted apple, we may accuse and berate each other, we are all in this matter, equally concerned, equally unfortunate, equally guilty. If the South has been the boisterous youth who solicited, and even demanded, what the blindness of passion made him think almost his right, the North has been the weak, willing, profligate maiden, who yielded—for money—what she knew to be wrong. We are all, slave-holders and abolitionists, citizens of the same community; nor is it possible for us to denationalize ourselves. Our state lines are fast sinking into little more than county lines; even the old state rights Democratic party has adopted the cry of—The Republic one and indivisible! We are all in the same ship, and must sink or swim together. We are slave-holders or abolitionists, not because we differ much either in moral character or intellectual capacity, either in sentiment or opinion, but mainly from differences of social and topographical position. So completely alike, in all fundamental points, are some of our most ardent abolitionists and some of the boldest of our southern defenders of slavery, that if they could, in a night, be made to change places, the one finding himself in possession of a cotton plantation and a hundred slaves, and the other the editor of a northern abolitionist newspaper, with a tolerable prospect of going to Congress on that interest,—and supposing, also, the memory of past com-

mitments to be at the same time obliterated,—there
is nothing whatever in their moral or intellectual constitution which would prevent them from exactly and
most conscientiously filling up each other's present
places. To the common eye, the moon appears, according to the relative position of the object and the
observer, a disc of light, or an absolute non-existence.
It is only to the philosopher that the new moon and the
full moon are the same thing. But in the present
age, we are all growing to be philosophers, and difference of position cannot long stand out against coincidence of intellect and sentiment. The abolition of
slavery is the great work of the generation now in
being. What thoughtful man doubts it? Mr. Calhoun
certainly did not. Our Revolutionary Fathers did
what they could. Peace to their ashes and honor to
their memory, spite of the diatribes of those content
with nothing short of every thing! The abolition
of slavery in the Northern States, wretchedly and
inefficiently as that matter was managed; its exclu-
sion from the great North West; and the abolition
of the African slave-trade, were things great in themselves, and in their consequences mighty. Who can
doubt that, if slavery had not been abolished in Massachusetts, some wealthy Boston supporters of the
law of 1850 would be, at this moment, exhibiting
their attachment to the Union by filling their houses,
perhaps their cotton factories, with slaves purchased
in the South? Who can doubt that, if the African
slave-trade had not been abolished as seasonably as it
was, negroes, freshly imported from Africa, would be
now selling in the New Orleans market for a hundred
dollars a head? And what hope would there be for
liberty, were the fertile states of the North West now
cultivated, as, but for the ordinance of 1787, they
would have been, by servile hands, not servile by consent, but servile by compulsion?

The abolition of slavery was desired, for their own
states, by all the more intelligent citizens of Maryland and Virginia, even more ardently than any where

at the North; but they had neither the courage nor the means to overcome the mountains of ignorance, prejudice, and interest which rose up before them. They were obliged to content themselves with repeating, after Lord Bacon, "Time is the greatest innovator," and with hoping from their children what they could not accomplish themselves. But the result has only served to confirm the philosophy of Lord Bacon, whose mention of Time as the great innovator is so generally quoted in a sense totally different from that in which he uttered it. "Surely," he says, "every new medicine is an innovation; and he that refuses new remedies must expect new evils; for Time is the greatest innovator; and if Time alter all things to the worse, and wisdom and council alter them not to the better, WHAT SHALL BE THE END?"

A pregnant question truly. What shall be the end? —a question the answer to which must make a part of An Inquiry into the Feasibility, Expediency, and Necessity of the Abolition of Slavery in the United States of America, with Outlines of a Practical Plan for its Accomplishment—a second treatise to which the present one is intended as an introduction.

APPENDIX.

In confirmation of the statement contained in the text, I give here some extracts from Mr. Webster's too famous 7th of March speech, (1850.) It has been attempted to glorify this speech by giving to it the title "For the Constitution and the Union." Less grandiloquently, perhaps, but quite as truthfully, it might have been entitled "A job for the presidential chair." As if to magnify the sacrifice he was about to make to the slave-holding Moloch, the orator prefaces his declaration of adhesion to the fugitive bill of 1850, "with all its provisions to the fullest extent," by some historical statements, such as might rather have justified an indignant opposition to that disgraceful piece of slave-holding legislation, and which even gives color to the conjecture that a large part of that famous speech was prepared before Mr. Webster had quite made up his mind to barter away his voice, and vote, and permanent reputation for the chance of southern votes in the presidential caucus.

"Let us consider for a moment," says Mr. Webster, "what was the state of sentiment north and south in regard to slavery at the time when this constitution was adopted. A remarkable change has taken place since; but what did the wise and great men of all parts of the country think of slavery then? In what estimation did they hold it at the time when this constitution was adopted? It will be found, sir, if we carry ourselves by historical research back to that day, and ascertain men's opinions by authentic records still existing among us, that there was then no diversity of opinion between the North and the South on the subject of slavery. [This is rather overstating the matter. There was at the time of the convention, and in the convention, a zealous pro-slavery party, but it consisted exclusively of citizens of Georgia and the Carolinas.] It will be found that both parts of the country held it equally an evil, a moral and political evil. It will not be found that either at the North or the South there was much, though there was some, invective against slavery as inhuman and cruel. The great ground of objection to it was political; that it weakened the social fabric; that, taking the place of free labor, society became less strong, and labor less productive; and therefore we find, from all the eminent men of the time, the clearest expression of their opinion that slavery is an evil. . . . The eminent men, the most eminent men, and nearly all the conspicuous politicians of the South, held the same sentiments; that slavery was an evil, a blight, a scourge, and a curse. There were no terms of reprobation of slavery so vehement, in the North at that day, as in the South. The North was not so much excited against it as the South, and the reason is, I suppose, that there was much less of it at the North, and the people did not see, or think they saw, the evils so prominently as they were seen, or thought to be seen, at the South.

"Then, sir, when this constitution was framed, this was the light in which the Federal convention viewed it, [i. e. slavery]. That body reflected the judgment and sentiments of the great men of the South. The question then was, how to deal with it, and how to deal with it as an evil. They came to this general result. They thought that slavery could not be continued in the country, if the importation of slaves were made to cease; and, therefore, they provided that, after a certain period, the importation might be prevented by the act of the new government. . . . It may not be improper here to allude to that, I had almost said, celebrated opinion of Mr. Madison. You observe, sir, that the term *slave*, or *slavery*, is not used in the constitution. The constitution does not require that 'fugitive slaves' shall be delivered up. It requires that persons held to service in one state, and escaping into another, shall be delivered up. Mr. Madison opposed the introduction of the term *slave*, or *slavery*, into the constitution; for he said that he did not wish to see it recognized by the constitution of the United States of America, that there could be property in men.

"Now, sir, all this took place in the convention of 1787; but, connected with this, concurrent and contemporaneous, is another important transaction, not sufficiently attended to. The convention for framing this constitution assembled in Philadelphia in May, and sat until September, 1787. During all that time, the Congress of the United States was in session in New York. . . . At the very time when the convention in Philadelphia was framing this constitution, the Congress in New York was framing the ordinance of 1787 for the organization and government of the territory north-west of the Ohio. They passed that ordinance on the 13th of July, 1787, at New York, the very month, perhaps the very day, on which these questions about the importation of slaves and the character of slavery were debated in the convention at Philadelphia. So far as we can now learn, there was a perfect concurrence of opinion between these two bodies; and it resulted in this ordinance of 1787, excluding slavery from all the territory over which the Congress of the United States had jurisdiction. . . . Three things are quite clear, as historical truths. One is, that there was an expectation, that on the ceasing of the importation of slaves from Africa, slavery would begin to run out here. That was hoped and expected. Another is, that, as far as there was any power in

26*

Congress to prevent the spread of slavery in the United States, that power was executed in the most absolute manner, and to the fullest extent. . . . Why, there it stands! The vote of every state in the Union was unanimous in favor of the ordinance, with the exception of a single individual vote, and that individual vote was given by a northern man. This ordinance, prohibiting slavery forever north-west of the Ohio, has the hand and seal of every southern member in Congress. It was, therefore, no aggression of the North on the South. The other and third clear historical truth is, that the convention meant to leave slavery in the states as they found it, entirely under the authority and control of the states themselves."

Yet, after all this historical detail, including the emphatic statement of the care taken, under the auspices of Mr. Madison, not to admit into the constitution the idea that there could be property in men, Mr. Webster has the inconsistency to speak, in the very next paragraph, of the establishment of the constitution of the United States " with a recognition of slavery as it existed in the states," apparently intending to concede that the Federal constitution expressly recognized slavery as an existing legal institution of the states; whereas the utmost that can be found in it is an obscure recognition, and that only by implication, of the existence in the states of a class of persons neither free nor bound to service for a term of years, and that a recognition of the fact merely, without the slightest acknowledgment of any legality in it. But this misrepresentation of the constitution was essential to afford Mr. Webster a colorable pretence for fishing after southern votes, with his favorite bait of devotion to the constitution and the Union—a very melancholy piece of fishery, as it proved on this particular occasion, —not even resulting in a glorious nibble. The cunning and voracious southern pike proved, indeed, altogether too nimble and adroit for a fisherman whose chief practice had been,—and a very successful practice too—in catching northern gudgeons with the same sort of bait.

The paragraph above alluded to is as follows, containing, along with the treacherous concession above criticized, and some additional historical mistakes, a good deal, however, of wholesome truth. " This was the state of things, sir, and this the state of opinion, under which those very important matters were arranged, and those three important things done, that is, the establishment of the constitution of the United States with a recognition of slavery as it existed in the states [this is the admission criticized above]; the establishment of the ordinance for the government of the North-Western Territory, prohibiting, to the full extent of all territory owned by the United States, the introduction of slavery into that territory, while leaving to the states all power over slavery in their own limits; and creating a power in the new government to put an end to the importation of slaves, after a limited period. There was entire coincidence and concurrence of sentiment between the North and the South, upon all these questions, at the period of the adoption of the constitution. [Mr. Webster here again ignores the existence, at that time, of the pro-slavery party of South Carolina and Georgia, which has since became predominant in the Union.] But opinions, sir, have changed, greatly changed; changed North and changed South. Slavery is not regarded in the South [it would be more correct to say in Maryland and Virginia, for North Carolina, even then, was undetermined upon this point] now as it was then. . . . What, then, have been the causes which have created so new a feeling in favor of slavery in the South, which have changed the whole nomenclature of the South on that subject, so that, from being thought of and described in the terms I have mentioned, and will not repeat, it has now become an institution, a cherished institution, in that quarter; no evil, no scourge, but a great religious, social, and moral blessing, as I think I have heard it lately spoken of? I suppose this, sir, is owing to the rapid growth and sudden extension of the COTTON plantations of the South. . . . The age of cotton became the golden age of our southern brethren. It gratified their desire for improvement and accumulation, at the same time that it excited it. The desire grew by what it fed upon, and there soon came to be an eagerness for new territory, a new area, or new areas, for the cultivation of the cotton crop; and measures leading to this result were brought about rapidly, one after another, under the lead of southern men at the head of the government, they having a majority in both branches of Congress to accomplish their ends. The honorable member from South Carolina [Mr. Calhoun] observes, that there has been a majority all along in favor of the North. If that be true, sir, the North has acted either very liberally and kindly, or very weakly; for they never exercised that majority efficiently five times in the history of the government, when a division or trial of strength arose. Never. Whether they were out-generalled, or whether it was owing to other causes, I shall not stop to consider; but no man, acquainted with the history of the Union, can deny, that the general lead in the politics of the country, for three fourths of the period that has elapsed since the adoption of the constitution, has been a southern lead."

See "Speech of the 7th of March, 1850, for the Constitution and the Union." *Webster's Works*, Everett's edition, vol. v. pp. 333–339.

How lamentable that, after thus exposing the moral and political weakness of the North, Mr. Webster should proceed to give a new, and, if possible, still more humiliating instance of it, by voting for Mason's unconstitutional and atrocious fugitive bill!

> Oh, what a fall was there, my countrymen!
> Then you and I and all of us fell down,
> And bloody treason triumphed over us.